Haunted Pennsylvania

Altoona, Cove Forge, Bedford, Merion, Douglassville, Philadelphia, Schellsburg, Reel's Corner, Lebanon, Williamsburg.... Towns, mountains, lakes, roads—many of these lethal locations are accessible to the public. Maps and photographs show you the way. Others may sound like tales to be told around a campfire, but be assured they are hidden family secrets, to be whispered about only at night. Just be sure to look over your shoulder before you start reading....

Patty Wilson has made a career of studying and writing about Pennsylvania. She worked for the Williamsburg Heritage Society for five years and wrote for various newspapers such as *The Shopper's Guides* of Blair and Bedford Counties, the *Bedford County Press*, and *Family: The Christian Perspective*. She is also a contributor to *Fate* Magazine. Mrs. Wilson lives on a farm in south-central Pennsylvania with her husband and three sons. She has collected folklore and ghost stories for most of her life and enjoys telling them in both the written and oral form.

"When my book Ghosts of Gettysburg *was first published, I was astounded at how many individuals had experienced the paranormal there but were afraid to talk about it. Patty Wilson's book* Haunted Pennsylvania *has every indication of opening up the fascinating subject statewide. Those who think they're alone with their ghostly experience should read Patty's book to see how universal and permeating the Other World really is."*
— Mark Nesbitt, Author of *Ghosts of Gettysburg, More Ghosts of Gettsyburg, Ghosts of Gettysburg III and IV*

Haunted
Pennsylvania

Patty A. Wilson

Belfry
Books

Haunted Pennsylvania
Copyright, ©1998 by Patty A. Wilson

ISBN: 0-9637498-7-0

Belfry Books logo designed by Lisa Wray Mazzanti
Original black and white artwork of small house and open door
Copyright ©1998 by Toad Hall, Inc., drawn by Kama Lee, 10 Salena,
Bentlyville, PA 15314.
Cover design and interior pages by Steven Dale Birch, 23420 Happy
Valley Dr., Newhall, CA 91321

First printing: November 1998

Belfry Books
A Division of Toad Hall, Inc.
R R 2, Box 16-B
Laceyville, PA 18623

Dedication

This book is dedicated to my husband, Gary, whose patience and persistence have kept me going even when I thought that I couldn't go on anymore. May he know that without his love and belief in me, I would not have been able to pursue my dreams. Thank you, Gary. I love you! And to Terry who always believed.

Author's Note

I am privileged to bring to you a sampling of the wonderful folk-lore and ghost stories from the home state I love so well. Pennsylvania has so many historic and contemporary tales to offer. Of course, it is totally impossible for anyone to capture all of the wonderful stories of the people and places of Pennsylvania in a single volume. So please do not feel slighted if I've left you out. I truly hope to visit you once more with more eerie and compelling stories.

If you have any stories to share, please feel free to write and send them to me. (My mailing address is listed below.) I would love to hear special family stories, historic hauntings, and any eerie or touching tales that you would care to share from anywhere. It is my hope that, with your help, these stories can be recorded to be remembered and enjoyed for many generations to come.

Throughout the book you will find an asterisk (*) at the end of some of the stories. This * marks a special note about the names of the people in the stories. Understandably, some of those who shared their stories with me did not want anyone to know who they are. In other cases, the families of those involved deserved their privacy—especially when they are still grieving the loss of a loved one (as in "The Woman In Blue.")

I'll leave you now to begin a journey through a special world that I call *Haunted Pennsylvania*. I hope that you enjoy the trip.

Patty A. Wilson

Patty Wilson

Patty A. Wilson
P.O. Box 98
Waterfall, PA 16689-0098

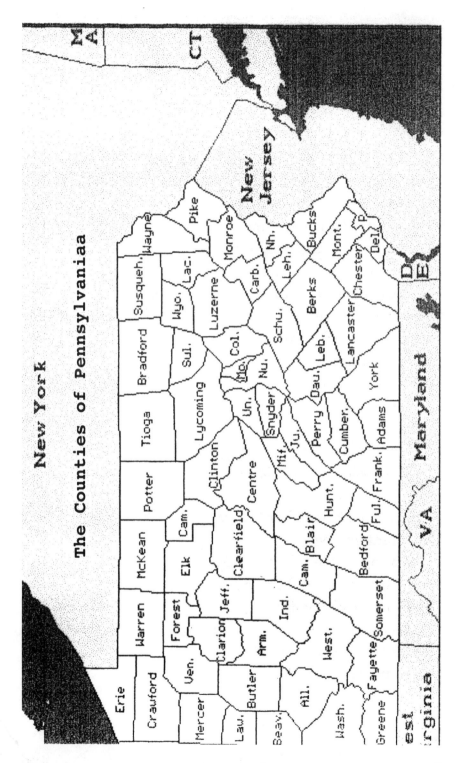

The Counties of Pennsylvaniaa

Table of Contents

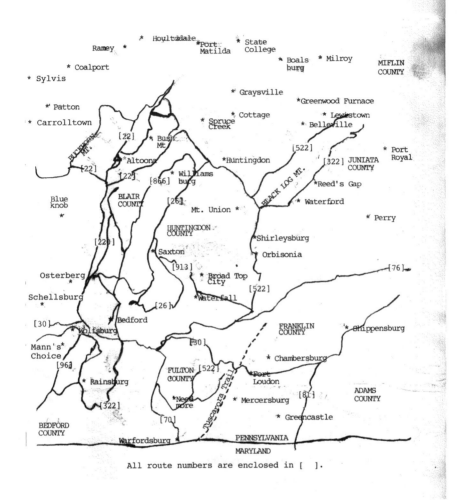

Ramey *
* Houltzdale
*Port
Matilda
* State
College

* Coalport
* Boals
burg
* Milroy
MIFLIN
COUNTY

* Sylvis

* Graysville

* Patton
*Greenwood Furnace

* Carrolltown
* Cottage
* Lewistown
* Spruce
Creek
* Belleville

[22]
* Bush
Mt

*Huntingdon
[522]
[322] JUNIATA
COUNTY
* Port
Royal
*Altoona

[22]
[22]
* Williams
burg
[866]
*Reed's Gap

Blue
knob
*
BLAIR
COUNTY
[26]
Mt. Union *
* Waterford

HUNTINGDON
COUNTY
* Perry

[220]
*Shirleysburg
* Saxton
* Orbisonia

[913]
[76]

Osterberg
* Broad Top
City
[522]

Schellsburg
*
*Waterfall

[30]
* Bedford
FRANKLIN
COUNTY
* Shippensburg

*Wolfsburg
[30]

Mann's*
Choice
* Chambersburg

[96]
FULTON [522]
COUNTY
*Fort
Loudon
ADAMS
COUNTY

* Rainsburg
*Mercersburg
[81]

[322]
*Nee
more
* Greencastle

[70]
BEDFORD
COUNTY
Warfordsburg *
PENNSYLVANIA
MARYLAND

All route numbers are enclosed in [ ].

This icon appears at the beginning of each new story and as a "filler" at the end of a story where there was not enough space to start a new story.

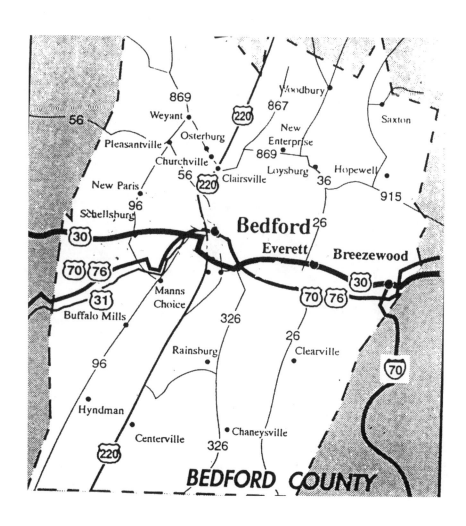

This icon appears in the heading of stories that are in locations accessible to the public.

The Girl On The Third Floor
(Williamsburg, Blair County)

In the small central Pennsylvania town of Williamsburg stands a house which at first glance seems like all of the other houses on that street. But upon closer inspection it is evident that the porch needs painting and the grass is a bit shaggier than the neighbors. There is an air of neglect about the property, even though the house itself is a beautiful structure inside and out.

The Burger family also found the house a rather delightful place, and in the beginning of the 1980s moved their three children into this pleasant, rambling structure.

The house had been built in another era, with large airy rooms and a kitchen with wall-to-wall cupboard space along the longest wall. The cupboards were broad and deep, reaching from ceiling molding to baseboard. The upstairs opened into spacious bedrooms, and the attic was a semi-finished room. The Burgers decided that the attic would be an ideal place for the children to have their play room because of its size and comparative seclusion from the downstairs. The only problem was that an open area of the attic bordered the stairs. It was a lengthy drop from the opening to the bottom of the stairs. The Burger family remedied this problem by installing a heavy railing across the opening onto the staircase below.

The Burger children—Ellie, age 5, Thomas, age 7, and Kelly, age 8—were pleased with the big, spacious playroom. Their parents were confident that they had taken all necessary precautions to make the room safe after the high railing was installed.

It was Ellie Burger who first noticed that something was wrong with her new house. She complained that when her mother left her alone in the kitchen to eat breakfast, a scary little girl would climb out of the bottom cabinets and stare at her. To her mother, Pat, this was ridiculous. She wondered what kind of stories the older kids on the block had been telling Ellie. And Pat was more convinced that it was a tale the older kids had told when Thomas stayed home from school one day and complained that he'd seen a little girl with dark hair and a long dress climb out of the cupboard.

During this time the children also complained that they saw the little girl in the attic playroom. One evening Ellie came downstairs crying and shaken—the scary girl had tried to push her down the attic stairs! Pat comforted Ellie. She wished that she could have blamed it on the older children, but they had been in the kitchen when Ellie had been frightened and pushed.

At last, Pat felt compelled to bring up the stories with her husband George. He didn't laugh as Pat had thought he would, but he was not ready to admit that they had ghosts either. George, who was usually outspoken and not afraid to state his mind on anything, was surprisingly noncommittal.

One afternoon Pat was entertaining her neighbor Lyla in the kitchen. She excused herself to run downstairs and switch the laundry from the washer to the dryer. On her way down the steps, she yelled back that Lyla was to help herself to some iced tea in the refrigerator. As Pat shuttled wet laundry into the dryer she heard Lyla cry out and then the sound of breaking glass. Pat ran back to the kitchen.

"There's a little girl in there. She opened the door and stared at me." Lyla pointed to the bottom cupboards—the same cupboards where the children had seen the scary girl.

Lyla was badly shaken and Pat took her to the living room to calm down. Pat questioned her closely about the child and was shocked to find out that the girl Lyla described was the same one that Thomas and Ellie had seen.

As soon as Lyla left, Pat phoned George at work. She begged him to come home. She was actually afraid to go into her own kitchen.

That evening George and Pat tore out all of the dishes and shelving in the bottom cupboards. George climbed inside, poked, pried, thumped the walls, looked for trap doors, anything to explain what Lyla had seen. There was nothing but solid wall, studs, and timbers behind the cupboards.

For the next few weeks no one mentioned the strange girl again. Pat and George were careful not to let the children alone in the kitchen, and soon they hoped that whatever had been happening was finally over.

The Burgers gave a dinner party one evening. After supper Pat sent all of the children to the playroom while the adults visited in the living room. The pleasant evening was shattered by screams from the attic, followed by the heavy thud of something falling.

Everyone raced upstairs to find that one of the boys was laying halfway down the attic stairs. He had sustained some nasty bumps and a broken arm, but was actually very lucky. If he had fallen further or landed differently he could have died. It looked as though the boy had somehow hoisted himself up on the high railing, lost his balance, and fell.

The child's parents took him to the emergency room. Pat and George questioned the other children about how the accident had happened. The children had a different story to tell. They all swore something lifted the boy over the banister. While they couldn't see who did it, just as the child had crashed to the steps below they saw the shadow of a girl looking over the stairs. Could it be that the children had been doing something they shouldn't have and then latched onto Ellie and Thomas' ghost girl to cover themselves? It was not very likely, but Pat preferred it to the alternative.

After that night the Burgers noticed that the neighborhood children would not go into the house, and their own kids refused to play upstairs without their parents. Pat still did not know what to make of what was happening in her home. She just couldn't swallow a bunch of superstitious nonsense about evil little ghost girls.

Several weeks after the accident, Pat finally convinced her children to spend a rainy Saturday in their playroom. She had a lot of cleaning to do and didn't want them underfoot. Besides, she told herself, there had been no accidents or even sightings of the little girl since the boy had fallen on the night of the party.

It was about two-thirty in the afternoon when Pat went upstairs to change the bed sheets. She listened to the children's noisy play from the floor above her while she worked. Suddenly there was a piercing scream. Pat dropped the sheets and ran up the attic stairs. Balanced on her back across the banister was Ellie, crying for help. She seemed to be struggling with some unseen force that pinned her precariously to the railing. Pat screamed and ran up the steps to her child. As Pat struggled to pull Ellie back from the edge, she felt invisible hands grasping the child, trying to force her over and onto the steps below.

Suddenly the hands withdrew and Ellie tumbled into Pat's

arms. She turned to her other children, angry and frightened. "How did this happen?"

The other children didn't hear her. They were looking past her to the far end of the banister. There stood a slim, dark child of about thirteen. She was dressed in period costume from the early 1900s. As Pat and her children watched, the girl's face filled with fear and she fell through the narrow rails of the banister to the steps below. Pat heard the girl's scream and the sick thud of the body striking the bottom of the stair well, but when she peered over the railing the stairs were empty. Pat had finally witnessed what the children had seen before. Now she could no longer deny that their home was haunted, or that the spirit child intended to do her own children harm.

Within a week the Burgers had left the house. The landlady didn't seem surprised by their sudden departure. She even refunded the unused portion of the rent.

It wasn't until weeks later that Pat Burger again met the landlady. By now Pat was determined to understand what had happened to her family in their former home. She questioned the landlady and learned that shortly after the turn of the century a young girl had fallen from the attic onto the steps below, killing herself. The landlady said that in the story she had heard, no one was sure just how the girl had fallen. Was it an accident or was she pushed? Pat never found that out, but she did learn that other families had heard the cries of the falling ghost, but her family had been the only ones to use the attic regularly.

Pat never found an explanation for why the girl had appeared from the kitchen cabinets, but she did learn that the child had led a difficult life. Perhaps the child had once sought refuge by hiding in those cabinets, or perhaps it had been a frequent punishment. Pat was never to know for sure.

This story was told to me by a young man who had spent time in the house in question. It was his aunt who had rented the place back in the 1980s. As a boy of ten, he had witnessed several incidents in the house, including the incident where the young boy had broken his arm. Several other family members, who also witnessed phenomena, believe that the ghost of the evil little girl tried to kill people in the attic.

Since my first recording of this story, I have been told by a friend of the family that now owns the home that there are still manifestations in the house, but that the family is very reluctant to admit it. The phe-

nomena is much less dangerous than what I have previously heard, but this could be in part because there are no young children in the home right now and because the attic is only used for storage.

*The names have been changed in this story.

On The Third Day He Will Return
(Ganister, Blair County)

This story is very personal to me because I knew and loved the woman to whom it happened. She was a wonderful neighbor for an eight-year-old girl to have. She never growled when kids messed up her house or plans, and she would play wonderful old world games that her family brought from Slovakia. Much of this story deals with the particular beliefs of her Slovenian ancestors and how this was combined with her Greek Orthodox background. I thought she was exciting, funny and exotic with her "strange" ideas. She kept pussy willow branches in her home for luck, a priest came at the new year (their year was different from the commonly recognized new year) to bless the house, and she did other things differently. Perhaps because of her differences, she was a wonderful friend who would tell delicious tales that my Mom would have frowned upon, but which stirred my imagination when I was young. Her name was Annie Homiac and she wasn't beautiful or well educated, but she was sweet and funny and filled with tales that tantalized me. This was my favorite story because it happened in the very room where she told it, and she swore that it was true.

Annie Homiac followed her mother from the small cemetery behind the church. Her brother John led their mother to his old blue sedan. Annie lagged behind, keeping pace with her twin sister Mary, and trying not to shiver in the cold, drizzly mist. It seemed appropriate that God had the world crying today for Annie thought her

5

heart was breaking. They were leaving behind their father in the cold, wet ground and going home for the first time without him.

Mary touched her elbow, startling her from her sad reverie. "You ride home with Ben and me, Annie. John and Marta are taking Mama."

Annie nodded and switched direction from the blue sedan to the more modern Chrysler that Mary's husband, Ben, drove. It was not a long ride home for they only lived three miles from the graveyard, and Annie would have walked it had it not been for the rain and the fact that she knew Mama would need her today.

Everyone was going back to the house, so Annie had made sandwiches and salads for them to eat. A cold roast beef was in the refrigerator to cut and home-jarred pickles, peaches, meats, and preserves were in the pantry. The neighbors had baked pies, cakes and other sweets, and Annie's best friend, Elsie, had come over early that morning with fresh bread. Annie busied her mind with practical thoughts so that she did not have to think about what they were leaving in the soggy ground behind the church.

At the house there were neighbors and friends who offered condolences. Annie slipped away from the group congregated on the porch and went into the house. The kitchen was cold and damp, so she hurriedly stirred the embers of the kitchen fire in the cook stove and set on a pot of coffee and a kettle for tea. She slipped an apron on over her dark blue dress and spread a cloth over the table. There were a million practical details to occupy her now and she allowed them to take over. She set the table with the foods; there were so many things that the settings spilled over onto the cabinets and counters.

The screen door squealed and Mama came in, looking worn and battered. She smiled sadly and sat down heavily in the chair nearest the door. Her eyes swept vacantly over the work Annie had done.

"I know they mean well, but I just can't take anymore." Annie's mother loosened her scarf, freeing her curly gray hair. "Annie, you've done a good job, but I can't eat right now."

"Why don't you just go upstairs and lay down for a while? Mary and John can make your apologies."

Mrs. Homiac glanced at the stairs wearily and shook her head. "I don't want to be alone up there right now."

Annie read the thoughts in her mother's eyes. "Go to the back room and lay down on the sofa. I can keep everyone out of there for today."

Mrs. Homiac nodded and got up. While the guests ate their fill,

Annie periodically checked on her mother. Some of the ladies washed dishes and put away the leftovers. Annie sat in the corner near the cook stove and watched as they worked. Normally she would have preferred to do the work herself, but today she was just too tired. Besides that, Mary and Ben were planning to stay the night so she still had to unroll the feather ticking on the spare bed in her room and make up the bed.

Finally Annie, Mary, and John ushered out the last of the company. There was a hush over the house now and Annie wondered if it might not have been better when there was noise to fill the void left by her father's passing.

"Has everyone gone?" Mrs. Homiac asked, coming from the back of the house. She looked rumpled and tired.

"We saved you a plate of food, Mama. Marybe you'd better eat something now." Mary busied herself by setting a place at the cleared table for her mother.

"Yes, I suppose I should." Mrs. Homiac eyed the food warily and then sat down.

During the evening things seemed almost normal. No one talked about the death, and Mrs. Homiac sat at her mending while Mary bathed her children at the sink and put them to bed. John turned on the television and Annie joined him to watch the program.

When bedtime finally came, Annie hurried to the linen closet for sheets to put on the bed for Mary. While she was there her mother called, "Annie, bring me the good basin and a new white hand towel." Annie obeyed, wondering why her mother had waited until now to wash up.

Everyone sat in the living room watching as their mother cleared off one of the deep window sills. She put the basin there and laid the hand towel beside it neatly.

"Go to the kitchen, Mary, and get me the best water pitcher filled with hot water."

"What for?" Mary asked.

"Just bring it here then I will explain." Mrs. Homiac fussed at the basin, arranging it perfectly in the center of the deep sill.

Mary hurried in with a metal pitcher filled with steaming water.

Mrs. Homiac took it carefully and sat it in the center of the basin. Stepping back she sighed, "There, now it's ready for your father."

"What?" John slid forward on the couch. "Mama, are you okay? Dad's dead."

Mrs. Homiac looked at her son disdainfully. "I know that, I'm

7

not daft. This is so your father can enter Heaven. He must come here within three nights to wash his hands so that he is clean of all sin to enter Heaven. This way God will know he's clean, and we will know he's in Heaven. It's a sign." She smiled proudly at her handiwork. "He'll come soon, so I thought we should be ready."

Mary took up the theme. "Mama, you don't really think that Dad's coming here tonight to wash his hands, do you?"

Mrs. Homiac stuck her chin out at a stubborn angle her children knew well. "I don't 'think' anything. I know that he will come tonight, tomorrow night, or the night after to wash his hands so that he can ascend to Heaven. He will come before three days are up, you will see. Now understand me," she flashed a glare at her children and their spouses. "No one is to touch that basin, no one but me, and I will not remove it until he does come. I will replace the water when it grows cold."

John could not help himself; he snorted. "Mama, that basin could be there a long time if you're waiting for Dad to wash his hands in it. That's just an old legend, a superstition from the old country."

"This is foolishness, Mama! I'm taking that stuff out of the window. Daddy's dead and he won't be washing his hands here tonight or ever. You have to accept that." Mary pulled away from Ben, who tried to stop her, and started toward the window.

"No!" Mrs. Homiac exclaimed, moving to block her daughter.

"Leave her alone." Annie's voice was soft, but firm. "If it brings Mama comfort, Mary, what will it hurt?"

Mary shrugged, rebuffed. "Fine, have it your way, but if Dad's coming to wash his hands I'm going to stay up to see it. Otherwise, you or her will have us believing it because of some towel you dampen yourself tonight."

Annie eyed her sister dispassionately. When Annie had been in the fourth grade her parents had made the decision to take her from school permanently to help with the work at home, and the other children often looked upon her as ignorant because of that. Still Annie had kept up the best she could and always made a habit of reading every word of the daily paper she purchased on her way home from work. Now she was ready for a fight. Mary had before thrown up Annie's lack of education to prove that she was smarter, but now Annie was angry. She thought it was stupid to have a basin of water in the window, too, but it hurt nothing—and it gave their mother some peace.

Mary huffed back down into her seat, and John smiled sardonically. "Well, if Dad's coming back, I'll have to stay for the big event too." He flipped on the television and settled in.

An hour passed, then a second one. Finally Mrs. Homiac gave in to her fatigue and went up to bed. Annie tagged along because she had volunteered to sleep with their mother so that Mary and Ben could put their children in her bed. John would lock up when he left. He only lived a few miles away so Annie knew that he would be back the next day.

Annie rose early and slipped downstairs to start the fire in the cook stove and began breakfast. She could not help taking the time to tiptoe into the cold living room to see if the basin had been touched. Annie did not know whether to be disappointed or relieved. At least the others had respected their mother's wishes enough to leave the basin alone.

That evening the family gathered in the living room once more. Mrs. Homiac sat quietly at her sewing and took the joshing her children dished out. Only once did she offer a rebuke. "You'll see," she muttered, leaning over to bite off the knotted thread of a seam.

It was late before the family drifted away to their various beds and just before Annie drifted off she heard the door slam as John left.

Early the next morning Annie rose as usual to start the fire and breakfast. The basin was still on the window sill undisturbed. By now Annie was having second thoughts. What would happen tonight when her father's ghost or whatever did not come to wash it's hands? She was beginning to worry about how their mama would take it. She knew that her mama honestly believed that he would come and this was the last night.

The day went fast for Annie. She had gone back to work the day after the funeral, so she was tired after walking home the four miles from the restaurant where she cooked. Mary had already started supper, and Annie was grateful for the help.

Before the table was even set, John and Marta pulled up, so Annie quietly set two extra places. The meal was a quiet one. By now the other kids had begun to see that the situation with their mother wasn't so funny any more.

Marta and Mary cleaned up after the meal so Annie joined the others in the living room. Mrs. Homiac had already refilled the pitcher with hot water and had put out another new, freshly washed, white towel in place of the dusty one.

The evening dragged on with television and sparse conversation.

Mary finally put her children to bed. Annie wondered how long she'd have to wait before she could slip away. Her legs hurt, she was tired, and most of all she dreaded the moment when her mama finally realized that her father's ghost wasn't going to come.

Annie couldn't keep her eyes open a moment longer. She got up and declared her intentions of going to bed. Mrs. Homiac looked at her daughter with sad eyes. "Aren't you going to stay up until your father comes?"

The others seemed to hold their breath, waiting for Annie's answer. She had been the weak link in condemning their mother's foolish idea from the beginning. "Mama, I don't think that Papa's coming."

Mrs. Homiac erupted from her seat. "Don't say that, Annie! *Kapisch!*"

Annie felt trapped. How could she get out of this without hurting her mother's feelings? Suddenly the problem was taken from her hands.

John leaped up, gasping. "Look!"

Annie whirled around to look at the window where John pointed.

The metal pitcher was shaking slightly—then it very slowly levitated upward. It stopped about a foot-and-a-half above the basin. Slowly the pitcher tipped over, pouring warm water into the pan. As carefully as it had risen, the pitcher floated back to the window sill. The water began to ripple and move as though some unseen person swished their hands in it. As the water settled, the white towel floated into the air and wrinkled as if compressed between invisible hands. Suddenly the towel dropped down beside the basin. The air rippled with cool electricity for a moment and then it was gone.

Silence filled the room. Brother and sisters started at each other.

Mrs. Homiac stood up slowly, tears flowing freely in her eyes. "Now your father is in Heaven. I knew he'd come. We just had to wait until the third day."

From that time on Annie believed in her mama's stories. Years later, when her mama passed away, Annie privately set a pitcher, a white towel, and a basin in the same window for her mother to wash with. This time Annie did not see the washing, but in the morning she found that the towel was rumpled and damp. At that time Annie knew her mother was in Heaven, because you see, Annie now lived alone.

Baker's Mansion in Altoona, Pennsylvania.

The Dancing Dress Of Baker's Mansion
(Altoona, Blair County)

Located in the city of Altoona, Pennsylvania, Baker's Man sion is run by the Blair County Historical Society. Baker's Mansion is also considered one of America's most haunted houses, at least according to an article which appeared in Life Magazine some years ago.

Elias Baker built his mansion after he made his fortune in the iron industry of Pennsylvania, and he moved his family into the 35-room Greek Revival mansion in 1844. He was a strict man and a snob when it came to things like class. It was because of this that the ghost of his daughter, Anna, is said to haunt the winter bedroom where she once lived.

11

Anna Baker cared very little about class, station, or being better than anyone else; she only knew that she had fallen in love with one of her father's laborers and she was going to marry him. Elias found out that Anna was secretly meeting his employee and was outraged. He tried to reason with Anna—marrying one of his employees was demeaning to the family.

When Elias realized he was geting nowhere with Anna, he went to the employee. At first the young man declared that nothing could come between him and Anna, but Elias knew that things were otherwise. He pointed out how ill-equipped Anna was for the life of a laborer's wife. Elias made it clear that he would cut them off, shun Anna, and he would make her entire family do the same.

He would never permit the young man to be his son-in-law. In the end Elias convinced the young man it would be better for Anna if he took the money Elias offered him and disappeared from Anna's life.

When Anna realized that her beau was gone, she was frustrated and hurt. It is not clear if she ever knew that her father bought off her lover, but she vowed that if she could not marry the man she loved she would never marry at all. Anna was true to her word and died a spinster.

Sylvester Baker, who is said to haunt the room where he died.

When the Edward Bell family donated a wedding dress to the historical society—worn by their daughter, Elizabeth, in the 1830s—it seemed to distress the ghost of poor spinster Anna. Elizabeth and Anna had been rivals at one time and she found the wedding dress, slippers, and parasol, now displayed in a heavy glass case in her room, both disturbing and fascinating.

According to the now retired curator Mrs. Emerson and to many of the tour guides, the dress sways back and forth in the locked glass case. The parasol and slippers change positions mysteriously, and the case has been found turned toward the wall many times although it weighs hundreds of pounds. An ex-tour guide, who worked there for several years, claimed that this fiddling with the wedding gown became commonplace. The ex-tour guide told another interviewer, "We booby-trapped the back of the airtight case to make sure nobody was playing tricks, and nothing was moved. But the dress kept right on moving whenever it felt like it."

But there are other people who believe that it is not Anna who moves the dress at all. Some claim that it is the spirit of Elizabeth Bell, who once wore the dress, and she is moving the gown around to show it off, and is taunting Anna with the fact that she had married and Anna never did. According to some local lore, Elizabeth truly did not like Anna and took every opportunity to tease poor Anna about being a spinster.

In the downstairs of the mansion, Anna's brother Sylvester died in the sitting room known as the single parlor. (So called because there is only one set of furniture of rather simple taste in this room. The formal parlor has a set of matching intricately hand-carved pieces and is known as the double parlor because there are two of each piece of furniture.) According to Mrs. Emerson (as quoted from a Tribune-Democrat Sunday issue, March 22, 1981), "'We had a problem with the burglar alarm system that even the alarm inspector couldn't figure out. There's an alarm plate here [under the carpet] and apparently there was a body

The sofa where Sylvester Baker died. This is the room where the police dog refused to enter, and where the electronic alarm goes off for no reason.

lying on it with sufficient weight to damage it. During the tour season this room is not open to visitors. It's chained off, so nobody could have walked on it.' According to Mrs. Emerson the alarm company believed that someone had dragged heavy furniture over the plate. She assured them that that was not the case."

Anna Baker, whose spirit seems most active in the house.

Before Sylvester Baker's death he had grown very mean. In his old age he was crippled and spent most of his time in his second-floor bedroom. If the servants were late with his meals, especially lunch, he'd bang on the floor with his cane for them to hurry up.

In the summer of 1979, G.D., then a tour guide and student at Juniata College, decided to bring a bag lunch instead of going out with the other guides at lunch time. While he was alone in the office eating and reading a book, he heard the dining room clock strike twelve. Within seconds he heard the sound of heavy banging from the second floor. According to G.D., "The sounds came from directly above me...from Sylvester's room."

G.D. searched for a rational explanation. Could someone have strayed away from the last tour? Was one of the other guides playing a trick? Or was it just that the shutters were not secured properly? G.D. laid down his sandwich and began making a systematic inspection of the mansion. He found that the shutters were all properly fastened back. He could not find anyone—but he certainly got a start when he entered Sylvester's room. Sylvester's cane, once used to pound on the floors for his meals and usually kept across the room, near the door, now was laying on the bed.

G.D. returned to the office where he waited for the other guides to return. He told them of the latest incident he had just witnessed and asked if one of them had been playing a trick. They all swore that they had not. In fact, they vouched for the fact that not one of them had ever left the rest of the group from the time they had left for lunch until their return.

At another time, radio station WRTA did a broadcast from the mansion. Gordon Hainer, a well known expert in supernatural ex-

The dancing dress in its locked glass case.

periences from St. Louis (identified in the Altoona Mirror, 9/5/80), went to the bathroom Mrs. Emerson recalls, "When he came out of the bathroom, there was about a 10-second pause, and then I heard him hit about every fourth step on the way down. He was white as a sheet and shaking like a leaf. He said, 'I felt a presence on the second step, starring down at me. It knew I didn't belong here, and I was very much frightened by it.'"

Mr. Hainer who was impressed enough with the ghostly phenomena to recommend it to writer Rosemarie Robotham. She reported on the Baker's Mansion and other haunted houses for an issue of Life Magazine in the early 1980s. Robotham and a crew of two showed up at Baker's Mansion to delve into it's otherworldly attractions.

According to Mr. Groskinsky, one of the two photographers that accompanied Ms. Robotham, in an interview that appeared in the Altoona Mirror 9/5/80, "We have experienced an incredible amount of problems working on this story. We have had our baggage and cameras arrive late several times, including today. I travel all the time, but I can't ever recall having the difficulties we've had on this one. Maybe these houses don't want the story done."

Mr. Groskinsky might have been joking but it seemed that he was right. He related that they had difficulties with the lights working to take their stills of the mansion. "The strobes had always worked perfectly before. When we set up to begin shooting, neither of them

15

worked. We couldn't get them to operate despite all our efforts, so we had to dismantle both and use parts from each to shoot."

The hauntings of Baker's Mansion have taken many forms. There is a foul smell of something rotting that first appeared in 1942 and recurs periodically. Mrs. Emerson once found a marble table in a second floor bedroom too hot to touch. The Regina Music Box ran down and stopped—and yet still played. A lap harp was thrown 20 feet when no one was near it. Doors lock or unlock mysteriously, a room that stays at a perfect 54 degrees even on hot summer days, and many other manifestations too numerous to mention.

Perhaps one of the strangest events was the night the alarms went off and a police officer brought his K-9 dog along to investigate. The dog simply refused to enter the room where the alarm went off. Nothing would induce the dog to cross the threshold. He just planted his paws firmly in the hall and growled into the room.

Oh, and there was the time that a skeleton handprint appeared on the one door, or when the Life Magazine crew were alone in the house and the doors shut and locked themselves, or the time that a young woman knocked on the mansion door after everyone had left for the evening and something knocked back at her.

Well needless to say, Baker Mansion has a well earned reputation not only as Altoona's most haunted house but as one of the most haunted houses in the nation. I have visited the mansion myself several times. Although I've never witnessed any active phenomena, the entire house is steeped in an eerie feeling. It is always preter-

The main staircase where a woman in black was seen and where other phenomena has been reported.

naturally cold, and there is a distinctly disturbing feeling in both the winter bedroom where the wedding dress is kept and in the room where Sylvester died.

I first went to the house as a child and was amazed that everyone else in my school group did not sense what I was feeling so strongly. I told the tour guide that a man had died on a particular sofa on display and she seemed shaken. Later I learned that it was Sylvester Baker who had died on that sofa. I kept feeling watched on the staircase and was terribly frightened of entering Anna's rooms.

As an adult, I've taken several friends and family members to visit the mansion. Each time I'm struck by how people react in certain areas of the house. In recent years there has been little publicity about the spirits that haunt the mansion; however, I can assure any reader who wishes to visit the mansion that they are still there. You may not get your tour guide to talk about them, but just stand back and feel the atmosphere of the house and soon you too will know that the living are not alone at Baker's mansion.

On my last visit to the mansion, as I wrote this book, I spoke with the present curator, Tim Van Scoyoc, who made two wonderful young tour guides and the mansion's documents about the hauntings available to me. Mr. Van Scoyoc has been the curator for five years now. Though he's not witnessed any otherworldly phenomenon himself, he described himself as, "an open-minded skeptic." However my primary guide, Julie, and another guide who joined us later named Brandon, informed us otherwise.

Julie confided that one evening in 1995 she and two other guides were in the nursery when a large ball of white light appeared on the wall. It stayed there despite their efforts to discover its origins. They ruled out both car headlights and pole lights because neither could reach that particular wall from the window. The ball of light left them shaken and they vacated the room quickly. Our second guide, Brandon, also witnessed the ball of white light and confirmed Julie's account.

Julie validated reports that the electronic sensor often went off in the single parlor when no one was in the house. The last time she remembered it happening was approximately a month earlier, in June 1996.

Brandon added an eerie story of his own. He said that once he had been in what is called the Lincoln Room (so named because this room is now used to house the historical society's collection of Lincoln memorabilia) when he heard footsteps behind him. Brandon was unnerved because there was no one else in the museum at the time. He said that he was standing before a large mirror but was frightened to look up for fear of what he would see. Instead, Brandon continued through the room quickly and left.

They also passed on a story about two other tour guides who were not on duty that day. It seemed that the female guide was in her familiar costume of a long black dress with bustles and ruffles on the day in question. She and the male guide were on the third floor where the servant quarters and Sylvester's study had been. The male guide went down to the second floor to do some work. A few minutes later he happened to glance down the staircase to see a small woman in a black dress and bustle hurrying down the stairs to the main floor. Thinking that this must be the female guide, he called out to her in a loud voice. A moment later the female guide appeared from the third floor to ask him what he had wanted. Shocked he told her about the other woman in a black gown and they searched the house. There was no one else in the house at the time and the doors were locked because it was before the museum opened. Many of the guides who heard this story believed that they had seen Anna's spirit because she was a very small woman with a tiny waist and would have fit the description perfectly.

I was also given an opportunity to look a journal kept in 1980 during the month of August when the ghosts seemed to be particularly active. Many of the entries were made by G.D. and were witnessed by other guides. Some of the entries read as follows:

"Sunday August 10, 1980: One strange thing—George noticed that the green rocker in the servant's room has been moved. Usually it faces the doorway into the room. Now it's turned toward the bed.

"Monday August 11, 1980: Earlier in the morning, approximately 8:45 [a.m.], George went to the second floor for paper towels and noticed the Wedding Dress case. The shoes had dramatically moved. [A diagram depicting the positions of the dress, shoes and umbrella followed.]

"Wednesday August 13, 1980: In the morning, footsteps were heard on the stairs, doors slamming, and a crash in the Ball Room by Sandy.

"Friday 15 [month name now dropped in journal]: On two separate occasions George heard a man's voice coming from the office. [The journal is not clear if this is Elias's old office on the first floor which is

A gown of Anna Baker's displayed in the master bedroom. Notice the hazy spot between the gown and the fireplace. There was no glare in this area and this did not appear in any other photos in the series of this room.

now used as the starting point for the tour or the business office on the second floor.]

"Saturday 16: At 10:30 [a.m.] the dress was noted that it moved. [Diagram followed.] About 12:30 [p.m.] after the guides stepped out to lunch the curator heard a loud crashing noise. [Many entries note that

19

the dress has moved.]

"Monday 18: Temps [temperatures] constant. However one strange occurrence happened. At approximately 10:00 a.m., Tim and George were on 3rd floor. Sandy came up to 2nd [floor] and stared at the dress—left the room—returned, and thought the dress moved a bit. Tim and George came down and went into the master bedroom. George sat down on the rocker. Tim stood by the bed. Sandy walked in—the three tried to get impressions from the room. Tim felt as if someone was pushing him backwards as he was standing. George felt as if he should put his head down as he sat on the chair for a minute. Within two minutes, Sandy saw a face appear by George—it was a man about 40 years old with short dark hair parted in the middle. He had deep-set, piercing eyes and a pointed chin. George was sitting there feeling depressed and alone. The face reached out hands and looked as if someone was going to put their arms around him. Sandy saw all this, repeated the Lord's prayer, and it disappeared.

"Wednesday 20: A thumping noise was heard from upstairs and a faint haze on the master bedroom chair."

The journal continued on for several pages noting dates, times, temperatures and happenings. Often voices, crashes and similar phenomenon were recorded.

Along with the journal was a hand-written account by an ex-tour guide, Naomi, about an incident with the wedding dress which she witnessed. The account states that a Ouija board was used by Naomi and the woman named Sandy who had witnessed the materialization of a face and hands in the journal entry above.

According to the account contact was made with an entity named Owen. (He claimed to be Anna's lost love. The history of the Baker family does not record the young man's name.) They spoke to Owen for a few minutes before the planchette began moving abruptly and they received a message from an entity that called itself Elizabeth. (Could this entity be the Elizabeth Bell whose dress is in Anna's winter bedroom?) Elizabeth was a rather negative spirit which stated that it was jealous of Sandy for having a living body. Elizabeth frightened Sandy a bit when she told the spirit that since it was not alive it could not hurt the living. Angered, Elizabeth repeated over and over, "Owen dead, Owen dead..." Then the entity told Sandy, "Sandy, go to Hell."

At this point the planchette changed its movements and became less jerky and slower as though changing personalities. The entity that now came through stated that it was Elias. (Elias had been Owen's earthly enemy if Owen really had been Anna's lover.) The entity spelled out, "Woman get a gown. He who was lord is now serf." (Here the writer states her conclusions about the message which are rather vague. It would seem to me that Elias—if it was Elias Baker—simply meant that he had been lord of Baker's mansion and was now a serf which is a servant or slave as defined in the dictionary.)

Elias seemed to be speaking to Sandy. He stated, "You know what is going to happen now, don't you?"

Sandy reported that she felt mentally conflicted and did not want to continue with the board. Sandy felt as if something was trying to get into her and she broke off contact and went upstairs.

Naomi reported that although she remained with the board on the main floor and tried to regain contact with the spirits by using two different people, she had no success.

About half an hour later Sandy came down the stairs rapidly and seemed agitated. She hurried through the house and out to the porch before she would even pause to answer questions.

Naomi wrote, "I asked her what had happened. [Sandy] told me that when she got to the second floor many people were in the Bell room [Anna's winter bedroom where the wedding dress of Elizabeth Bell's is kept] concentrating on the wedding dress in the case. [A large glass case that is locked with two locks and weighs several hundred pounds.] But [Sandy] felt drawn to the Lincoln room down the hall. Immediately outside the Lincoln room Sandy felt an ominous force which she had noticed before in other parts of the house at various times. Always before she would obey her urges not to enter the areas and avoided them until the feelings passed. This night she acted in defiance and entered the Lincoln room and looked around. Suddenly an unstable inrush of energy flowed through her from the crown of her head and out through the lower portions of her body. A sound in her ears like the crackle of a high voltage wire hitting water...she felt herself loosing consciousness but shook herself and left the Lincoln room and walked over to see what was happening in the Bell room.

At the same time, in the Bell room, a girl named Debbie had her back to the wedding gown and was lighting a set of candles in crystal candle holders at the far end of the room when Mrs. Emerson told her to look at the gown. [Debbie] turned and watched the gown on the hanger swaying from side to side and those in the room who had been skeptics

21

gasped and stepped back from the case. A parasol in the case, with its tip on the bottom placed very close to the back against which it leans, remained undisturbed while the dress continued to sway agitatedly for some minutes."

Naomi went on to state that on another occasion she, a woman she calls Claudette, and Sandy were working on the third floor when they heard "a muffled thud in the next room." Sandy and Claudette investigated the sound while Naomi remained to watch that no one was playing a trick on them. Sandy and Claudette came back frightened and Claudette seemed to have difficulty moving. Later Claudette told Naomi that Sandy's voice was faint as if coming from a distance. When they left the area where the noise was, the temperature jumped by about ten degrees. Naomi related that the air in the room was oppressive and almost claustrophobic. Later that feeling in the room was gone.

Naomi recorded yet one more happening in the house at another date. She wrote of her experiences when a psychic came to the house. (A psychic named Mrs. Elizabeth Sherman of Langhorne, Pennsylvania, did visit the house and left behind several drawings of her impressions of the entities in the house. Naomi's written account is the only one left on file at the mansion to describe the psychic's visit. Naomi always refers to the psychic as "the woman" or "psychic lady" so I can not verify that Mrs. Sherman's visit is the same one which Naomi recorded; however, Mrs. Sherman's visit is the only one known to the staff.) Naomi's account is startling for several reasons including the fact that she indicates that there is some belief that Anna once bore a child out of wedlock. She wrote:

"This evening a number of guests were visiting the mansion to see if they could detect or learn anything about what caused the strange phenomena. One of the people was an experienced psychic. I only observed her for a short while during which we were seated in the Bell room. Sandy and the psychic lady were operating the Ouija. I and the lady's husband had been talking in the hall and Sandy called me into the room too as she said to take notes. Sandy later told me that she needed someone to break the intensity of the session. Sandy said that before I entered the room the lady had been in a semi-trance and was speaking as Anna (?) saying, "Such pain, terrible pain." This coinciding with Sandy's receiving mental flashes of Anna delivering a baby.

"While I was in the room the woman seemed to be in communication with a spirit guide named White Bear, whom she described as

The ice room where David Baker's body was stored until he could be buried. Tour guides say there has been a lot of activity in the basement near this area.

being the chieftain of the healing spirits. This benevolent spirit said that it was not good for all of the young people to be in the house because the malignant force which exists here feeds on their energy. He said that he would help. His message was, 'Afraid are U. I shall help. I kindly ask each youth in house leave immediately.'

"The woman also received a message from Owen and Anna. Anna was very upset, insulted that she must look at wedding dresses on the two mannequins in the master bedroom which she had used during her life as a summer bedroom. And she wanted them removed immediately. At the time both mannequins were clothed in wedding dresses. Those were changed by the staff the next day.

The theory which is most accepted as an explanation for the phenomena in the mansion is that because the mansion was constructed with sheet lead it forms a non-conducting box through which the energy that is generated in the mansion by humans or machinery, and which enters though the unleaded roof, cannot escape. So when any strong-willed being—either human or spirit—focuses its energies, for some reason the additional energy held within the mansion facilitates the manifestation of things like the swaying wedding dress. The lead box theory tends to be supported by the fact that the day of the WRTA broadcast both the radio technicians and the T.V. cameramen experienced unaccustomed difficulties with their equipment."

Besides the spirits of Anna and Sylvester, the house is said to be haunted by their brother David. David died in a steamboat explosion and his body was stored in the icehouse (a dark section of the basement accessible only by a steep set of stairs on the outside and a rickety ladder on the inside) until the ground thawed enough to bury him. Julie and Brandon both related incidents of bumping, crashes and footsteps heard by guides in that section of the basement. Several of the guides believe that the noises are made by David's spirit.

There were many other incidents related to me of crashing sounds in rooms that were investigated. Nothing was ever broken or knocked over. There were other stories of footsteps on the main stairs and in several rooms. Doors slam on their own and smells have been reported throughout the mansion including the scent of Anna's favorite perfume.

There can be little doubt that Baker's mansion is indeed haunted—and haunted by more than one spirit. This house has truly earned it's reputation as one of America's most haunted homes. Anyone who takes the time to tour the charming mansion will find it's well worthwhile, and they just may see, hear or smell something that will be added to the growing catalogue of incidents that make up the lore of Baker's mansion.

I wanted to add a postscript to this story. While doing the research on Baker's mansion, I took several rolls of film at the house. I was aware that there have been many reports of mechanical malfunctions—the Life Magazine crew had difficulty in getting their equipment to work at the mansion—but I never thought that I'd experience any such trouble. Still, I took the precaution of taking along two new cameras which I had used several times before. Both cameras worked well, however many of the pictures I took at the mansion did not come out. Let me be clear about this, the camera took pictures, the film advanced (I used 35mm Kodak film purchased the same day I used it and new batteries also purchased the same day) and everything seemed to work fine. However, when the films were developed I received a note that one whole film of the mansion pictures did not turn out. There was absolutely nothing on the film. It was as if the pictures had never been taken. In fact, all of the pictures on that film were completely blank. Perhaps the ghosts of Baker's mansion have once again interfered with the world of the living by playing tricks with my cameras.

The Woman In Blue
(Saxton, Huntingdon County)

Sarah Reese had raised her family of four children in the small shack outside of Saxton, PA. She'd never been wealthy, but she had tried her best to raise her children well. Throughout her life, God and church had always been important, and she had made it a practice to go to church whenever she could. Sarah never learned to drive, so she either walked or relied upon friends and relatives to take her places. But she rarely had to walk because friends often stopped for her, particularly another church member, an elderly woman named Jesse Tate. As a result, Jesse and Sarah became friends.

That fall evening in the early 1970s, Sarah bustled about the shanty where she lived, hurrying to get ready before Jesse pulled up. They were going to revival at the local Pentecostal church. It was only the second night of revival and already there were few places left to sit. Jesse always hated to be late so Sarah tried to be ready when she pulled in, but tonight her arthritis was slowing her down. Her legs ached abysmally and she thought that she'd ask to be prayed for during the alter call.

Sarah pulled on her shabby dress coat against the cold rain and penetrating damp of the late fall night. It was only six o'clock and already it was fully dark. She seated herself in the rocking chair near the front window to wait on Jesse.

Car after car went by, but Jesse never pulled in. Church started at 7:30 p.m. and by 8 o'clock Sarah was very worried. An oppressive feeling pervaded her small shack. A cold wind touched her spine and she shuddered, pulling her coat close. The house was suddenly icy cold.

25

Sarah waited a little while longer, telling herself that perhaps Jesse had a flat tire or the car had broken down. But deep in her heart she could feel the crawling fear that something was seriously wrong.

At last she could wait no more, Sarah struggled up on arthritis-twisted legs and shambled toward the phone. She called Jesse's home first, and then she called the church. No one was in the office at night, but perhaps the church secretary would be there counting the offerings or working on the bulletins for the next service. There was no answer at the office so she put the phone down to think. She could not go out to look for Jesse herself, but perhaps Frank, her teenage son, could drive around and look. That thought cheered her slightly so she dialed the number of the house where Frank was visiting a friend.

Quickly she filled Frank in on her thoughts and "feelings." Through the years Frank had learned to take his mother's "feelings" seriously. She was often uncannily correct in her convictions. And as Frank grew older, he too was becoming more and more accurate in his own"feelings" and he had a very bad "feeling" about Jesse's disappearance.

First Frank tried the church parking lot. He drove around the lot looking for the old brown Ford sedan that Jesse drove. Next he drove the route she would have taken to pick up his mother for church. There was no sign of the Ford anywhere. Finally, he drove back to Jesse's house to see if she might have had an accident or had never even started her trip that night. At the house he found the door tightly locked, the old Ford gone from the driveway, and no sign of anyone stirring anywhere.

At last Frank went home to comfort his mother. But Sarah was very apprehensive. She went to her room and cried because of the overwhelming sadness that pervaded her. It was well after midnight when she tried Jesse's number for the last time. There was still no answer so she phoned the town police. Saxton was a very small town, but they had a decent-enough police force. Quickly she advised the officer who answered of the situation. But he was only slightly concerned and promised to have the duty officer, who had out the only police car, drive around and look for Jesse's sedan.

With a heavy feeling in her heart, Sarah said good night to Frank and went to bed. She was exhausted, but sleep came slowly that night. Once she thought she heard something near the house, but when she got up to look out the window there was no one about, only a sliver of moon shining down upon bare, wet tree branches.

It was late the next morning when Frank ran in, out of breath and screaming for his mother to call the police. He had been across the road at the little creek that ran through the area and there, hidden behind a screen of bushes, he had found Jesse's sedan. The driver's door was open and one of Jesse's dress shoes was still on the floor of the driver's side.

The police came quickly and confirmed that it looked like Jesse had been abducted. They found tire tracks that matched Jesse's car at the muddy end of the semicircular driveway that ran along the side of Sarah's house. It appeared to them that Jesse had begun to pull in the driveway and was either accosted or highjacked from there.

Sarah couldn't help shuddering. Things looked worse than she had ever imagined. She had thought that perhaps Jesse had an accident or a heart attack, but who would kidnap an old woman who just barely managed to live on her Social Security from month to month?

A cold, slow drizzle began shortly before lunch, and that hampered the police search. They tramped through the woods for a while but, finding no further clues, began to suspect that Jesse must have been transferred from one car to another.

During the following week, Sarah lived in agonizing suspense. She spoke daily with Jesse's daughters who were nearly frantic for word of their mother. By the week's end there was still no news of Jesse.

It was over the weekend that the snow began. It was a hard, dry snow that stung the skin and forced Sarah and her family to stay indoors. On Saturday Sarah's other son, Dan, came to visit and the topic turned to Jesse. The boys mulled over the idea of kidnapping, but Dan, who was twenty-two, scoffed at it. Kidnapping Jesse made no sense, and even if someone had been crazy enough to kidnap a penniless woman, where was the ransom note? No, something else had happened to her.

After lunch Dan and Frank went outdoors to chop wood for the night and to fill the coal buckets to feed the fires and keep them warm until morning. It was while chopping wood that Dan suddenly stopped and turned to Frank.

"Frank, did anyone ever search the old playhouse?" His voice was excited.

Frank stood so fast he nearly dropped a billet of wood on his toes. He knew exactly what Dan was talking about. Way back in the woods behind their home was an old shanty which had been falling apart even when they were children. It was well over two miles away, and they had

often slipped back there to play, over their parents' protests. The secret playhouse was a rabbit warren of rooms with doors hanging open,
gaping, glassless windows, and a roof that had partially fallen in. He
doubted if many people still remembered the old place. And it was far
enough away so that the police probably never saw it.

"I'll bet they didn't," he said excitedly. "Do you want to walk out
there?" Frank shuddered. He almost felt compelled to go the playhouse
now that Dan had reminded him of it.

"I think we should. Who knows, some nut may be living out
there, and with you and Mom here alone all week...." Dan left the sentence trail off, but Frank knew exactly what he meant.

Quickly they finished their chores, talking quietly all the while.
They decided not to tell their mother because they knew she'd veto the
idea. Instead they got their hunting rifles and told her that they were
going to a friend's to shoot target. They parked the car down the road
just out of sight of the house and slipped into the woods.

The snow stung their faces; a bitter wind pushed them forward.
Despite gloves and boots they were soon freezing. The further they went
into the woods, the stronger the cold feeling in Frank's heart grew, but
he knew better than to say anything to Dan. Dan had always scoffed at
their mother's "feelings" and Frank didn't blame him. He might have
doubted them too, except that apparently he inherited the strange trait
from their mom.

The old playhouse was located behind two hillocks that hid it
from view of the casual observer. It had been reclaimed by creeping vines
and the woods' vegetation to such an extent that even from the top of
the hills it was hard to tell that there a structure was there.

Dan and Frank paused behind a small copse of trees and decided
on a strategy. Who knew if there might not be some crazy man down
there right now, just waiting for someone to show up? Frank suggested
that Dan creep around the house and carefully peek into the gaping
windows from the front side while he did the same from the back.

Carefully, they crawled low through the snow and dead brush
to the house. Dan peeked through cracks and peeped above window sills
while trying to keep himself low. Frank worked his way just as carefully along the back. He peeked into the abandoned kitchen, but the only
dead thing there was a coon which was grotesquely bloated and distorted.

Frank was feeling silly, creeping along below window level and
peeking into the ruined, abandoned rooms, but then he raised his head

to peer into what had been a bedroom. His breath caught in his throat and he threw himself down hard into the snow to keep from screaming. Quickly he scrambled around the side of the shack and waved frantically for Dan's attention. Dan spotted him and crawl-walked toward him. Frank met him halfway.

"Did you see anyone?" Dan's voice sounded loud even though Frank knew that his brother was whispering.

"She's in there! Jesse's in there—dead!" Breath hissed out of Frank as he tried to maintain his voice. Frank turned and retraced his path. He did not want to see the ruined body of the old woman, but he made himself look again before he motioned to Dan. "In there."

Dan peered into the window and thought that he'd be sick. There was his mother's friend laying in a pile of rubble on the floor of the shack. Her legs were splayed out obscenely, her girdle, hosiery, and panties cruelly ripped away, and her dress and blue coat with ship's anchor buttons was twisted up above her hips. Her body was twisted cruelly, with her hands and arms wrapped around her head as though to ward off blows. He could see one side of her face, her blue eye staring up blankly, with ghastly wounds wreathing her throat and wrists, and her skull crushed on that side. Someone had raped her and mercilessly killed the old woman.

Frank and Dan made their way back to the copse of trees and then they both jumped up and ran. The cold wind stung their lungs, and pain caught at Frank's side, but he didn't stop until they broke through the trees near the road and made it to their car. Dan jumped into the driver's seat, digging for his keys, and Frank threw his rifle into the back seat as he slammed into the car.

The official police report stated what they already knew. Someone had accosted Jesse when she stopped to take the sharp turn into the driveway, probably with a gun, and forced her to drive across the road to the place where Frank had found the car. Then they walked back to the old playhouse where he had raped, sodomized, tortured, and then murdered the old woman. Although the police believed that whoever did this had to be local to know about the abandoned house, they never found the killer.

This was a tragic story that reminded people that even sleepy little towns are not immune to the violence of the times, but the story did not stop there.

In the summer following the murder, folks began to see an old

29

woman with a blue coat walking toward the Reese house. Friends of the family more than once were shocked to be approached by an old woman in a blue coat when they were getting in or out of their vehicles. The woman would draw close and then just vanish.

Late that summer a family friend had a fight with his wife and asked if he could sleep in his truck in their driveway. Sarah had agreed. In the middle of the night this friend claimed to have awakened with a cold feeling. It was in the middle of a late summer night, with a full moon that made it nearly daylight bright, and there, staring into the truck cab, was an old woman in a blue coat. She was startled when he woke up and just disappeared.

Another time, church friends were shaken when they stopped to pick up Sarah only to see Jesse walking down the driveway past them, and up the steps into Sarah's house. These people recognized Jesse well for they had known her for many years.

And yet once more, Frank and his girlfriend were necking in the driveway late one night when his girlfriend began to shriek. Frank turned and saw Jesse, in her blue coat, watching them. She turned when they made eye contact and walked up the steps to the porch. He scrambled out of the car and ran after her, but she was gone. There was a wooden banister around the high porch and the front door was locked, but still Jesse had simply disappeared.

Does Jesse haunt the place where she died? Many people seem to think so. I only know that when I drive by the Reese house, I often find myself expecting to see the specter of Jesse walking placidly down the driveway, her blue coat swinging, as she tries to get to her old friend.

*   * The families involved in this story have asked that their identities be protected.*

The Witch Of Rehmeyer's Hollow
(near Hanover, York County)

The story of the Witch of Rehmeyer's Hollow is unique to Pennsylvania. If the characters in this story were not possessed, they were at least obsessed by the unique blend of superstition and religion known as Hexeria. In the counties of York and Lancaster, Hexeria is still particularly strong. It is a combination of the Amish, Mennonite, and Judeo-Christian faiths combined with the strong Germanic and Dutch traditions.

Hexers were known variously as brauchers, powwowers, necromancers and witches. Hexeria still exists today, but it has been driven underground by law enforcement officials due in large part to this case. Hexeria is now a closely guarded secret, not spoken of to outsiders, but if you know the signs to look for and listen closely, you will find that it still exerts a control over certain people.

When reading this story, please bear in mind that there are small religious sects in these areas that do not follow "modern" ways. Children are only educated through the junior high grades. These sects run their own schools and are outside public control; they are distrustful of modern education, modern medicine, and modern attitudes. None of this is meant to denigrate these faiths, only to help the reader to understand how these ideas grew to prominence and why they continue to persist today.

In the early 1900s, sections of Pennsylvania were filled with hexers—witch doctors who combined Biblical teachings with superstition and witchcraft to come up with a system of faith healing for profit. Many of the local residents preferred the powwowers, as the hexers were called, over trained medical doctors. Local physicians could recount horror stories of needless sufferings and even deaths that were caused because of powwowers who undertook to heal diseases about

31

which they knew nothing. They would offer vials of foul-smelling mixtures for love potions, or a disgusting rubbing potion for tumors that needed medical attention. Powwowers often argued that they could cure diseases which medical doctors had given up on. They also cost much less than physicians, and powwowers didn't write prescriptions that had to be filled.

John H. Blymire was a fourth generation necromancer (powwower) who believed that he had "the power." John believed he should have been respected, feared, and loved, but his powers did little to help him gain either good health or respect. He was an unassuming little man, sickly his whole life, who often had to refer clients to more powerful powwowers for he could not heal stubborn illnesses.

As a young man, Blymire became convinced that he had been hexed by a more powerful witch. This belief consumed him, eating away at his precarious state of mind. He worked diligently at trying to find out who his persecutor was.

At one point John Blymire got married, but his wife divorced him when she suspected that he was planning to kill her. She was probably right. John mentioned to the people he worked with that he thought she was the one who had hexed him. He ignored the fact that if he was hexed, it had begun years before he had even met his wife.

John took a factory job in order to pay for his many visits to other local necromancers who "tried" for him, that is, tried to discern who had laid the hex on him. Many of them told him that it was someone he knew, someone he had once been close to, but none could name the person who was ruining John's life.

John was steeped in Hexeria lore and his bible was *The Long Lost Friend*, a book which area witches swore by. He collected himmelbriefs, letters containing Bible verses interwoven with words to ward off disasters from home, family, or self. All of this did not help lift the curse from John, though.

People who knew John testified he was a strange man, but he never entirely quit trying for other people since it brought in a small additional income. He would sometimes even try for people where he worked, but he rarely made any friends. Perhaps it seemed strange to others that John would be drawn to a fifteen-year-old boy, John Curry, and that Curry was equally enamored of Blymire, but history proved that theirs was a bond of need.

John Curry lived a miserable existence, beaten by an alcoholic stepfather. Barely able to gain any attention from his over-worked, abused mother, Curry needed the attention that Blymire showered on the boy. In turn, Blymire needed to be put on a pedestal. As a braucher or powwower he should have commanded respect, but John Blymire never had. Blymire enjoyed the boy's adoration, and they became inseparable.

The third member of the fatal trio was seventeen-year-old Wilbert Hess. His brother first brought Curry and Blymire to the Hess farm. The Hesses were good Pennsylvania Dutch who believed strongly in their local braucher. In each room of the Hess house was a himmel-brief juxtaposed with a picture of Christ to maximize the himmel-brief's power. The Hesses were impressed that their son had brought home a fourth-generation braucher who should have been very powerful.

During one of Blymire and Curry's initial visits, Blymire told the Hess family about his curse. The Hesses commiserated with Blymire's account of his search for his hexer. They, too, had been recently hexed. Mrs. Hess in particular was upset because she could not find out who her tormentor was.

Blymire's friendship with the family grew rapidly, and one evening when he was tried for by yet another braucher named Mrs. Nell, Blymire finally found the solution not only to his hexing, but to the Hess hexing as well. Mrs. Nell was a well-known and very powerful necromancer. Her fame had spread throughout the counties for many years. Blymire never doubted it when she told him that he had been cursed by Nelson Rehmeyer who was himself a powerfully feared braucher whom Blymire had worked for as a youth.

Blymire and Curry made their way from Mrs. Nell's to the Hess farm with the news. Blymire explained that as a boy he had worked for the fearsome, self-proclaimed witch on his farm. He had been terrified when Rehmeyer had gone into the room under the kitchen through its trap door in the floor. Blymire knew, even in his youth, that Rehmeyer practiced both white and black magic. He could not understand why Rehmeyer would curse him, but he knew in his soul that it must be true.

Blymire also knew that in order to lift the spell he would have to get a lock of Rehmeyer's hair and his book of magic spells. He would have to bury the hair eight feet deep and burn the book to break the powerful magic. He told all of this to the Hess family who now believed they were also under a Rehmeyer spell.

Blymire, Curry, and Wilbert Hess agreed to go to the Rehmeyer farm to feel things out. They later said that they roused Rehmeyer from his bed and that he willingly let them in for a while. Eventually he even asked them to stay the night, which they did. They never worked up enough nerve to get either the hair or the book from its cubby hole under the floor.

On the second evening, one of the Hess boys again drove the three men out and dropped them off near Rehmeyer's hollow where the old witch lived alone. (His wife and two daughters lived in another house further down the hollow because, by their own admission, Rehmeyer was hard to live with.) This time the trio jumped the old man, wrestled him to the ground, then bludgeoned him to death with a length of wood from the kitchen wood box.

Despite the fact that the curse supposedly had been lifted by the death of witch Rehmeyer, Blymeyer and Hess did not see their luck change for they were quickly apprehended. Curry, too, was arrested and along with his partners confessed to the brutal murder of the old man. In their minds, Rehmeyer's death was not really a murder. After all they had to break the curse against them somehow.

The three were tried separately and the judge and prosecutor refused to allow any mention of the powwowers, necromancy, hexing, or of Blymeyer and Rehmeyer's unusual occupation to surface in court. Instead the court preferred to focus on the fact that the three men took a small amount of money from the house—though it was ridiculous to believe that these three hex-infested men robbed and murdered a reputedly powerful witch for ninety-seven pennies each.

The court could not fathom that three men could spend so much time chased by imagined spirits and hexes. Reason demanded that murder had to be committed for some profit. Even when Blymeyer's attorney brought forth a medical witness, who stated that Blymeyer had the mentality of a child of eight, it was impossible for the court to allow Hexeria to surface.

In further testimony it was suggested that Blymeyer could not be held responsible for his acts because his mind had been stunted by his close association with powwowing as a child. None of this washed with the court or the jury. Blymeyer and his cohorts were all found guilty and sentenced.

But the strange story behind the murder spread around the world as reporters from all across the United States and Europe poured into the small town of York. Some reporters took on the highbrow attitude that York was filled with dumb Dutchmen and this greatly hurt the image of York County.

No matter the reason for the murder of Rehmeyer, he was still dead. But—as some have whispered—he may not be gone. Since that November night in 1928, Rehmeyer has been sighted in his home and in the hollow where he lived, worked and practiced his magic both white and black.

Little Boy Lost
(Ganister, Blair County)

Above the little village of Ganister, in Pennsylvania, there was a farm in the 1850s. It was not much more than a plot of land where the family could grow what they needed, but to the man who settled it, it was everything. The house sat high on the hillside. Below it was a crude barn with a chicken coop tacked on the far side nearest the woods. Below the coop was a small stream that forked just beyond the barn to make a small island of land during dry years.

The family had several children, the eldest of which was a ten-year-old boy. His main chore each day was to gather the eggs and feed the hens morning and night. At first he didn't complain about the job, but after a short while he started to put it off. To his parents it was not just the normal forgetfulness of boyhood, but rather a dread of going down to the coop alone. He often waited until he would see his father go down to milk the cow or slop the hogs. He would even lie if it was growing dark and the hens were not yet fed.

The boy's father and he had several conversations about responsibility, and the boy had promised that he would not lie about feeding the hens anymore. Still, as the summer dragged on he seemed to grow more and more fearful of going down to the barn alone. With the coming of fall the days shortened; the boy was now forced to go down near dusk to feed the hens after school.

He tried to tell his parents why he hated going down, but he just didn't know the words. It was scary. There was something down there that frightened him, but he could not explain it and his parents were not the type to accept vague feelings as fact. By late fall, his parents were just about at the end of their ropes. Feeding the hens was not a hard job, but their son needed to learn about responsibility and work so they insisted that he continue doing it.

When the boy's father heard at supper one night that his son had not yet fed the birds and gathered the eggs, he was furious.

"Get down there right now!" his father roared, kicking back his own chair.

The boy was almost in tears. "Don't make me go," he cried.

The fear in his son's eyes softened the man's tone. "I'll wait for you on the porch and watch you, how's that?"

It wasn't what the boy really wanted, but it was better than nothing so he picked up the granite basin his mother used to collect eggs and shambled off. He checked several times to be sure that his dad still stood on the porch before he disappeared around the edge of the barn.

His father followed his progress mentally. There was the sound of the coop door snapping shut, and the sound of grain being poured into the basin. He heard the door thump open again as the boy stepped into the chicken yard, calling the birds. He heard the normal excited clucking that accompanied feeding time. Suddenly, he heard the birds give out frightened squawks as they fluttered about on inefficient wings. He heard his son let out a scream that was instantly cut off.

He yelled for his wife to get his gun and took off down the hill. As he ran, there was a metallic thunk from near the stream. He ran even faster, but he saw nothing.

He rounded the corner and skidded to a stop in front of the coop. There was a pile of spilled grain near the door, but no boy. He raced back around the barn and fumbled lighting the lantern. Even with the light from the large lamp, he saw nothing out of the ordinary. He called for his son, and his wife walked back and forth yelling, too, but there was no reply.

He began walking along the stream looking for the prints of something—human, animal...something. He saw nothing. As he neared the little island, the lantern light glinted off of the blue granite of the egg basin.

They searched all night but they found nothing else. Finally the farmer had to saddle up a horse and ride into Ganister for help. Others joined the search, but the child was gone.

Folks whispered that Indians, wild cats, bears, even gypsies had stolen the boy, but none of the explanations were reasonable. There had been no Indians or gypsies in the area for years, and no mauled carcass ever was found to prove that an animal was responsible.

There have been stories similar to this one from all over the state, and perhaps the most frightening aspect of them all is that they are true enigmas because none of the children have ever been found.

If there is one thing that I have learned by having listened to the haunted tales of Pennsylvania, it is that adults should listen to children and their fears. Perhaps it is because they have not yet learned to control their imaginations, or perhaps it is because they still have faith, but children seem to often know that something bad is afoot before the adults do. The children may not be able to tell adults in clinical terms what is wrong, but believe them or you may be sorry that you didn't.

The Monster Of Broad Top
(Broad Top City, Huntingdon County)

Monsters have been stalking us since the beginning of time— they are a common theme among the human race. There are sea monsters such as the ones in Loch Ness and Lake Champlain; big hairy ones like the Sasquach and Abominable Snowman; and even the crocodile man of the Florida Everglades. Monsters come in all kinds.

Their shapes, sizes, and characteristics are determined by the minds of the seers and sometimes by nature itself. Some monsters have turned out to be unidentified but natural species which scientists are only now categorizing. Others are more mysterious and we can speculate about them for a long time.

Monsters are often in the eye of the beholder. I once read a description of a monster a 15th century Englishman saw in Pennsylvania. This man was writing a report to the English king, and the monster he described was truly horrible. He said that it was as huge as a healthy young tree, and thicker than a man's waist. It made a fierce sound that numbed the human brain. It was a creature that had no legs and yet it moved faster than a human could. It was known to fasten itself to a nursing woman's breast while she slept or to steal and eat young children. This creature was so hideous that its description was more than a paragraph long. What was this creature? It was a rattlesnake.... I have always harkened back to that description of a snake when I heard people talk about the monsters indigenous to their local areas. I thought that they were all exaggerating...but that was before I heard of the monster of the Broad Top.

In the winter of the 1984 I married and moved to a rural area of south/central Pennsylvania known as Waterfall. Soon after moving there I learned that the area atop the mountain that surrounded the valley where Waterfall lay was known as the Broad Top. It's called that because it is actually a broad spot atop the mountain range where a small settlement was built. Broad Top, I soon found out, was the focus for various mysterious activities. From the people of Broad Top I first heard of Tommyknockers, small beings who mined the local coal mines at night, and who knocked upon the stone walls of the mines if there was the danger of a cave in for the miners.

I also found out that there was a large slithering creature that lived in the woods surrounding the Broad Top. This snakelike creature was described as being approximately 20 feet long with a girth about half the thickness of a telephone pole. Hunters claimed to have come upon it the local woods actually trying to swallow a young deer. Others have claimed that it attacked cars or even hunters.

In the fall of 1987 I met a woman I'll call Judy Parks. She and I struck up a fast friendship. We had known each other a couple months when I brought up the subject of hunting season. During buck hunting season companies shut down for the first day, the local schools have a two-day holiday, and even hospitals are manned with skeleton crews so that the doctors can hunt. It is attended with all the pep and joy of Thanksgiving itself, so mentioning that my husband had to work on the first day of buck season was a natural thing.

Judy shuddered at my mentioning the season. This surprised me because she was an avid hunter herself as the various trophies on her walls attested. "I'm not going this year. Pop wanted me to go out with him, but I just can't make myself do it."

"Don't you like hunting anymore?" I queried.

Judy screwed up her expressive face and brushed back her carroty hair. She eyed me oddly, as though I had touched a nerve with her. "I just don't want to go hunting on Broad Top."

Various ideas ran through my mind. Was game scarce? Were careless hunters hunting the area? Was the terrain too rugged and difficult to climb? I asked her those questions, but she seemed to withdraw. At last I changed the subject and we moved on to talk about something else.

Without warning Judy brought the conversation back to hunting the Broad Top. "I'll tell you something if you promise not to laugh," she said. Her voice and her eyes showed her nervousness.

I quickly gave my promise. I rarely find things that upset my friends funny.

Taking a deep breath, Judy stared past me to the window and began. "About four years ago Dad, Jim (her husband), and I went hunting on dad's farm up on Broad Top for the first day of buck season. Jim and I had scouted the place earlier and had built a stand back in the trees beyond the last corn field. We knew that every night the deer just polluted that field trying to eat the last of the corn stalks and the bits of corn the picker had missed. Dad had his stand off to our right and further back in, where their trail led back toward a small stream. We figured that we'd get into our stands before dawn and then if we heard Dad shoot or if he heard us shoot it would warn the other one to watch the trail and field for more deer.

"We saw a few does and Jim saw one buck but he was too far off for a clean shot and so we let him go. By late afternoon we were all stiff and cold. I was getting really disgusted with the whole thing. I told the guys that I was going back to the house and help Mom get supper on. When I left them, Dad was heading back up the deer trail to try another place further back in the woods.

"Jim came back about dusk, but Dad was still out there. He knew better than to stay in the woods after dark. First of all you can't shoot anything after sunset, and secondly you're likely to get shot. When Dad didn't get back, we started getting worried. There are been shots from the direction he'd gone earlier in the day. We couldn't help worrying that he might have been shot.

"Jim and I got flashlights and started back across the fields to look for Dad. We hadn't gone far when we heard a crashing in the bushes to our left. We flashed the lights in that direction and there was Dad staggering toward us for all he was worth. His face was a pasty white, and he had one hand pressed against his chest. I thought he had a heart attack.

"Jim and I got Dad back home quick. He refused to let us take him to the hospital, but after he had rested he told Jim and I not to go back to our stand anymore. His face was still that funny pasty color and he shook when he tried to pick up his cup. He finally told us that he'd seen the monster. We all knew what he meant; hunters have been coming out of the hills for years with stories of that monster. He said that it was draped over some rocks and was nearly 20 feet long. It was a scaly dirty tan color with variegated markings. It was swallowing a rabbit when he stumbled across it. It swallowed it in a second and then took off fast slithering toward him. He had taken off running. The last thing he remembered was falling over a pile of brambles and smacking his head.

"When he woke up it was dark and he was alone, thank God!"

Judy shivered as she finally shifted her gaze back to me. "You may not believe it but Dad did see that thing, whatever it is."

I didn't call her a liar, but I had to wonder at a snake-creature that did not hibernate in the winter. In late November Pennsylvania is usually one very cold place.

Later I heard others describe seeing the snake-creature. One old couple came from a drive over Broad Top mountain with a story of seeing the creature laying in the road, stretched all the way across both lanes and its head over the berm. They claimed to have stopped their car to watch it cross because it was so thick that they were afraid that running over the creature would damage the car. In coloring and size it resembled closely the thing Judy's dad had seen, and this couple had been so shaken by the experience that they reported it to the local police.

Interestingly, later that same day another man reported seeing the same thing slithering across the road again.

I do not know if the creature of Broad Top is only a very large snake (an escaped python perhaps?), or even a practical joke that someone plays. I have never seen it myself, so I can only pass on the story. But for those who have seen it, Broad Top has become a very scary place. If you go there, be sure to be very careful....

The White Lady Of Buckhorn
(Buckhorn Mountain, Cambria County at the border of Blair County)

Like so many stories of Pennsylvania, the White Lady of Buckhorn has mellowed into a local legend. Forgotten are the real names of those involved, and even the time frame changes. The white woman has been said to have died variously in a buggy accident or in a car accident depending upon who tells the tale. I have chosen one version and have given the characters names, although the names of the real people involved have long been forgotten. Despite the lack of detail every so often there is a spurt of sightings that drift down from Buckhorn Mountain to keep the old story alive. The white woman has frightened many young couples over the years and has been blamed for a few accidents, too.

1932

Marcy Martin set a little feathered cap atop her head at a pert angle, and nodded at the reflection in her bedroom mirror. She looked pretty in her white dress suit and matching cap

41

adorned with small feathers along the side. She glanced at her bedside clock and sighed. She still had time to kill until she was to meet Danny in the woods beside her home.

Around her the house made little settling sounds. She could hear her father's heavy snoring, and the squeal of her brother's mattress as he turned over in the next room. Her heart was beating hard because in a few moments she would be leaving them all behind—perhaps for good.

Marcy sat quietly in the rocking chair and touched her long blond hair. She had done it carefully in a sweeping bun to be sure that not one strand would come loose.

She glanced at the clock again and closed her eyes trying to control her breathing. She had to steel herself for the next few minutes of activity.

It was time. She stood up and reached out for her purse beside her on the bed. She opened it up and felt in the small pocket for the handkerchief that she had tucked in there in a wadded up ball. With fingers that shook slightly, she opened the hankie and took out the engagement ring it held. The ring was old and slightly tarnished. It was of gold, with one small stone that Danny had told her was a real diamond. She put the ring on her third finger and snapped her purse shut.

Danny would be waiting for her by now so she had to hurry. She padded to her night stand and turned out the small light. In the darkness she picked up her small suitcase and tucked her shoes under her arm. She took one last look at her old bedroom laying warm and familiar in the soft shadows. She loved the room so much and her throat hurt as she gently shut the door on her childhood.

Marcy quietly negotiated the hall and the narrow stairs without a noise. Then suddenly she bumped into the chair her mother had left pulled over near the back door.

Biting back the pain that sang up her leg from her shin, she stood frozen in the darkness, waiting. There was no sound from above. After what seemed a long time, Marcy realized that she was holding her breath and left it out in a low sigh. Her heart was beating furiously now.

Quietly she set down her case, shoes, and purse before she lifted and moved the chair from the doorway. Then she felt for the lock and gingerly twisted it open—but the bolt shot back like gunfire; she bit her lip. Still she heard no sounds from upstairs so she pulled it open, picked up her bags and stepped out onto the porch. She eased the door shut, leaving it unlocked.

The night air was cool against her hot skin. She could feel the rough wood flooring of the porch against her stockinged feet, and set her shoes down. They were her first pair of real lady's shoes. Black heels with a smart bow across the toe. She had loved them at first sight, but her mother had to argue with her father to get them for her.

Marcy's thoughts turned briefly to her father asleep in the house. He would be furious with her for running away. He treated her like such a baby; her could not accept that she had gown up. She was a woman now, and she wanted to marry Danny. For a second she felt a twinge of regret about sneaking off. What if her father never forgave her? What if he never allowed her family to speak to her again? In that moment the possibilities loomed frightfully before her, but then she saw the flash of Danny's light on the wooded path, and her thoughts turned to him.

The light bobbed in the darkness for a few steps, then winked out as Danny stepped into the back yard. The moon was shining nearly full. He steered his way through the toys her younger brothers and sisters had left laying in the pale light.

Danny met her at the bottom of the steps, and took her case. He leaned down to kiss her deeply then whispered, "I love you."

Her heart soared. Marcy was suddenly brave. She would do anything for Danny, even face her father's wrath.

Danny took her elbow with his free hand, leading her around toward the front. Marcy hesitated. He was supposed to be parked at the other end of the woods path where her father would not hear Dan's old Model-T start up. Dan sensed her hesitation.

"I had to park 'round front," he whispered. "It's too wet back there." He indicated the woods path with a toss of his fair head. "I was afraid that we'd get swamped. We're parked down the road a little way."

When they got around to the front, Marcy picked up the pace, running toward the old car in the shadows down the road. Dan stayed close beside her until they reached the car. Quickly he stowed the small suitcase in the back beside his own bag, and closed the door for Marcy.

Dan hurriedly cranked the car until it turned over. He rushed around, folding his lanky frame behind the steering wheel, and started the car before it cut out on him. They had made it. Now nothing would stop them. They would drive over the county line and get married at a Justice-of-the-Peace in the morning.

The car gave out a small, choked pop of backfire as Dan eased it into gear. Dan didn't hesitate, he pulled out onto the dirt road and started for the county line. They were on their way.

Now he risked a glance at Marcy in the glow of the moonlight. She looked beautiful, her dark eyes glowed with excitement and her hair, pinned neatly up, made her look like a child playing dress up. She was so small and lovely that his heart almost burst with joy. He reached over and took her hand. His fingers felt the warm, hard circle of the engagement ring he had given her, and he smiled, rubbing it with his thumb.

"You're finally wearing it."

Marcy offered him a smile. "I'll never take it off again." Her eyes promised a wonderful future, and Dan was caught up in the moment and his driving.

He never noticed the old truck until the lights were blazing in on them.

"What's wrong with that guy?" he muttered, releasing Marcy's hand to gain better control of the wheel.

Suddenly the driver began honking his horn furiously, and trying to force his way around the car on the narrow mountain track. Marcy whirled around in her seat to look. She grabbed Danny's arm.

"That's my father!" she cried in a trembling voice.

A look of fear haunted her eyes, and Dan stepped on the accelerator. He'd be damned if Mr. Martin was going to keep them apart now. His mind filled with thoughts of their life that he'd loose if they were caught. He pushed on the gas pedal harder.

"Slow down. You're going too fast." Marcy was gripping the dash and holding on in fear.

The old car careened along as it bumped up the side of Buckhorn Mountain. Behind them, the truck kept pace thundering angrily on the horn and flashing its lights.

At the top of the mountain, Dan was sure they'd make it. His car was in better shape than the old truck. He applied his foot to the gas petal even harder and the car sped on. Now he was forced to brake briefly for the hazardous turns that twisted down the mountain side. The road sped by in a blur, and Marcy was deathly quiet. He risked a glance at Marcy, her face shone pale and tight in the uncertain light.

Grimly, Dan bit his lip and applied the brakes again. He had driven this old road many times, and he knew that a series of dangerous curves lay just ahead. The brakes bit in; the car jerked with the force of his foot stomping down. The car was not slowing fast enough. Within a second the sickening realization hit him, they'd never make it through the curves if they didn't slow down.

Behind him the truck had dropped back. Dan barely even noticed. All of his energy was concentrated on slowing the car before they hit the curves. His foot worked the brake desperately, but the car didn't slow enough. The car left the road, becoming airborne, as it failed to make the curve. He heard Marcy's terrified scream, then there was a sickening crash.

Dan woke up in the hospital days later. His body was wracked with pain, and he could not move his arms. It took him a while to find out what all had happened, and why he was there. His mind had been numbed by the drugs and the pain, but he finally remembered Marcy's pinched, little face and her screams as the car flew through space.

No one would answer him at first when he questioned them about Marcy. He didn't need their answers. Their pitiful stares and false smiles told him that she was dead. He had killed her on that mountain road as they had tried to elope.

The stories about the ghost of a young woman appearing in cars along the Buckhorn Mountain on Rt. 36 between Altoona and Ashville started shortly after the accident. Young couples driving over the mountain late at night would suddenly realize that there was someone else in their car. They would turn to find a lovely young woman in a white dress sitting there, staring. She'd look at the driver until he turned, then she'd sigh and disappear.

Soon people began saying that it was Marcy looking for Dan. Dan heard the tales but he could never bring himself to drive that mountain again. He didn't want to see her pinched little face, or the pained look in her eyes when she realized that they would never be together now.

Even today couples sometimes report seeing the White Lady of Buckhorn in their cars, and she had even been blamed for several accidents along the Buckhorn.

Through the years the details of the elopement have been lost; some folks claim that the young couple weren't in a car but rather in a buggy. Still the particulars are always the same, and the hapless young woman died along that mountain road one night on the way to her wedding. People have been sighting her for many years, and still claim to see her yet today.

Maggie Graeme's Calling
(Blair County)

E tta Colins loved the little cabin she had been given as part of her salary at the Detoxification Center where she now worked. Etta thought that perhaps she was one of the luckiest people alive. Six years ago she had been addicted to drugs and alcohol, had been a prostitute, and had wanted to die—but that was before she had met Clinton Marks. Marks was a millionaire who had lost his own son to drugs and alcohol. His loss had made Marks compassionate toward those who were also addicted. And so he had started a center where others addicted, as his son had been, could get help. Etta had been lucky enough to get placed there after her suicide attempt.

At the Drug & Alcohol Rehabilitation Center, Etta fought her demons. She spent time first as a client, then as a ward, and finally as an assistant counselor at the center. She became friends with Marks who watched over the facility himself. Now he had started a Detoxification Center for teens, and he offered Etta a job as a counselor at the new facility. It was a way for her to get back into the world, and a way to pay back a dear friend who had given her back her life.

Etta couldn't believe how beautiful the little cabin Clinton Marks had loaned her was. She could see only good things in her future now. In fact, she was excited that day as she began setting things to rights in the cabin. By next weekend she would be hosting some of Marks's other hand-picked counselors when they came to tour the facility that was about to open. It was a far cry from the world she had once known.

The cabin was small, only two rooms with a bath, but it suited her needs. She had accumulated very little over the years so it took her only a little while to get unpacked. By evening she was as settled as she would ever get, and as she fixed herself a simple supper, she couldn't help humming.

While she ate supper the phone rang and Etta jumped up to get it. Few people knew where she was, only Clinton, a few rehabilitation friends, and her folks. It would probably be Clinton settling the last minute details about the other counselors arrival.

"Is Janet there?" The voice on the other end of the line was definitely feminine, but something about it sent a chill through Etta's spine.

"No. Wait! Do you mean Janet Ramsey?" Etta referred to one of the counselors Clinton Marks was sending up. "She's not here. She won't be here for a couple days yet. Can I take a message for her?" Etta couldn't explain it but she was suddenly cold, and that faraway woman's voice frightened her.

"Tell her that Maggie Graeme is calling." The phone went dead.

Etta was left holding a silent receiver. Quickly she jotted down the name. She hoped that whoever Maggie Graeme was, she would not call again. That woman gave her the willies.

Etta's hopes were in vain for the next evening at about six o'clock the phone rang and immediately Etta recognized the faraway voice of Maggie Graeme.

"I'm sorry, but Janet is not here. She won't be here until Tuesday." Etta could feel shivers creep up her back.

"I want to speak to Janet." The woman didn't seem to understand.

"I'm sorry, she won't be here until Tuesday." It took all of Etta's control to keep from dropping the receiver.

"I need to talk to Janet. Tell her Maggie Graeme is calling." Again the phone went dead.

The next night the call came again.

"Is Janet there?"

Etta felt panic grip her stomach. "I told you she won't be here until Tuesday ."

"I have to tell you something about her. Can I come see you?" The woman's voice seemed to send chills through Etta.

"I don't think so. I'll tell Janet you called." Before Etta finished talking she knew that the line was dead once again.

On the next night the phone rang at the same time and Etta would not have answered it if she had not promised Clinton that she'd be responsible for the center until the other counselors arrived.

"I must tell you something about Janet," the far-off voice said.

"What do you want to tell me?" Etta fought to keep her voice from cracking.

"I must see you first." Why was this woman's voice so insistent?

"You can just tell me. I don't know you."

"I'm Maggie Graeme. Janet knows me." The line fell silent and Etta hung up.

Two more times, each around six o'clock, Etta answered the phone only to find the eerie voice of Maggie Graeme on the other end. The last call ended with Maggie saying that she'd come on the night Janet arrived. Etta tried to argue but the line went dead and she was left shivering with fear.

On Tuesday the other counselors arrived in a flurry of baggage, and there was excited chatter as Etta took them on a tour. Then they cooked a noon meal in the large facility's kitchen. While they were eating, Etta thought of the strange phone calls she had been getting.

"Janet," she called to the woman at the other end of the table. "You've been getting some phone calls here already."

Janet, a twenty-four-year old woman who had been clean of drugs for nearly three years, turned to look at her quizzically. "What? I couldn't have. I didn't even know the number for this place until Clinton gave me my papers this morning. I haven't had time to give it to anyone—even my mother."

A shiver passed over Etta, but she thought of that cool voice and persisted. She certainly was not hallucinating. "Well, someone's been calling every day and asking for you, so you must have given someone the number."

Janet shook her head. "Did they leave a name?"

Etta didn't need to refer to the memo she had written the first night; she would never forget that voice saying, "Tell her Maggie Graeme is calling."

"It was a woman named Maggie Graeme..." Etta paused, seeing Janet blanch at the mention of that name.

"That's impossible," Janet exploded, jumping up and nearly knocking over her chair.

Now Etta was uncertain if she should persist. The other counselors were staring at them. Still, she had taken those calls. "Well that's what she said. She always called around six o'clock in the evening and asked for you specifically. She said, 'I need to talk to Janet. Tell her Maggie Graeme is calling.' Then in some of the other calls she said she wanted to talk to me about you. I told her I didn't want to, but she said she'd be here tonight."

"Maggie Graeme?" Janet was holding one hand against her chest and Etta could see agitation in her huge eyes. "Maggie Graeme is dead!"

Etta was confused. "I'm sorry. She must have called before she died."

Janet shook her head. Her breathing was rapid and Etta was beginning to fear the girl would faint. "Maggie died over a week ago in a car accident. She was my mother's friend and they were in the accident around six o'clock in the evening. My mom's fine, but Maggie died..." Her voice trailed off and Etta tried to suppress the shudder that shook her.

She tried to stop the words that came to her bloodless lips, but they slipped out. "She said she'd be here tonight...."

That night Etta and Janet stayed far away from the cabin and the facility. The others slept in the facility and said that nothing happened. But Etta and Janet felt that, if Maggie Graeme came, it would have been to the cabin.

On Wednesday morning Etta called Clinton and asked if she could move to another cabin. He agreed but when he asked why, Etta refused to say. It was only a couple years later that she was able to tell him about the calls she had received in the cabin... calls that she believed were placed from Maggie Graeme's grave.

* The names of those involved have been changed because several of those involved felt that their professional standing would be jeopardized if their part in this story came out.

The Legend Of Captain Jack
(The Shirleysburg area, Huntingdon, County)

In 1750, one of the earliest settlers of the Shirleysburg area of Huntingdon County was a fellow known as Captain Jack. Captain Jack was something of an enigma from the very first when he refused to let anyone know his full name. Rumors went around that he was British royalty, that he was related to the royal family, that perhaps he was a bastard son or a shamed son of a royal person, but no one ever knew for sure just who Captain Jack had been.

If people wondered about Jack's history, they didn't have to worry about his present. He had come from the East with a wife, a small son and a daughter. Jack was a devoted family man and he spent a great deal of his time providing for his family. While he was out hunting one afternoon in 1752, his family was attacked by Indians. Jack returned to find the cabin was in flames and the bodies of his family laid on the ground where they had been mutilated.

Some say that Jack went mad on that day. The history books say that he dedicated himself to the extermination of the natives after that. Stories were told of Jack saving settlers and appearing from nowhere to warn local folks of Indian attacks. Many credited Jack with saving their lives.

When Chief Pontiac began his rebellion, the settlers formed a group and chose Jack as their leader. Jack earned a reputation for his boldness and cunning, risking his life time after time, doing whatever was necessary to protect his charges. He never faltered in his single-minded determination to save others from the fate that befell his own family.

Jack formed a group of rangers who dressed in Indian garb. They studied the ways of their enemies and often lived like the native people. Under Captain Jack's command, a deal was forged with the British who supplied them with food stuffs, powder and weapons. In exchange, Jack and his rangers protected British colonies; providing safe passage for British troops traveling between forts.

With time, Captain Jack became a local legend. He was also known as "The Wild Hunter of the Juniata," "The Half Indian," "Black Rifle," and "the Black Hunter." Eventually Captain Jack faded from history as easily as he had floated in. Rumors and theories abound, but no one is sure whatever happened to the mysterious Captain Jack.

There is one legend that says he finally settled in a community at the foot of the mountain which still bears his name (Jack's Mountain). For years settlers in town told tales of seeing his ghostly spirit wandering the mountains every night. Others claimed that the old mountain man was often seen relaxing on the rocks near the spring where he had loved to sit so much in life.

The mystery surrounding Captain Jack makes him one of Pennsylvania's most romantic characters, and even his death is shrouded in the mystery of where and why his spirit still roams.

"It's Not For Sale!"
(Blair County)

The car in this story belongs to my brother so I am one of the witnesses to what the car tried to do to him. Terry is a sensible man, not given to imagining things. In the beginning he did not fear the car, but now he is so frightened of it and of what it wants to do, that he keeps it housed in a locked garage. Often when people find out that he has this car in storage they will ask about buying it, but even when he lost his job and was completely broke and had to scrounge for money to pay the garage rent, he told those who offered to take the car, "It's not for sale." After you read this story you will know why.

51

W hen Terry saw the car on the lot of the used car dealer, he knew that he would have that car. It was a cherry-red 1968 Mustang coupe and it was in great condition. It was not the type of car Terry had gone to the lot to look for—with five children he had planned to buy a big car—but it was beautiful and he fell in love with it.

For the first few weeks Terry showed the car off to his family and friends. Everyone smiled indulgently about the little car filled to bursting with children and predicted that Terry would not keep the car long. He surprised everyone, though, when he still had the car several months later as winter began.

A 1968 Mustang coupe was not the best car for a man to drive when he had to travel nearly twenty miles every day to work. Still, Terry insisted that the car did well in the snow and ice. He was actually very proud of it. In fact, he often boasted about its abilities.

Terry is a very kind, giving man and he often gives away the things he loves most. Perhaps that was why he promised the car to his fifteen-year-old sister, Georgette, when she grew up. He told her that he'd maintain the car until she was old enough to take on the responsibility of insurance and maintaining the vehicle. She was thrilled with the gift for she also had an affinity for the car. Having been born in 1968 herself she looked upon the car as some sort of friend.

Things went well with the little red car for nearly a year, but then there was some repair work being done on the road Terry took to work. He was forced to detour around the shorter mountain and take a road that ran through the town of Hollidaysburg, PA. This detour also led him through a place where the road literally ran through a graveyard on Route 22 East from Frankstown to Geeseytown. Years ago the state had moved some graves from the center of a local graveyard, built retaining walls and guardrails to protect the other graves from shifting with time, and had run a major road right through the old cemetery.

Terry didn't think anything about the detour except that it would cost him time. That is until the first morning he took that route. The car responded to Terry's control just as it always had until he hit the stretch of road that ran through the cemetery. Suddenly, he later related, he thought that he had hit an ice patch. The car seemed to slide around on its own accord and the wheel jerked around in his hand. Desperately, Terry saw the cement retaining wall loom up before him.

With a tremendous effort Terry jerked the wheel to the left and brought the car to a stop just inches from the wall. He eased the vehicle back into the traffic lane and proceeded only a few feet until he could get past the retaining walls. He stopped and shakingly lit a cigarette. He had never been so close to death in his life.

Terry tried to tell himself that the car had skidded, but somehow that didn't seem right. He'd been driving for nearly twenty years and he knew how a skid felt, but this had been different. His mind whispered that someone had jerked the wheel from his grip, but of course that was ridiculous. Perhaps, he thought, there was something wrong with the steering column.

That evening Terry passed through the cemetery without incident and this reinforced his idea that it had either been ice or a fault with the steering. By the time Terry reached his home he was sure that the steering mechanism worked fine.

In the morning Terry bundled up and began his daily trip to work. He was more cautious as he drove, fearing the smooth icy patches that had formed over night. He was nearly crawling along by the time he reached the cemetery. He eased into the cemetery grounds and suddenly the steering wheel jerked from his hands once again.

He fought it, but the wheel twisted around until he saw the cemetery retaining wall filling his windshield once more. He tapped the brakes, fearing that he'd spin out of control on the ice if he jammed his foot down too hard. The brakes did not respond. Instead the car seemed to accelerate and he knew that he was going to hit the wall. Desperately he brought his foot down hard on the brake, stomping instead of pumping. The car lurched forward and then jerked to a standstill only inches from the wall. Terry quickly righted the vehicle and once again pulled forward until he could stop where he had the day before. What had happened?

Terry refused to admit what he really thought. Instead he told his brother that night that there was something wrong with the steering. Together they tore the entire thing apart. Both men were excellent mechanics, but Terry's brother, Jerry, was better than most professionals. He had an ability with vehicles that bordered on being a God-given gift.

After two days of working and reworking things, Jerry had to admit that there was nothing wrong mechanically with the car. He had checked everything possible. He now reconnected the steering and took the little, red car out for a ride himself. Terry sat in the passenger's seat, and as they rode the back roads without incident, he suggested that they take a route that would lead them through the cemetery and past the retaining walls. He was half-hoping that the car would once again go out of control, but at the same time he prayed that nothing would happen.

One of his prayers was answered. The little car responded to Jerry's lightest touch and they passed through the cemetery without incident. Now Terry was thoroughly confused, perhaps it had been something wrong with the steering, or had he really slid on ice twice in the same spot in as many days? Why had the car not acted up for Jerry, and why, for that matter, did it never slide when he was going through the same stretch on his way home?

The next morning, Monday, Terry got into the little car and started for work. He passed the detour signs and followed the arrows along the road that led to the cemetery. His heart pounded in his chest as he neared the cemetery. He tapped the brakes and slowed down to a crawl. There was almost no ice this morning, thanks to a thaw over the weekend, so he felt better about passing through the cemetery, but just the same he would be cautious.

The car responded to his slightest touch until he was halfway through the cemetery. Suddenly the wheel was jerked from his hands by a strong force. He wrestled it, but it was almost more than he could control. He lifted his foot to tap the brake, but suddenly he felt what seemed to be another foot or a hand forcing his foot back onto the gas pedal. The force tried to jam his foot down hard, but Terry jerked it away barely, tapping the gas in the process. With his left foot he hit the brake hard, causing the car to grind and jerk spasmodically. Then the car began to accelerate on it's own and the wheel wrenched itself to the right toward the wall. The gray cement wall filled his vision and he desperately tried to stop his acceleration. Suddenly there was a terrific jolt and the scream of metal on stone. The vehicle had hit the wall. With a last shudder the engine died.

Terry never knew how he got the car started, but he managed to back it away from the wall and pull over onto the berm just beyond the cemetery. He got out to look at the damage done by the collision and because he was frightened to stay inside the car. He found himself avoiding standing directly in front of the car. It was silly, he knew, but he had the distinct impression that it could come to life and run him over. He almost believed that it was sorry that it had not managed to kill him.

With a shock Terry stared at the right front side of the car. There was barely a scratch and no dents at all in the metal, yet he had distinctly heard metal buckling as he had collided with the wall. How could this be? Fearing that his perceptions were off, Terry walked back until he saw the place on the wall where he had collided. There a large stain of red paint showed that he had impacted hard. There was a gouged-out place in the wall that was rimmed by red paint flecks. To Terry the red paint seemed like blood, as though the car had hurt itself and had bled on the wall.

Shaking himself, Terry turned around and went back to the car. Now the car of his dreams was a nightmare. He quickly tied a bright orange cloth swatch on the car's door handle and left the car there. He'd hitchhike to work.

A couple miles from the accident site, a fellow he knew picked him up. Terry gave very little detail about why he was walking to work. He never mentioned the accident to his friend, he simply said that the car wasn't working right.

That very night Terry stopped at a car lot and bought a cheap clunker to get him back and forth to work. He made arrangements to have the Mustang towed back to town, and he rented a garage where he could keep it locked up.

Terry is not to this day a superstitious man, but he refuses to sell or give away his car. For perhaps the first time in his life, Terry broke a promise. When his sister, Georgette, grew up he did not give her the car. He did tell her and myself the story of the little Mustang that he keeps housed behind locked doors. His brothers both know the story and I'd venture to say that they don't believe it. But I have never known Terry to purposefully lie, and I've never known him to break a promise, so I must believe that he really fears that car. He truly believes that it tried to kill him several times on the same stretch of road. Why, we will never know. Perhaps there was some force in the cemetery that responded to the car, perhaps a previous owner, but no one can be sure.

All I do know is that no matter how bad things have gotten for Terry that car has stayed locked up. He's afraid to junk it, afraid to drive it, and afraid to sell it. No matter how often, or how much is offered, Terry always insists, "It's not for sale!"

The Man With Cloven Hands
(Williamsburg, Blair County)

1927

For sixteen-year-old Daniel Berk and his family, times were often hard. His father farmed a little, worked the mines some, did odd jobs when they were available, and generally tried to make ends meet any way he knew how.

One of the jobs his father did was to cut mine props to sell to local mine bosses. When times were tough, his father could usually figure on some money from the sale of mine props. Dan and his younger brother, Curt, would get pulled out of school to help with the cutting and hauling, which was just not a job for a single man. His father worked them hard, but he was fair with the boys and worried about getting them back to school as soon as possible.

In the fall of 1927, the Berk family was already feeling the financial pangs of what would soon become the depression. Work had been hard to get, so Dan and Curt set off with their old man into the woods to cut mine props for a couple weeks. They had an order that would get them through the next several months if they could fill it. The boys hitched the mule to the log-pulling chains. They tied the provisions to the mule, setting off after their dad into the hills near their farm to cut and drag logs back for mine props.

For a week the three of them worked hard from sunup until sundown. At night the boys would listen to their father tell stories of things that had happened in the Allegheny hills where they lived. There were stories of Indian ambushes, of haunts that kept certain areas free of settlers. He told stories of disappearances, and of the little men who lived in the coal mines. The boys loved listening to the tales, but they didn't take them all that seriously. They were just something to kill the hours until they could unroll the bed rolls and fall asleep.

. One afternoon, as they worked, a man walked into their camp where Curt was hauling the cut brush and small logs. Curt yelled for his father and Dan who came on the run. The fellow wasn't anything special; he was a small, dirty man with a dark scruff of beard, hair that was shaggy and needed washed, and he smelled bad. He asked if he could work for some food. It was a common request and Berk had never been one to send a man away hungry, especially if he'd offer to work.

"I'll tell you what," Berk said, rubbing his arm across his forehead to wipe away the sweat. "You see that pile of wood there?"

The stranger nodded, looking at a large pile of wood that needed sorted. There was a lot of brush mixed in with some logs that could be split for fire wood.

"You separate the brush and drag it off over there." Berk pointed to a pile of brush already filling a small clearing. "And you cut and rank what's left, and you got yourself a deal."

The vagrant nodded. "Sounds good to me."

Berk picked up the provision bag, water jug, and his ax as he nodded to his sons. "We'll be back in a bit. Got a few trees to cut yet before we quit for lunch. You be done by the time we get back and you can join us."

As the boys followed their father down the hill toward the creek, Dan looked back. The vagrant stood at the top of the hill smiling and watching them go. For some reason Dan shuddered. He thought of a story he had once heard about some fellows who had been done in by a crazy man. He couldn't help thinking that he'd not turn his back on that bum, and he'd keep his ax handy, too.

Berk kept his boys busy for the next couple hours. Every once in a while he'd pause and listen for chopping sounds from the camp. They never heard a sound.

Finally Berk ordered the boys to quit and wash up. He had just figured that the bum had run off when he saw that he'd not get a free lunch and there was nothing up there to steal. Berk filled the water jug at the creek, then washed up himself. The cold water felt good on his face and neck. There was a burned place on the back of his neck where the deceptive October sun had caressed him all morning.

"Curt, you finish dragging and cutting the brush after lunch. Sounds like our friend ran out on us."

Curt laughed at his father, but Dan could not help thinking that it might have been for the best.

"Well, I'll be!" Berk stopped dead on the trail. There sat the vagrant leaning against a neat rank of wood. The ax was propped along side him. Berk looked at the clearing and saw that the brush had all been dragged just like he had said. He looked at the bum again and his mouth opened. The fellow looked just like he remembered except that instead of hands the fellow now sported two cloven hooves that jutted from the ends of his rolled-up shirt sleeves. Berk tightened his grip on his ax.

"Dad..." Curt breathed.

Dan just stared, blinking and trying to make sense of what he saw.

Berk put a protective arm in front of his boys. "Stay here."

He walked toward the wood pile. As Berk got close to him, the bum threw back his head, laughed, and simply faded away. Dan had seen it all, the bum, the cloven hands, and how the vagrant had faded away, but he didn't know what to say about it.

That evening, they sat around the campfire and heated a jar of their mother's home- made soup. Berk took the bowl Curt offered and hunkered down opposite his sons. "You know, boys, there's some things a fella just never talks about. I believe we might just keep this to ourselves."

The boys followed their father's advice, except when they were alone. For the rest of the week they wondered exactly what they had seen. They came up with some disconcerting ideas, but their father refused to even entertain such thoughts.

As the week ended, Berk told the boys that they were going into town. It had been a while since he'd spent any money on alcohol, but he thought that he could use some strong drink, and he thought that seeing other folks would calm the boys nerves.

Calmitt was a dry town. It had a booming rail road station, however, and to accommodate those who had money and a thirst for drink, a bar had been built across the Juniata river from the town proper. The local folks called the area across the bridge The Addition, and tolerated the bar because it brought folks from the trains into the town to spend money. It was to The Addition bar that Berk headed when he got to town.

As Berk and his boys entered the bar, they were struck by the noise and confusion going on at the far end of the long room. There were poker tables over there and Berk had once or twice sat in on a game himself, but he'd rarely heard such fussing over a simple card game. Curiosity got the best of him, and he pushed his way to the edge of the crowd gathered around the table. The boys tagged along, unwilling to be separated from their father. Berk caught the words "card shark" and "cheat" being muttered by the crowd.

At first, Berk didn't see what all of the fuss was about. It was just some local boys playing, then he caught sight of the player who had his back to him. Berk pushed around to the other side of the table to get a better look. He could feel the boys bumping along behind him but he didn't give them a thought. He could swear that he knew that player, and if he was right...

Berk felt his stomach knot up into a tight ball of fear. There, sitting at the poker table, was the vagrant he'd offered a meal to. The bum was holding a hand of cards, and had a considerable pile of money on the table at his elbow. Berk felt Curt clutching his arm as he cried out, "Dad, that's him!"

Dan thought that his legs would buckle. The vagrant was sitting there smiling at them from across the table. Dan's eyes sought out the hands but they looked normal. No, they were blurry. There was a sudden ruckus as chairs fell back and someone screamed, "Look at those damned hands!"

Dan blinked his eyes but nothing changed. He was staring at the vagrant who was pressing his cards between two cloven hooves. The vagrant looked at the crowd staring at him, laughed, and just disappeared. Dan found himself staring at a vacant chair. Now he knew that people would believe his story, but he was too shaken to speak. He just sat down and listened as his father told of their first meeting earlier that week with the man with cloven hands.

This story was taken from an interview with one of the sons who had seen the man with cloven hands. He told this story while in his late seventies; however, he was very alert and had told the story before. One thing is certain, the man believed that what he had seen was real.

It would be easier to discount his tale if not for creatures such as the Jersey Devil which has been sighted by many honest people over the years. This creature is said to have cloven feet and is supposed to wander freely in the wild ranges of the remote Jersey woods.

Then there was the case of a small English village that awoke one morning to see in the snow a single set of cloven hoof prints walking through their village. The prints kept a straight line over cottage roofs, passing through fences unimpeded, and going over miles of open country totally unseen. No other prints disturbed the hoof prints, and they finally ended at the coast.

There are other cases of cloven-hoofed creatures being seen or bipedal cloven prints sighted, although there are no natural bipedal cloven-hoofed creatures. At best, I can say that perhaps no one but God knows who or what the Berk family saw in the Pennsylvania woods that fall week in 1927.

* Because those involved have died, and I could not find their family to request permission to use their real name, I have changed the name of the family involved.

Covatta's Brinton Lodge
(Douglasville, Berks County)

In 1927 Caleb Brinton bought the old lodge located at 1808 West Schuylkill Road in Douglassville and turned it into a private club for the rich and famous. For many years he lived in the lodge and ran the club along with his companion, Lillian Moore. In 1972 the house was significantly damaged by Tropical Storm Agnes, which drove him from the house. Because Brinton loved the lodge so much, it is believed that after his death his spirit returned to his home.

After his death, Brinton left the lodge to Lillian Moore. Ms. Moore had become an invalid by this time and only used the first floor of the house. But neighbors began to notice lights burning on the second and third floors of the lodge. A figure was seen walking past the windows and they commented on it to Ms. Moore. She was a bit

Top: The entrance area and front of Covatta's Brinton Lodge.
Below: A view of the back of the lodge.

surprised because she knew that no one other than herself was in the house and she certainly could not climb the stairs—but the idea that ghostly entities were walking the upper floors did not truly disturb her. She had spent many years at the lodge and already knew that it was very haunted.

Ms. Moore finally sold the lodge but lived next door in another house. In 1980, the lodge was sold again to Robert and Sandra Covatta, who turned into a restaurant.

The Covattas loved the lodge from the very first. It was a very beautiful structure. The white stone building was trimmed by reddish

61

woodwork and the landscape around the lodge showed off the building well. Inside it still was filled with the grace and beauty of a simpler time.

The Covattas moved into the third floor of the lodge. Although they'd been told the building was haunted, that did not deter them. Previous owners said there were strange noises they could never explain, that the doors of the once private club kept closing themselves and that both employees and customers commented about feeling chilly drafts passing them in places where no draft was possible. So it was not surprising that very shortly after they moved in they began to experience odd phenomena. There were footsteps which moved around though no one was there. They heard a baby crying. And then they would see someone moving around from the corners of their eyes.

One day in 1981, Sandy Covatta bought a portrait of Andrew Jackson to hang over the fireplace in one of the dining rooms. She had the picture hung and liked the effect it gave the room. The next morning she was a bit surprised to see that the picture was laying against the fireplace screen. She checked the wall but the hook was in place. The picture's hanging wire was also intact. Puzzled, Sandy rehung the picture.

The next day she was surprised to again find the picture leaning against the fireplace screen. Sandy hung it once more.

On the third day that the picture was in the lodge, she again found it against the fireplace screen. This time she wondered if the cleaning woman was removing it at night for some reason and not replacing it? She spoke to the lady who assured her that she had not touched it. She informed Sandy that when she came in to clean, the picture was already off the wall and leaning against the screen. She had thought that Sandy Covatta had been taking it down nightly for some reason.

Sandy was perplexed by why it was removed. The cleaning lady offered a theory. Andrew Jackson had been a Southerner and perhaps the spirits in the restaurant resented a southern general being hung above the fireplace in a northern home. What a thought!

Eventually Sandy did seem to get her way for the picture has now hung at the lodge for sixteen years, but this incident made her aware that she was sharing her home and business with others who had definite opinions about what happened in the building.

Sandy has also experienced a problem with the dimmer switches in part of the older building. In the one dining room the dimmer switches kept being turned up on high. Sandy spoke to the waitresses about this because she wanted the lights dimmed to create a softer atmosphere. The waitresses have said that they never touched the dimmer switches.

In the President's Room and in the 1700s Room, they would find lights turned on when they shouldn't be.

The Rustic Room was lighted by candles until recently. There were candles on the mantel and at each table. Recently the Covattas had to have electric brass wall sconces installed in this room because the candles keep being blown out when there is no one in the room. In the same room, a large crock that Sandy had placed on top the mantel keep being moved down to the floor. When the cleaning woman was asked about this, she said that she thought that was where it belonged because when she came in it was always there.

In the dining rooms in the older part of the lodge, people often feel as if someone is gently putting their arms around them or that a hand has been placed on each arm. Others say they have been hugged softly on the shoulders by someone.

Through the years there have been several pictures moved, doors closing by themselves, and drafts or cold spots are often felt.

Sandy has never doubted that Brinton's Lodge is haunted by several spirits, but she has come to know them quite well. She feels they are good, protective spirits. And so she is always considerate of them and welcomes them there.

One evening one of her employees named Bonnie and Sandy Covatta were walking up the main stairs of the lodge, talking and telling jokes. As the ladies chuckled over something funny, they caught sight of a man's pant leg just behind them. They were a bit embarrassed because the joke had been private, so they moved back when they reached the landing so that the gentleman could pass by. To their surprise there was no one there.

Sandy asked Bonnie what she had seen and Bonnie confirmed that she had seen a man's pant leg made of tweed just behind them. They had seen the same thing.

Through the years the Covattas and their employees have often glimpsed a person coming through the lobby that they took for a customer only to realize a few seconds later that there was no one there.

One of the hostesses at the lodge is Betty Effinger. Betty has lived beside Brinton's Lodge for many years and knew Caleb Brinton. She was a good friend to Caleb in his last years and came in to help him when he needed it. She also knew Lillian Moore well. Betty told me that she and others have heard parties going on in the private club. There is the clink of crystal glasses, the tinkle of laughter, and the sound of conversation—but no one can be seen.

Sandy told me that employees have reported being pinched on the rump, tapped on the shoulder, and have felt someone blow in their ear as they were working on both the first and second floors.

Sandy made friends with Lillian Moore and the elderly lady confirmed that she had known of odd occurrences in the lodge for many years. Sandy also made friends with Betty Effinger who had known and cared for Mr. Brinton. Betty reported taking the spirits in the house in stride, and offered information about them. She told Sandy that one of the spirits she recognized as Mr. Brinton. He was just as sweet in death as he had been in life. It was Mr. Brinton who touched people and even gave them hugs from time to time.

The Covattas have had several psychics and others come to the Lodge. One group told them that there are five spirits haunting the house. One is the woman in white who is often also referred to as "The Bride." Betty Efinger recognized the woman. She said that the woman is a young lady, a twenty-six-year-old Miss Witman, who had died in the lodge of the flu in 1917. Sandy said that Miss Witman's spirit is usually seen coming down the main stairs in a long white dress. From time to time customers have approached her to ask about the wedding that is going on the second floor. They comment on how pretty the young blond woman looks in her white lace gown with its high lace collar. When this happens, Sandy must explain that there is no wedding going on upstairs and often tells them about Miss Witman.

Until the lodge was remodeled, customers had to use the restroom on the second floor and from time to time they would see Miss Witman walking in that hallway. And several customers have been given quite a start by Miss Witman's spirit. In particular one gentleman customer who frequents the lodge was startled quite a few times. When the gentleman went upstairs to use the restroom and wash his hands, he was surprised when he glanced into the mirror to check his appearance and saw Miss Witman staring back at him instead . This has happened to three or four other guests who have told Sandy about it.

There is also a spirit that described as a roly-poly gentleman in a derby hat. This man is believed to be Mr. Brinton. According to Betty this is Mr. Brinton who died on the first floor of the house. Betty says that Mr. Brinton sometimes touches her on the arm as she cleans the rooms alone. His touch is warm and she believes that he is just saying hello to an old friend since she cared for him in his later years.

There is the spirit of an old lady who guards the third floor staircase. The stairs are steep and the railing could be dangerous. Mrs. Covatta believes that this is why this old woman seems to stay in this area.

Then there is the ghost of a little girl whose spirit is seen around the house. She seems to have suffered and was confined to a room at the lodge. A psychic told Sandy Covatta that the little girl had been mentally retarded, and that was why she had been kept in one room. The little girl wears a long dress from a past age, and has not been as active recently as she used to be.

One day Sandy Covattas niece came to visit and brought along her five-year-old son. The little boy walked up to Sandy in the main lobby area and took her hand. He pointed toward a little alcove under the stairs near the doorway to the waitress's dressing room, and asked if she could see the little girl sitting there.

Mrs. Covatta looked but saw no one. The little boy, however, seemed very sincere and Sandy knew that a girl ghost haunted the building. The little boy went over and hunkered down to show how the little girl was sitting and pointed to the spot. Still Sandy saw nothing.

"Don't you see her pretty eyes?" the little boy asked.

To Sandy there was nothing visible, but she had a sudden feeling that the child was there. Softly she said to the little boy, "Tell her that she's welcome here for me."

"Oh, she knows that," he said matter-of-factly. Then he just got up and wandered off to play. The ghost child didn't scare him. He had just wanted to know if others could see her pretty eyes as she watched the comings and goings that have surrounded her since her death long ago.

There is yet one other spirit that seems to frequent the lodge and that is a tall, thin man with a watch bob in his vest pocket and black garters on his arms. The Covattas call him "Dapper Dan," and he seems to stay in a certain downstairs area around the Meeting Room dining area.

Betty also said that Mr. Brinton saw the spirit of his Quaker mother in the house carrying a lantern from time to time. This elderly Quaker woman seems to prefer to stay in and around the bedroom she had used in life and is always seen with her lantern.

The psychics have told the Covattas that although only five spirits stay in the house, the building is a gateway for many other spirits which pass through. Other psychics have spoken of seeing a Continental soldier in the old part of the building.

In recent years the Covattas decided to convert one of the porches into an additional dining room and to add a first floor bathroom that was handicapped accessible. They hired a construction firm to complete the renovations.

During the remodeling the men often complained that their tools were being moved about. A senior stone mason always brought along a radio to play classical music while he worked. He confessed to the Covattas that he and the other men would see the station knob moving by itself while the radio was at the lodge.

One day Sandy was upstairs, sleeping in one of the second floor suites. She awoke and went to the bathroom, then fell back into bed. As she lay there trying to forget that she had to get up, she felt the bed move as though someone had sat down on it. She sat up and looked around, but she was alone.

She felt the bed give a second time as if the person had just stood up, but still she was alone. After she laid back once more, she felt the bed depress beside her once more. Again she looked around but was alone.

Once more she felt it give as if someone had gotten up, but still she saw nothing.

It seemed that nothing further was going to happen so she laid back and relaxed again. Suddenly the bed shifted once more and she turned over not expecting to see anything. This time she saw what she called "a blob of fog" at the end of the bed.

She sat up and asked it, "Who are you?"

The fog disappeared.

Because the Covattas lived at the lodge for a long time, there were a lot of pictures taken there. In many of the family photos are light streaks or light blobs which they cannot explain. What Sandy finds odd is that through the years she has noted that the blobs or streaks would appear in one picture taken in an area but not in a second one taken a few minutes later. The light streaks would reappear in yet a third picture taken in the same spot a few minutes after the second one. It is as if the light moves about on its own.

Sandy and her husband have moved out of the lodge, and recently their son and his wife, Lori, moved into the attic apartment with their two small children. Lori works at the lodge as well, and has had several incidents happen to her. She tries hard to take the hauntings in stride, but she's a bit unnerved by them when they occur.

Lori said that when they first moved into the building her oldest son, Shawn, who is three years old, did not at first like his new room because it was "scary." Now he seems to have adjusted.

One day Lori came in after the boys had taken their nap to find that Shawn was a bit upset. He wanted to know who the old man was who had been in his room. Lori was at a loss because there had been no one on that floor except the boys and herself.

Two weeks later Shawn again woke up from his nap and asked his mom about the old man who came into his room. Lori still does not know who it was, but perhaps it was old Mr. Brinton just checking on the little boys.

Recently, one night Lori and her husband were in their bed when they heard music through the baby monitor in the boys' room. Her husband thought that Shawn must have gotten up and pushed the button, so he got up to put the boy back to bed.

In their room both boys were sound asleep but the cassette player was playing softly.

In late January of 1997, Lori was standing in the boys' room looking out a window when she felt someone touch her on the shoulder. She turned but found that other than her one-year-old baby she was alone.

When she and her husband first moved back into the third floor apartment, they noticed that every night after they tucked the boys in and had gone to the living room to watch T.V., someone's shadow would pass the doorway of the living room. It came from the direction of the children's room, but when they checked no one was ever in the hall. They had the impression that someone walked from the boys' room, down the hall, and passed through their bedroom door. This occurred for quite a while after they moved in.

From time to time Lori has found that the boys have trouble sleeping in their room. One day she took out a Bible and laid it on their dresser, then she addressed the spirits in the house aloud. She asked them to watch over her children and to protect them. She believes that now they do care for the children especially, and she noted that the boys no longer have trouble sleeping in the room.

Lori often senses that she is being watched throughout the lodge, and there are areas in the building that make her so uncomfortable that she avoids them if she can.

There seems no doubt that Covatta's Brinton Lodge is indeed a very haunted building. From the customers to the family which lives upstairs, everyone has experiences to relate from time to time. Perhaps the reason that the spirits at the lodge are so kind and protective is that the family truly accepts their presence there. Lori Covatta seemed to put the family's feelings about their spiritual residents best when she said, "There is definitely something there. They (the ghosts) don't live with us, we live with them."

Dreaming Of The Lost Cox Children

(Pavia, Bedford County)

It has been nearly one hundred and fifty years since two little boys wandered from their home near Pavia, but their story has reached over the years to touch people who would never know them. This is a well documented story that almost everyone from Central Pennsylvania has heard of. Parents have told the tale to scare their children into staying out of the woods, and grandparents have whispered the tale to delight older kids. But few ever talk about the most extraordinary part of the story, a visionary dream that brought home the two little boys and ended the uncertain suffering of their parents. Even death could not stop the lost Cox boys from coming home, but they needed the help of a sick man to bring them back.

S amuel Cox stood in front of his cabin near the small town
of Pavia and breathed in deeply of the crisp, clean spring
air. It was April 24th in the year 1856 and Samuel was looking forward
to the spring planting. It was almost a physical thing, this need to plant
his crops each spring. He smiled as he studied the woods surrounding
his home. A flash of white caught his eye as a deer crashed into the deep
underbrush, an owl cried lazily from the old oak where it rested, and the
farm animals called for his attention.

Samuel picked up the milk pail from its peg on the porch and
the egg basket off the front steps and started down the familiar trail to
the barn. From inside the crude structure came the lowing of the heifer
urging him to hurry; she needed her full udder emptied and her breakfast fed to her. The hens squawked frantically when he came within view,
and his rooster let loose with a series of earsplitting crows from atop the
wood pile. Samuel laughed at the cock's antics and hurried to measure
out their grain. As he scattered it, the hens dashed in near his boots for
a bite and then fluttered away on nearly useless wings to keep out of
his reach. He hurried inside and checked for eggs. There were only a
few so he'd wait and send the boys for them later in the day.

In the barn the cow's plaintive cries greeted him. Samuel patted the heifer on the rump. She replied by sidling as close as her tether
would allow. Samuel forked hay from the loft and poured a measure of
grain into the trough before the cow. She munched contentedly on the
golden grain while he stripped her slowly of her milk. Finally she was
dry, and he put up the milk pan on a shelf long enough to turn her loose
in the corral. She could rest there until later. It was too early to turn
her out in the fields.

Samuel picked up the egg basket and stowed it on a high shelf,
then taking the foaming milk pan he plodded back up the path through
the crisp air to the cabin. He walked slowly so as not to spill a drop of
the steaming milk, with four children he needed every drop of it.

At the cabin the door was opened by his seven-year-old son,
George. George was tall and thin for his age, with dark hair that fell in
a shock over his forehead, and flashing blue eyes like his own. George
grinned at his Pa and took the milk pail. He carried the heavy pan carefully to the kitchen nook and handed it to his mother.

Samuel watched as his wife placed a steaming platter of hot
cakes on the table and hustled the children to their places. He washed
his hands in the basin of cold water on the dry sink and took his place.

Mrs. Cox was bustling about, straining the milk and setting it in a pitcher. Samuel helped the younger children to cut up their hot cakes, but Joseph, his five-year-old, insisted on doing it himself. He made a bit of a mess but Samuel admired his independence.

Mrs. Cox nearly tripped over the family's coon dog as she rinsed out the milk pail quickly. "George," she snapped. "I told you to put that dog out. The house is no place for that beast."

George looked up sheepishly and sighed. "It was cold out, Ma." He caught the warning glance from his father and got up to put out the dog.

Mrs. Cox sat down at her plate. "Please pass the hot cakes, Samuel."

Samuel passed the nearly empty platter. "Those hot cakes were good."

She smiled and spread a pat of butter over the last hot cake. "It's the weather. Hot cakes always taste good in cold weather."

"There's not much cold weather left. It will be time to plant the garden soon."

Mrs. Cox sniffed. "At least here we know how and when to plant. Not like out in Indiana. I think folks bragged that place up too much. It was so cold and damp, the children would have caught their death if we'd have stayed longer."

Samuel was about to reply when the dog's frenzied barking stopped him. The hound bayed loudly to get their attention, then it went back to barking and growling. Samuel pushed his plate away and stood up.

"Sounds like Beast's got something treed." He winked at George and Joseph who were just finishing up their breakfast. "Maybe that's supper he's got up there, and maybe there will be another tail to add to your collection."

The boys looked at each other excitedly. They had been collecting tails for a while now, and had them in a box under their bed. They wondered what kind of animal the dog could have treed.

Samuel went for his gun, not paying much attention to the boys, and left. The boys took their plates to the sink and hurried into their jackets. They ran for the door telling their Ma that they were going after Pa and were out the door.

Mrs. Cox didn't worry about them. They had wandered the woods with their father many times and it was exciting for them when he brought game back.

Samuel followed the sound of the dog's barking until he came to a snarled hickory tree where a fat coon sat snapping and hissing at the dog. He reached out to pull back the hound and took aim. Just as he pulled the trigger the coon leaped to the next tree. He hit it, but only enough to wound it. It bounded off leaving a trail of blood. Samuel did not know that the boys were hiding behind some bushes watching and following him.

He took off after the dog who was following the blood trail of the coon. Samuel cursed under his breath as he followed. He was a good hunter and did not like to wound animals. He only took good clean shots, but even then something could go wrong. Now he had to find that coon and put it out of its misery.

Behind him George and Joseph followed at a slower pace. Their little legs just couldn't keep up with their father. Joseph wanted to stop; they were not to go this far into the forest, but George grabbed his hand and urged him on. They wanted that coon's tail.

Despite his bravado George knew that he was going to get in trouble if his parents found out he had taken Joseph so far into the woods. There were dangers among the trees. Wild animals and strangers who could hurt them, but George kept going until he had to admit that they were lost. Joseph was crying that he wanted to go home, that he was tired, so George took his hand and started walking the way he thought home might be.

The knowledge came to him by degrees as the day wore on. George would see something that seemed familiar, but when they reached it he would realize that he didn't recognize it. The day warmed slightly, but still their coats seemed thin when the wind blew. It was cold for April. Joseph's hands were cold and red and his face was chapped from crying. The crying faded into a terrible silence.

Samuel got back home around noon. He had gotten the coon so he took it to the barn, skinned it, and tacked the hide to the barn wall. He snipped off the tail for the boys and went to the house.

Mrs. Cox was surprised when Samuel came in alone. She had expected that the boys would have been back long ago, cold and hungry. She was ready to chide Samuel for keeping them out too long, but she knew immediately from Samuel's blank look that the boys were not with him.

Immediately her stomach dropped. She dashed outdoors to call them. Samuel followed close behind her, adding his voice to the calls. Silence. The sickening feeling spread as the minutes mounted. Where were they?

Samuel tried to reassure her as he shouldered into his coat and started back along the trail the coon had led him on earlier. He hunted and called until his throat hurt and his feet were numb with cold. The cold only spurred him on, though, for how could two little boys survive in the dank, raw Spring cold?

Finally Samuel headed for Pavia. The day was growing colder and he had to find the boys. In Pavia there were others to help him look. Surely if they all hunted for the boys they would soon be found.

The townspeople tried everything they could to help. Over the course of the next days they searched constantly. Big bond fires were lit so that the boys could spot them. For fourteen days men hunted in the damp and cold. There had been a lot of rain that spring and Bobs Creek, the nearest stream, was swelled so badly that no man could cross it so the searchers felt sure that the boys were in the strip of woods between their home and the creek. This is where they concentrated their search but they were unable to find the boys.

Mr. Dibert woke from the dream sweating and shaken. This was the third night that he had dreamed of the lost Cox boys. He tried to write the nightmare off as just his guilt at being too sick to search for them himself. Of course by now everyone had realized that the boys had to be dead and would probably never be found. Still, he could not shake the feeling that his dream was significant. But being a logical man, Mr. Dibert tried not to place any significance on his dream.

It was nearly two weeks after the boys had disappeared before Mr. Dibert mentioned his disturbing dream to his brother-in-law, Mr. Whysong. Dibert described the dream in depth. "After you pass a certain point on the mountain you'll see a dead deer," he explained. "The dead deer is next to one little shoe. You must go on further; you'll see a little beach tree that's fallen over the creek. The children passed there. Go further on and you'll come to a big birch tree. Near that birch is a hemlock in a deep ravine near Sayn Run and that's where I keep dreaming the children are." Despite himself, Dibert was clearly shaken by the visions. He wished that he was well enough to stomp the woods and check on his dream himself.

Whysong listened attentively and then decided that he'd give his brother-in-law's dream a chance. He started out near where the boys were last known to have been. By now the hunt was called off, but there had been so many people tramping through the area that Whysong could hardly imagine anything could have been missed.

Still, he walked on, just tramping around partly for his own benefit, and partly because the dreams had really rattled Dibert.

Whysong almost stumbled over the dead deer. Dead deer were not uncommon but it gave Whysong a start. He rooted around in the dead, wet leaves around it for nearly twenty minutes before he found the little shoe. It was a tiny, black boot like the one Mrs. Cox said her boys had worn.

Whysong tucked the small shoe in his pocket and walked on. He came to the creek and walked along it a while before he found a small beech tree that had fallen over Bobs Creek. He crossed there and continued on. He could not help feeling led. It was as though Dibert had been there to see the boys walk by.

Whysong passed an old birch tree and stopped. Within several yards was a hemlock that led to a deep ravine he would later learn was called Sayn Run. Whysong searched the ravine and there he found the bodies of the little boys. Joseph was laying with his head pillowed on a rock while his brother George sat nearby. They seemed to have paused to rest and had never gotten up again.

Whysong made his way back to Pavia and told of his finding the brothers. He led the way back to them. They made a pitiful sight in the solitude of the forest. It was speculated that Joseph had died first, then George had died while he sat waiting for his very tired, dead little brother to awaken. Perhaps George would have survived if he had pressed on, but it was not in the little boy's heart to leave his brother to awaken alone in the woods.

Whysong was questioned by the authorities and confessed that he only found the boys because of Dibert's dreams. This led to Dibert's being questioned. At first no one believed that Dibert had dreamed of the boy's location, but it was proven that he could not have had any part in their disappearance. The loss of the Cox boys left a scar on the heart of Pennsylvania that time has not been able to heal. But no one was more touched by their deaths than a man named Dibert, who dreamed a vision that finally brought the little dead brothers home.

In 1906, the Perry Lumber Company, on whose land George and Joseph Cox were found, donated the ground for a small memo-

rial. From across the county, contributions came in to build a monument to the lost children. On May 8th of 1906, the 60th anniversary of finding the boys, the $120 monument was erected. People come to Pavia to this day to lay flowers before the monument and to remember an all-too-human tragedy.

Those who make the pilgrimage along the little dirt road near Pavia will find the monument at the end of the path. There is also a simple plaque which is dedicated to the "Lost Children of the Alleghenies": George and Joseph, who remain together in death, are as they were in life.

The Baby Cried
(Williamsburg, Blair County)

This story took place in my own family when I was a child. I remember my aunt's fearful trips to my grandmother's house. I remember the strange silences and the frightened whispers. And I remember the day when all of the whispers turned to tears and I learned the secret that had sent my aunt running from her home once more. It wasn't until nearly twenty years later that yet another relative found proof that my aunt had truly heard what she had claimed to. Well, you read the story, and you be the judge.

In the spring of 1974 Shannon Riley saw that half of the double house beside her mother's home was empty and for rent. She was thrilled to find out that the old couple who owned the house, and lived in the other side, were willing to rent it for a reasonable rate. It took her a little time to convince her husband, but in the end Shannon

The house, now a feed store, where the body of the baby was found in the basement.

managed to convince him that moving to the vacant place was just what they needed.

Shannon's marriage had been a difficult one. She had met David Gifford in high school and, despite her parent's warnings, she had been enthralled by him. He was sort of an "outlaw" in that his family that had a bad reputation, and David seemed to thrive on making his own even worse. Perhaps it was the danger, or the fact that David was devastatingly handsome, or that Shannon had never had serious attention from a man before, but it wasn't long before Shannon became pregnant.

At eighteen years of age, she had few options so she told David that he was going to be a father. Far from being impressed, he simply stopped seeing her. It wasn't until her father had found out and gone to speak to David's father that a marriage had been arranged. Shannon felt like a fool, but after David agreed to the wedding she built herself a dream world where she and David would live happily ever after.

Reality had not been so kind. David was lazy, only taking occasional work, and the reality of motherhood had been hard for Shannon. Now she saw the move as a new start. She would be near her mother. She could go to her for support, for help when things were bad. And the new home would be so much better than the shack they had lived in out in the woods.

It seemed at first that David shared Shannon's desire for a new start. He took a job in town at a local factory making good money. Now Shannon could meet the rent payments, so one weekend the young couple and their infant son, Davy, moved in.

The house was wonderful. There was a small living room and a kitchen with a breakfast nook. There were two small bedrooms and a real bathroom with hot and cold water all of the time. Shannon was grateful for both after the hardships of the shack.

Each morning Shannon got up early to make David his lunch, then stumbled back into bed until Davy's cries roused her again. She never seemed to get enough sleep now that she had a child.

Davy seemed difficult since the move, but Shannon tried to console herself with the thought that soon he would be used to the new house and he would relax. Often she would awaken to hear cries only to find him sleeping or playing contentedly when she got to his room. She could not understand it.

It was only after they had been in the house for a few days that a chilling fact dawned on her. The baby she was hearing crying was not always her own.

One evening she sat alone in the house playing with Davy while David worked on the old beat-up Chevy he drove. She heard the sound of an infant crying. It was not the healthy crying of her son, who was giggling on her lap. This was the sound of a newly born baby. It was a sound that sent shudders through her.

Shannon grabbed Davy and shot out the door. She tried to tell David about that strange crying but he only laughed. She was just being a fool he said.

As Davy began to sleep through the nights, Shannon began to catch up on her own rest. Now she was able to stay up all day cleaning and playing with her little son. One afternoon she was startled to hear the same thin crying filling the house. She ran to check on Davy, who was having his afternoon nap, but her mother's instincts told her that it was not her son's cry.

Davy was sound asleep she saw as soon as she entered his room, but in the hall by the stairs the crying grew stronger. Shannon felt compelled to figure out what was happening in her new home. She followed the sound down the stairs. The crying seemed to fill the kitchen. It was coming from the open basement door.

Shannon stared at the open door in horror. The basement was cool and damp so she had left the door open to help air it out. Now she darted to the door and slammed it, shutting off the cries.

She was shaking and the only thing in her mind was getting away from the sound. She ran back up the stairs and grabbed her son. Within seconds she was crossing the short distance to where her mother lived. Shaking and crying she poured out her story to her mother. Her mother listened closely but said nothing for a while.

At last Shannon could not take the silence anymore. "Do you believe me, Mom?"

Her mother turned kind eyes on her. "I believe that you believe that you heard a baby crying in your basement. You know, Shannon, childbirth can cause some women to...imagine things. You've been under a lot of stress with a new marriage, a baby, a move to a new house. It's all been too much."

Shannon shook her head stubbornly. "I heard a baby cry in that basement," she whispered faintly.

During the next few weeks the frantic trips to her mother's home became almost common. Always Shannon stood the crying as long as she could, but at last the thin wails would drive her from her new home. How, she wondered, sitting at her mother's home, could her dream home have turned into a nightmare so quickly? Just what had happened in that basement.

She was frightened to suggest to David that they should move again, but after David went on night shift she did not have to make the suggestion. It took him only a few days to realize that Shannon's stories were true.

One afternoon Shannon took Davy over to visit with her mother so that David could sleep undisturbed. That was when the crying filled the house; it seemed to climb inside his head. It was a terrible sound that he couldn't stand. David quickly got up and went to the basement door. Shannon was right, the crying came from the basement.

Within a few weeks Shannon and David found another house and moved.

Not until nearly eighteen years later would Shannon turn on the television one evening to watch the news and get the shock of her life. The local newscaster was standing outside of the double house where Shannon had lived long ago. It had been bought and turned into a feed mill store. The new owners had been digging in the basement to trace a broken water line when they had made the gristly discovery. Buried beneath the dirt floor in an old feed sack was the body of a baby.

Shannon nearly dropped her coffee cup as she listened. The reporter walked to the side of the house where Shannon had lived and pointed down to indicate a ditch that ran directly into the basement where Shannon had once heard the cries. She remembered the frantic trips to her mother's house, the terrible crying, and she wished that her mother was still alive to know that she had not imagined the dead baby. There truly had been a baby buried in the dirt of her basement, a baby that had continued to cry from its terrible little secret grave.

* The names have been changed in this story.

The Demon On The Pump
(Acosta, Somerset County)

So many of the stories told about the supernatural are tales passed down from generation to generation. There is no way to prove them, but deep in our hearts they strike a common cord that tells us that they are somehow true. This story was often told by my grandmother, Helen Koke, and was often confirmed by her older sister, Mary, who had also witnessed the event. As a child, it was a treat to get my grandmother to tell this tale. As an adult, I can see that it is almost a parable about the supernatural, still those present on that warm spring night claimed until they died that they had seen the demon on the pump.

The revival service had let out late partly because Reverend Porter had preached such a hellfire-and-brimstone sermon and partly because of the massive response to the alter call. For fifteen-year-old Helen Koke and her friends, the sermon had been enthralling. Rarely had they ever had a traveling preacher who could paint such vivid pictures of Hell and it's demonic inhabitants. As the group of young people stepped from the flickering lantern light of the open tent, it was the most natural thing in the world for their conversation to turn to demons.

Grant Harland, one of the oldest boys in the group at the age of seventeen, sneered at the girls who were declaring that demons were real. "You can't be serious about this! Demons can't be real. This is 1937 not the Dark Ages. My father told me that all of this religious stuff is nonsense."

Helen's sister Mary turned a horrified face toward Grant. "You can't mean that you don't believe in God?"

Grant shook his head in frustration. "God I do, but not in demons. They are the figment of someone's imagination used to keep children in line."

As the others began rapidly exploring the idea, Helen Koke remained quite. She merely looked at Grant. She had seen demons before. In fact, demons were very real to her. She had seen them that very night as Reverend Porter had prayed over several people. She couldn't believe that Grant hadn't seen them, too.

"I know they are real, I've seen them."

Helen jerked her cornflower eyes up from the darkened path. For one horrified second she thought that she had spoken aloud her thoughts. Quickly she realized that the voice had been that of Elizabeth Worley, Mary's best friend.

"Didn't any of you see anything tonight? They were like shadows running from the alter back through the congregation." Elizabeth's voice was quiet, small like her slight frame but she held the gaze of the older teens defiantly.

Grant opened his mouth to make a scathing retort but one of the other boys, Jason Wright, spoke up uncertainly. "I saw something...."

Others looked away while some of the teens just stared at him. They too had seen something. They had seen nebulous shadows detach from those being prayed over. They had seen the dark shapes run among the pews looking for those whom they could enter. Had they not all seen it? Had they not all sought the refuge of the alter and the preachers because of the shapes?

Grant looked around defiantly. "I saw nothing by a lot of hysterical people," he declared.

Elizabeth stuck to her guns. "You'll be sorry that you said that, Grant."

Grant snorted. "Really, Elizabeth, you didn't buy into that dog and pony show, did you? I'll not believe in demons unless I see one with my own two eyes."

Another boy named Hank laughed. "Be careful what you say, Grant."

Helen walked along with the group, growing more and more appalled by the turn the conversation had taken. It seemed somehow blasphemous to deny that something the Bible said was real was not.

By the time the group reached the Koke home the conversation had turned to the next day's school work. Mary invited the group in for tea and they accepted.

Although Helen and Mary came from a good family, their folks had grown poor over the years and their mother was ill. The house had a sad air of having once been in better shape. Helen knew that Mary hated their stand in society and was surprised by the invitation, but she decided to make things as nice for Mary as she could while the guests were there.

Mary settled in the parlor with the guests and Helen excused herself saying she needed to fetch a fresh bucket of water from the pump out back.

Hank stood up to volunteer to get the water, but Grant took the bucket from Helen's hand and smiled at her. "I'll get the water, little Helen." He leaned over to make himself heard only to her. "So the demons don't carry you away."

Grant walked through he hall, laughing at his joke, and disappeared through the door outside. Several minutes went by before the scream came. It was followed closely by the sound of a bucket being dropped and the thud of footsteps on the stone path around the back of the house.

Grant burst through the door. He was shaking and pale. He did not resemble the cocky young man who had scoffed so about demons on the way home from church. He no longer had the bucket, but he grabbed at one of the other boys.

"Come on. Out there at the pump. You've got to see it." He pulled mercilessly on Hank's arm, forcing him to come along.

The others trooped after them and Helen found herself running to keep up. She nearly plowed into two other girls as they came to a dead stop around the corner of the house.

The pitcher pump was a large one with a graceful, curving handle several feet long in its curve. There, leaning against it, stood a creature that made Helen's skin crawl.

The creature was nearly three feet tall and of a greenish pallor. It resembled a man except that its skin had a scaly look and it had a tail that it flipped up as it stared back at the teens. Even from Helen's distance, she could smell the thing's odor. It was the sharp stench of burning sulfur that clogged her throat, gagging her.

The creature smiled at the teens and turned it's gaze directly upon Grant. His eyes flared like green fire. "I am real. Believe!" It's voice was low, raspy and horribly intense.

Grant staggered back toward the house. He didn't say a word; he just stared at the little creature that smiled back on him with insidious mirth.

Hank yelled, "It's a trick!" He lunged forward to grab the little man, but the man simply disappeared. He was there leaning against the pump handle, then he was not.

Helen jumped as Hank's screaming began. He staggered away from the pump holding his hand. "I'm burned," he yelled.

One of the other boys went forward to help him. He reached for the pump handle to sluice cool water over the blistering skin of Hank's burned hand but pulled back quickly in alarm. The handle radiated heat. Hank sank to his knees nearly crying with the pain, and holding out his hand—on which was burned a perfect imprint of the pump handle!

Some of the group went over and helped Hank back into the house where Mary got out the salve jar and applied her mother's burn salve to the brand. Grant was gone. He had never stopped once he got around the house. He ran home and he never argued about religion or demons again. In the future he refused to discuss that night with anyone.

Hank made up a story to explain the awful burn, but Helen and Mary never forgot the night they saw a demon leaning on their pump, and they carried this experience for the rest of their lives.

The Haunting Of Elmhurst
(Cresson, Cambria County)

O ff Route 22, three miles east of Ebensburg, near the town of Cresson, stands the stately 255-acre estate of Elmhurst. The estate was the summer home of the Thaw family of Pittsburgh who made their fortune in railroading and coke-making for the steel mills of Pittsburgh and Johnstown.

The "summer cottage" is actually a 23-room English Tudor mansion surrounded by woodlands and an orchard. The house was built especially for the Thaw family and no expense was spared. From its imported wallpapers to its European woodwork, Elmhurst is a shining example of how well the other half lived in the first part of the twentieth century. The beautiful, exclusive estate is now privately owned.

Elmhurst housed many rich and famous people during its time. Writer Edward Stratemeyer, who wrote many famous book series under pseudonyms such as Frank W. Dixon and Carolyn Keene (the Hardy Boys and the Nancy Drew books), visited Elmhurst. Helen Keller visited the estate, too, but the most famous, or rather infamous people to ever visit Elmhurst, were the Thaw family's own son Harry and his wife Evelyn Nesbit Thaw.

Evelyn Nesbit left her home in Tarentium, PA near the turn of the century to make her fortune in New York City at the age of fifteen. By all accounts the dark-haired beauty never lacked confidence, nor the ability to turn a situation to her advantage. She was fascinated by the theater and modeling and began working at small parts. She was "discovered" when artist Charles Dana Gibson immortalized the young

Evelyn in pen-and-ink. Evelyn's pictures, along with many of Gibson's other works, were featured in magazines such as Life and they became the standard for the Victorian "glamour girl."

Evelyn's beauty drew many to her, and soon she began a long-term sexual relationship with famous architect Stanford White, who was nearly thirty years her senior. White was already a famous figure, the designer of Penn Station, Madison Square Garden, and the Vanderbilt residence in New York City. He spotted Evelyn when she starred in the Broadway musical Florajora and was enchanted.

The stories of the torrid romance between the 49-year-old White and young Evelyn shocked even jaded New York City. White enjoyed watching Evelyn pose for him, so he had a red velvet swing constructed in their love nest. She would swing either naked or partly clothed while he watched and photographed her. She also posed nude on fur rugs while White snapped shots of her in various provocative positions. He decked out their retreat with a vulgarity that was almost shocking. Their apartment featured the red velvet swing suspended from the ceiling, a great canopied bed with vast overhead mirrors, and floor-to-ceiling draperies to hide their escapades.

The couple flaunted their affair in public for several years. So all of New York was surprised to learn that not only had Evelyn Nesbit gone on a cruise with Harry Thaw of Pittsburgh but the couple had come home husband and wife. Thaw's family was shocked at his reckless actions but Harry, too, had a dark sexual appetite. He was so bizarre that he had been blackballed from the high-brow clubs despite his vast wealth. Stories of his fetish for black snake whips and various sexual implements added an even more lurid appeal to the tales that followed Evelyn.

By all accounts, Evelyn's marriage to Thaw was less than idyllic. Thaw had a notorious temper. Once he angrily drove a car through a large display window at a department store. And Thaw was infuriated by his wife's relationship with Stanford White. White's name could not be spoken within his hearing, and he regularly beat Evelyn.

During their brief marriage, Evelyn was forced to attend summer parties and stay for extended visits at Elmhurst with the entire Thaw family. The family made excuses for Harry's behavior and turned a blind eye to Evelyn's abused features. She was neither wanted nor welcomed by her in-laws, who barely tolerated her presence for the sake of propriety. In later years, Evelyn would write a biography in which she would state that she hated her visits to Elmhurst. When one thinks of how terribly painful and desperate her time there must have been, hidden from public view, where Harry could devise perverse pleasures and beat her at will, one can understand why she despised the beautiful estate.

Eventually Evelyn and Harry Thaw went back to New York City to see and be seen by the "right" sort of people. Rumors began to surface that not only had Evelyn resumed her affair with Stanford White, but that it had never really ended. The stories, of course, quickly reached Harry Thaw.

One night Thaw and Evelyn attended an event at Madison Square Garden. White was in attendance at a nearby table. Throughout the evening Thaw fumed over the rumors; he believed Evelyn was flirting with her lover right under his very eyes. At last he could stand it no more. Thaw rose from his table and stalked directly to where White sat alone. The chorus began singing, "I Could Love A Million Girls" as Thaw stood over White. Thaw pulled a small gold handled .22 from his pocket and shot White three times in the head.

The subsequent trials were a circus. Thaw's first trial ended in a hung jury. The second jury sent him to a hospital for the criminally insane where he would spend several years. Because of Thaw's wealth, life at the asylum was not so bad. Thaw had a car at his disposal as well as a specially decorated suite with rugs and furniture from his home. He went on trips and generally lived a normal life.

Evelyn divorced Thaw. But she now was so notorious that she was not taken seriously when she applied for acting jobs. She was reduced to doing burlesque in second-rate dives. She died in a California nursing home at the age of 82 in the fall of 1968.

The Elmhurst estate was sold off and became the property of the Westminster Presbytery of Pittsburgh. The property was purchased primarily to be used as a retreat camp. A young couple named Hoover were hired to maintain the house and grounds, and to care for the retreat groups. The couple was given a mobile home on the property to live in. In the late summer of 1968 the couple moved their three small children onto the premises.

The Hoovers began noticing that there was something unexplained happening in the fall of that year. The couple would go to bed with the thermostat set at a certain temperature only to wake up to a chilly trailer the next morning. The first time this happened Mr. Hoover tore apart the furnace in the mobile home to see what was wrong. Since he and his wife were the only two people in the home tall enough to reach the thermostat, it never occurred to him to check it first. Mrs. Hoover discovered that it had been turned off as she hustled the children back to their warm beds. Throughout their long time at Elmhurst, they would periodically have this problem of a thermostat that readjusted itself.

Mrs. Hoover was in the habit of staying up after the rest of her family went to bed at night. She used that quiet time to get the last of her work done, and to relax without three small children for a little while. One night she slipped into bed and was laying there thinking of what she planned to do the next morning when she heard footsteps in the hallway.

At first she assumed that one of the children had gotten up to use the bathroom, but the steps continued in the hall. At last she got up to see who was wandering back and forth, and put them back to bed. The hall was empty. She checked the children and found that they were all sound asleep. She shrugged off the incident and went back to bed.

The Hoovers would hear the footsteps up and down the hall of their home many times.

A few nights later, she retired late and just as she began to relax she heard someone knocking hard on the back door of the home which opened into the hallway. Her husband heard it, too, and woke up. The pounding sounded again, and he jumped up, grabbing a gun and his flashlight. He dashed to the door and threw it open. There was no one there. According to the Hoovers, it would have been impossible for anyone to cross the lawn and make it into the security of the trees before they had gotten to the door.

This incident was unnerving but the couple locked up securely and went to back to bed. They were very much aware now of the fact that they were on alone on a 255-acre estate with no neighbors close at hand if there was a prowler.

The next afternoon Mr. Hoover was out working on the grounds, cutting brush; Mrs. Hoover was cleaning up the mobile home and folding laundry. The two oldest children were in school and the baby was asleep in her bed. Suddenly, Mrs. Hoover heard a loud male voice call out her name. It startled her, but she thought it must be her husband right outside. She went to the door and looked out. Her husband was not near the house. Instead, he was down in a field far enough away that it could not possibly have been him clearly calling her name.

85

That same night Mrs. Hoover went to bed late and found that she was restless and unable to relax. She felt that she was being watched. Frustrated with herself for feeling that way, she flopped over to face away from her husband and froze. Directly on the floor beside her was a column of gauzy white fog. It stood as tall as a human and, as she watched, it seemed to be taking shape.

Fear gripped Mrs. Hoover and she rolled over trying to wake her husband so that he could verify what she saw. By the time she got him awake, the fog had disappeared. Mrs. Hoover would later say that her first impression was that the figure in the fog was male, but later, as she thought about it, she couldn't be sure. It seemed to her that the figure had been assuming the shape of a woman wearing a wide-brimmed picture hat.

During their days at the main house, the Hoovers began to notice many unnerving things as well. They would turn out the lights before they left each evening, but there would be lights burning when they returned in the morning. Finally, they tried leaving on the lights since someone or something seemed determined to turn them on anyhow, and found to their consternation that the lights were turned off the next morning.

They often found the front door standing open, stove burners turned on mysteriously, furniture moved about when the house was empty and locked, and the sound of footsteps or the thud of loud knocking often rocked the otherwise silent house. At times it got so bad that Mrs. Hoover refused to be there alone.

Throughout the first winter, the Hoovers kept experiencing unnerving events. At first they tried to explain away the phenomena, but it kept happening. Explanation by explanation, they ran out of excuses for lights that seemed to turn themselves on and off and heavy feet treading where no one could be. It seemed that the longer the family stayed at Elmhurst, the more the spirits there tried to get their attention.

Mrs. Hoover found that at times she grew so unnerved or was so frightened that she would have to flee the house. Once outside she'd walk about the driveway trying to convince herself that she had not felt someone touch her, or that a man had not just called her name clearly while she knew she was alone in the house. They tried to explain away the feeling of being watched, the odd feeling that someone was right there beside them, and the cold spots, by saying that it was just the effects of a large, old house. The couple tried to keep the phenomena to themselves for fear that someone would think they were crazy, but in time the sheer volume of the events grew until they had to tell someone.

Local people always seemed curious when the Hoovers mentioned that they were the caretakers of the old Thaw estate, and many times they were treated to rumors of ghost stories which they refused to confirm. At last the Hoovers began confiding to a few relatives just what they were experiencing, but still they would not admit that they worked in a haunted house.

After the Hoover's had been at Elmhurst for a while, the previous caretakers came to visit and the Hoovers worked up their nerve. Now they had a chance to learn if anyone else had ever experienced what they were going through at the beautiful mansion. Carefully, they began steering their conversations around to unexplained events at the house.

At last they asked the questions that had been troubling them. Had the previous caretakers, who had been there for almost four years, ever experienced anything unusual? Immediately the couple knew exactly what the Hoovers were trying to say.

The caretaker's wife laughed. "Goodness," she said, "Many a night my husband got up with a shotgun thinking someone had gotten in." They confirmed that the opened front door, moving furniture, the crashing sound of glass breaking though no broken glass was ever found, and all of the other things the Hoovers were experiencing had happened to them as well.

In large part this revelation soothed the Hoovers. They were not alone in the hauntings. Others had experienced them as well. It was unnerving, but the Hoovers loved their work and they had never had dangerous or evil experiences, so they chose to stay on.

In time they would learn from the West Minster retreat guests that some of them had experienced hauntings at Elmhurst, too.

It wasn't long after this, that stories about someone being seen in the empty mansion began. People who came to see the Hoovers, not knowing that the family was not home, often stopped on the mansion porch to peer into the house in case one of the Hoovers were home but hadn't heard their knock. Many times their friends would come back later and ask who was the pretty young woman in the long white dress who had been in the house earlier. They related that they had knocked, but she refused to answer the door. They always described her as young with dark hair piled softly atop her head, standing in the entry hall or on the stairs, looking back at them. Some said that she simply walked by the door ignoring their knocks and calls.

The Hoovers assured their friends that no such person could have been at Elmhurst, but after this happened several times they grew concerned. How could someone be getting into the house when they were gone?

Mrs. Hoover had a nagging feeling that the young woman in the white summer dress was not mortal but admitted that was frightening. Until now the hauntings had usually been the moving of things when they weren't about. Other than the figure in the column of fog, she had never seen any apparitions. Who was this woman in white?

Mrs. Hoover went to the local historical society and began to do research on the house. It wasn't hard because the Thaw family had been very wealthy and there had been many files of clippings kept on them throughout the years.

She read the story of Evelyn Nesbit and Harry Thaw and wondered what had happened to Evelyn. Eventually she learned that Evelyn had died just after they had come to work at Elmhurst, and just before the woman in white had been seen for the first time. Mrs. Hoover was confused, though, for Evelyn had been an old woman when she had died, but this white woman was young with dark hair and always described as very pretty. Could Evelyn have been forced to return to the scene of her brief unhappy marriage after death? And if she had returned to a place she had admitted she had disliked in life, had she come back looking as she had back then? It seemed that it was a possibility.

The possibility turned into certainty for Mrs. Hoover when she came across a picture of young Evelyn in a special issue of Life Magazine. The photo of young Evelyn Nesbit fit the description others had given of the woman in white perfectly.

Mrs. Hoover spent a great deal of time in the kitchen at Elmhurst and one afternoon, as she prepared for a retreat group, she brought her small daughter along. To entertain the child, she had brought crayons and coloring books. She sat the child up on a stool at the counter and began her work.

For a while the child chatted with her mother and colored. Suddenly the little girl cried out. The stool tipped over and the child hit the floor, spilling crayons as she scrambled for something to hold onto. Mrs. Hoover ran over to pick up her child and make sure that she was okay. The little girl was fine, but she was upset because she claimed that someone had pulled her hair.

Mrs. Hoover knew that this notion was ridiculous because they were alone in the room and she had been on the other side of the big kitchen working at the stove. She set the child back up and began to work again. Once more the child resumed coloring.

A few minutes went by, then suddenly the little girl cried out in pain once more. The stool tipped over again and the girl fell once more. Again she insisted indignantly that someone had pulled her hair and pushed her stool over.

Mrs. Hoover still insisted that the child was imagining things and calmed the child. Once more she set the child on the firm stool and instructed her to color. She went back to work, and for a while the incident seemed forgotten. Suddenly the child cried out again and the stool tipped over.

The child was crying and insisting against reason that someone had pulled her hair hard, then pushed her over. This time Mrs. Hoover believed her little daughter. The child's expression was frightened and she was genuinely upset. It wasn't a game or a childish prank that had her daughter shaking and sobbing in her arms. She picked up her child, turned off the stove and left the house. She decided that she'd just wait in the driveway until someone else came along to enter the house with her.

One Monday afternoon Mrs. Hoover heard a car drive up to the mobile home and saw a young woman get out. The girl introduced herself as Julie and explained to Mrs. Hoover that she wanted to do a story about the history of Elmhurst for a school project, and asked for a tour.

At first Mrs. Hoover refused. She was exhausted from having cooked all weekend for a retreat group of nearly 110 people, but as the girl left Mrs. Hoover felt badly. After all, hadn't the girl wanted to do the story for a class project? Quickly Mrs. Hoover called the girl back from her car and explained that she was very tired but would take her on a brief tour.

The girl agreed to be brief, and Mrs. Hoover got into her car. Together they drove up to the main house, and Mrs. Hoover unlocked the front door so that they could go in. Once inside, Mrs. Hoover began to feel very nervous. She said that in all of her many years in Elmhurst she had never before nor would ever again experience that terrible feeling that seemed to be permeating her that afternoon. As she walked up the stairs to the second floor explaining the history of the house, every cell in her body seemed to be screaming to her mind that she had to get out of the house now!

In the second floor hall she paused, trying to fight the terrible panic that gripped her. She forced herself to look around but saw nothing amiss. Suddenly the feeling got much worse and the weight of her conviction that she had to leave immediately was staggering. She turned to Julie and interrupted the girl. "We've got to go now," she muttered heading for the stairs.

Julie followed, demanding to know what was wrong?

Mrs. Hoover turned to her, and it was as if her panic suddenly infected the young girl, too. "We have to leave now," Mrs. Hoover exclaimed, and began running down the stairs.

Julie followed quick upon Mrs. Hoover's heels. They literally flew through the door and slammed it shut behind them.

Once outside reason seemed to return, but Mrs. Hoover admits that she wouldn't have gone back into the house right then for anything.

As they stood in the driveway trying to catch their breath, Julie took an old black-and-white Polaroid camera from her car and snapped a picture of the front of the house for her report. The old-style film had a covering over the picture and it took approximately three minutes to develop. So Julie tossed the picture and the camera back into the car without even looking at the photograph and took Mrs. Hoover back to her trailer.

About a week later Julie returned with a story to tell. After she had gotten home, Julie had tossed her school books and the picture of Elmhurst onto the kitchen counter, then went back out. Her father had come home and discovered the picture.

When Julie returned, he asked about the photograph. Julie explained that it was of Elmhurst mansion and was for a school project.

"Have you looked at the picture?" her father asked.

"No," Julie explained. She had been late for another commitment, so she had just left her stuff and had gone back out.

Her father handed her the photograph and asked her what she saw.

As Julie stared at the black-and-white photograph of the front of Elmhurst, she saw the porch, the heavy front door, the second floor where there were three full windows and part of a fourth. The first two windows were dark and empty as was the partial fourth window, but in the third there appeared a white misty face clearly looking out. The face had no distinguishing marks to tell if it was male or female but a white face, almost like a mask, was clearly looking out.

Shaken, Julie had brought the photograph back to the Hoovers. Did they have any idea what had caused the image?

The Hoovers were baffled. Not only was there no one in the house at the time of that photograph, but the room where the face appeared at been locked because it was being used for storage. There were no curtains on the window of that room, and there was nothing in the room that could have reflected such an image onto the glass.

Julie would later return with an enlarged 8 x 10 black-and-white of the picture along with papers from Polaroid stating that they could not determine what the image was, but that their lab had determined that it was neither a fault in the film nor a deliberate touching up of the original. The Hoovers still have the framed 8 x 10.

The Hoovers enjoyed their life at Elmhurst despite the hauntings which they were learning to take in stride. They had begun to accept them as just part of their lives. There was never anything dangerous, and they had come to believe that whatever haunted Elmhurst meant them no harm. Despite their acceptance of the hauntings they were a bit surprised when the church approached them about removing the mobile home from the grounds. The church wanted to have the family move into the third floor of the mansion so that they would be closer for retreats. The Hoovers agreed to live on the top floor of the mansion.

One of Mrs. Hoover's many jobs at Elmhurst was cooking for the retreat groups that often came. One night in 1976 she was preparing a meal for a youth group when there was a knock on the door. Mrs. Hoover answered it and found a woman on the other side who seemed fascinated by the house. She asked if she could possibly tour it? Despite the fact that Mrs. Hoover was very busy, she agreed to show her around. Mrs. Hoover truly enjoyed the beauty of Elmhurst and loved sharing it with others.

As the ladies walked about, Mrs. Hoover offered bits of historical information about the house but was very careful not to mention anything about the hauntings. As the women walked back toward the door at the end of the tour, the stranger turned to Mrs. Hoover and asked if the house was haunted. She said that it should be haunted with its colorful history.

Surprised, Mrs. Hoover, admitted that well there were a few little incidents which could be taken to mean it's haunted. Delighted, the woman listened to the tales, then thanked Mrs. Hoover and left.

Mrs. Hoover thought nothing more about the stranger's visit and went about her work.

Nearly a week later the strange lady returned with another woman. She introduced the second lady as Nancy Coleman, a reporter for a Johnstown newspaper, The Tribune-Democrat. Ms. Coleman wanted to do an article about the hauntings at Elmhurst for her paper. At first the Hoovers did not know what to do. They were after all only caretakers of the property. Perhaps the church that owned it would not like that type of publicity for their retreat.

Eventually the couple agreed to tell some of what they knew, and Ms. Coleman and her friend left with enough material for an article. The Hoovers told of the male voice that they often heard in the house calling out clearly their names. They described being touched or stroked on the head, and spoke of repeatedly hearing a muted male and female voice in the second floor room above the dining room arguing quietly. The voices seemed loud enough to distinguish that it was a man and woman fighting, but never clear enough to tell who they were or what they were fighting about.

During their stay at Elmhurst, Mrs. Hoover described the family often hearing a loud crashing that sounded to her like a piano dropped from the third floor. During one of her mother's visits Mrs. Hoover's mother confessed that her sleep on the second floor had been disturbed by a terrible crashing. Mrs. Hoover was surprised because she had not heard a thing in her third floor apartment that night.

Another morning she entered her mother's room to find that the lady was still in bed with the sheet pulled completely up over her neck. She seemed agitated and Mrs. Hoover asked her what was wrong? Her mother confided that someone had been touching her cheek off and on throughout the night. Mrs. Hoover suggested that perhaps it was just the sheet brushing her mother's cheek. The older lady bristled at the notion. "I'm quite capable of telling the difference between a hand stroking my face and a piece of cloth," she told her daughter.

Mrs. Hoover was to experience something similar herself only a little while later. One evening she was in the kitchen making sticky buns for a retreat group when she was startled by someone taking their finger and twirling her hair and touching her scalp. She jumped and whirled around. She was alone.

Mrs. Hoover tried to convince herself that she had imagined the touch, but as she turned back to the stove it happened again. Again she whirled about, but there was no one else there.

Mrs. Hoover took a deep breath and willed herself to be calm. Again she turned back to the stove, then froze. Fingers moved across her hair, twirling it, and she felt the pressure of fingers pressing her scalp. Panic set in and she flipped off the stove as she rushed from the house. She took refuge in the driveway until someone else came to accompany her back into the house.

During their time at Elmhurst, the Hoovers learned a lot about the spirits haunting the house and came to believe that there was more than one. There seemed to be a man who moved throughout the building and called out their names quite clearly.

Second was the spirit of a young woman they believe is Evelyn Nesbit. She has appeared with her wide-brimmed picture hat, and seemed to Mrs. Hoover to be trying to tell them that the house was evil and they should be careful.

They also felt a more malevolent spirit at the mansion at times. This spirit seemed evil to them and they tried to avoid it. They attributed the more upsetting incidents to this spirit.

There was also the couple that fought forever above the dining room.

Many of the things that happened at the house could have been attributed to one or more of those spirits. From the mysterious movement of furniture to the fickle lighting system which seemed to always do the opposite of what they wanted, there were many incidents which they felt were the work of a spirit trying to get their attention. Mrs. Hoover put it this way, "It was as if they wanted our attention."

Mrs. Hoover believed that at least one spirit at the house looked out for them.

By now Ms. Coleman's article on the hauntings at Elmhurst had been published. The Hoovers thought very little about it. They were busy raising their children and living their lives. One thing that they had learned by living at Elmhurst was that a person can adjust to just about anything and make it a normal part of their life. They simply accepted that something had happened and moved on.

Eventually the church decided to sell the estate, and the Hoovers saw an opportunity to start a business at Elmhurst. They became partners with three other couples in a year round complex called Elmhurst Village. The Village offered a book store, a dining room which serve lunches and dinners, horseback riding, a figure salon, a gift shop and a lovely atmosphere for those who chose to enjoy it.

The Hoovers still resided in the top floor of the house, and they did much of the immediate work since they were always there. Along with their partners, they set about making their new venture a success.

One afternoon Mrs. Hoover answered the door and found a man and two women waiting on the porch. The gentleman began to introduce them, but the one woman seemed to be standing there staring intently directly behind Mrs. Hoover. Suddenly the woman commanded, "Don't move!" to Mrs. Hoover.

Mrs. Hoover stood still. The gentleman explained that he and his wife had brought his sister-in-law from Altoona, PA to see the house because they had read the article in the newspaper and they wanted to see if the stories of hauntings were true. His sister-in-law was psychic and she would know as soon as she had toured the house if it was really haunted, or if this was just a story to entertain the newspaper's readers.

Suddenly the psychic interrupted. "Okay, you can move now," she said relaxing and smiling at Mrs. Hoover.

She picked up on what her brother-in-law was saying about being psychic. Mrs. Hoover invited them in and allowed the group to walk around for a bit while the psychic seemed to be absorbing the atmosphere.

When they were done, the psychic told her that there were seven spirits in the house. She said that there was a young woman who haunted the house along with a man she described as "tall and slender, with slicked-back hair."

She said that one of the spirits had been very upset about Mrs. Hoover having moved a gray chair from a certain second floor room. The spirit had contacted the psychic and told her that it wanted the chair put back.

Mrs. Hoover couldn't believe her ears. How could this woman have known that a few weeks ago she had had her husband take a tattered gray chair out of one of the second floor rooms because it was so shabby it ruined the decor of the area?

As the psychic and her family prepared to leave, she paused to explain her odd actions when they had first come.

"You must be wondering what I was doing when you opened the door," she said to Mrs. Hoover. "Well, there was the spirit of a man standing just behind you with his hand held just behind your head, open palm near but not touching your hair." She demonstrated what she meant, and Mrs. Hoover felt shivers quiver across her. How many times had she felt someone touch her hair in the house?

In October of 1978, the Hoovers were contacted once more by Ms. Coleman of the Tribune-Democrat in Johnstown. She wanted to know if she and a group of four other ladies could spend Halloween night in the house. She was hoping to write another story about their adventure.

The Hoovers agreed and the ladies were put up on the second floor. Mrs. Hoover explained to them, however, that the bathroom on the second floor was out of commission. They had been having some plumbing problems with it and the flooring in the room was partially torn up so that the pipes could be repaired. As an added precaution so that no one would be hurt, the bathroom was also locked. If they ladies needed a rest room, they'd have to use one on one of the other floors.

Mrs. Hoover took the ladies on a tour of the house and imparted some recent incidents that had happened at the house. She said that she was always awakened at 4 a.m. each morning by a feeling that some-one was in the bedroom. This impressed the ladies and they decided that 4 a.m. would be the best time for them to hold their seance. Mrs. Hoover also said that a Ouija board used in the house had spelled out a mes-sage about a little girl's murder happening nearby soon. Unfortunately, a child was murdered nearby within days of the prophesy. A gentleman visiting the house from the Midwest saw a woman in white walking in the library. There had been a horrible scream at 4 a.m.the previous Tuesday which had awakened both Hoovers. As Mrs. Hoover spoke, the women had a growing sense that they were being watched.

Mrs. Hoover saw that the ladies were settled in room #3 for the night, then went back to her home on the top floor. In the morning she went back down to the second floor to see how the ladies had fared. It had been a quiet night and she thought that the adventurous women had been disappointed.

Instead the ladies seemed very excited. The women quickly told her that they had awakened at a quarter to four, but as they prepared to go back to the library for the seance, the noises began. Loud creak-ing noises suddenly broke the silence. The women were surprised be-cause there had been no noises like that before, and there were no such noises during the rest of the night.

The ladies had lain there awake, listening to the noises until finally one of them called out to the others. The creaks seemed to be coming down the hall and right into the room. One lady asked if the others were hearing the noise, and they confirmed that they were. They felt that there was definitely something unseen in the room with them suddenly. They had not felt that way only moments earlier.

The women got up and began searching, but they found no one nor anything else that could account for the sounds.

Two ladies felt very cold and they reported a tingling feeling. One lady felt a cold spot pressed against the corner of her mouth suddenly. Was it the spirit that had touched others actually kissing her or caressing her lips?

By now the ladies decided that they no longer wanted to have a seance. Eventually the coldness seemed to leave the room, and the women felt that they were no longer being watched. They relaxed and slept the rest of the night.

In the morning the women had all been out in the hall when one of them had glanced at the bathroom door of the locked bathroom that was out of commission. The bottom half of the door was made of wood, but the top half was a large piece of white frosted, pebbled glass. It was the glass that now held the women's attention. Etched into the frosted glass was the image of a woman in a wide-brimmed picture hat, her hair piled high beneath the hat. It was a perfect silhouette of Evelyn Nesbit from the shoulders up.

Mrs. Hoover knew perfectly well that the image had not been there the night before, nor had it ever been there in the past. She quickly fetched a cloth and cleaner and tried to wipe the image from the glass. It remained despite her efforts. She unlocked the door and cleaned the inside of the glass but that did not remove the image either.

After that morning, many people would see the image at various times. Some people, though, never seemed able to see it. One man who could not see it was professional photographer Larry McKee, of Altoona who came a few weeks later to take some pictures of the house. Mrs. Hoover showed him the second floor glass and tried to get him to see the etched image. He could not see it, but snapped a picture of the door anyhow. Later he contacted the Hoovers and showed them the photograph he had taken. In the picture the image of Evelyn Nesbit appears clearly in the glass.

As for Ms. Coleman and her friends, they certainly did not feel disappointed by their experiences in the house. One of the women would later confess that she had felt drawn to the room that had once been Evelyn's bedroom. She said, "I felt Evelyn come into that room and say

'Thank you for coming. I never liked it here.'"

The Hoovers lived in the house from 1969 until the early 1980s, and they found much about their life at Elmhurst which they loved, but Mrs. Hoover said that though she missed the house, the grounds, the seclusion, she knew that she could never live there again. She had had her share of invisible entities standing behind her as she played the piano or cooked, and of items being moved from their proper places in an eternal game of cat-and-mouse which always ended when someone got truly exasperated about having to look for something they had left in plain sight. The family had had it's share of unexplained events.

The family that purchased the house from the Hoovers was very skeptical when the Hoovers tried to warn them of what they might expect in the house. The man was rude and abusive to Mrs. Hoover. He said that she was a nut who had imaged the entire thing.

There was nothing else the Hoovers could do, so they simply moved on. However, Mrs. Hoover was not surprised to find out that less than a year after purchasing Elmhurst, the family had fled the premises in the middle of the night. She wondered if the nasty disposition of the family might have empowered the evil spirit she had always sensed there during her tenancy. She had always felt that her family's faith and its wholesomeness offended and weakened that spirit.

The present owners are nice, private people who have made the estate their home. Whether they are still being visited by the spirits or not I do not know, but I do know that for many people Evelyn Nesbit, Harry Thaw and several others are still around and in residence at Elmhurst.

The Possession
Of Etta Mae
(The Altoona area, Blair County)

E tta Mae had just turned nine years old a few weeks before she met Ruby Varner. Ruby lived in an old house off the main street. It was a little blue and white cottage that had seen better days. The grass and bushes were always overgrown, and the paint was peeling from the gingerbread woodwork of the front porch in long, ugly blisters. Etta had often heard of Ruby; the kids in school said that old Ruby was a witch. Etta didn't believe that. But she did believe the stories that Kelly Hogan told about candles and strange moaning and chanting sounds coming from the Varner house. Kelly should know, because her house bordered the Varner yard.

When school let out one warm September afternoon, Etta slipped away from her brother, Billy, who was supposed to meet her at the grade school and walk her home. Kelly had told her another story about the weird sounds coming from that "old witch Varner's" and Etta thought that she wanted to see if old Mrs.Varner was as spooky as Kelly said.

The bright early Fall leaves made her feel brave as the sun streamed through the various colors. Surely nothing could happen to her on such a resplendent, warm day, with the town buzzing about its business along the main street.

Etta looked up and down Main Street to see if anyone she knew would see her before she slipped between two houses and down a narrow concrete path that widened into the alley. It was cooler there in the shadow of the large trees, and the town's sounds faded slightly. She tucked her long, dark hair behind her ears and started up the graveled alley toward the Varner house. This end of town was bordered by railroad tracks and beyond them a wide curve of the Juniata River. The river wrapped itself around the edge of the town and curved away into the countryside. Here, in the alley, gravel crunched underfoot and the river chattered over rocks, making Etta feel more and more alone.

She had almost decided that it would be better for her to turn around and go home, when she saw the peeling front of the Varner house. Her sense of adventure forced her to plod on and see the witch.

The house looked abandoned. It sagged sadly in the front and the porch steps had been replaced by cement blocks. Boxes and bags were stacked in haphazard fashion all over the porch leaving only a narrow path to the torn screen door. The whole property was overgrown, with untended bushes and late summer roses still offered their last blooms as they trailed over the sadly sagging porch front. The entire yard was surrounded by a gray, weathered board fence. There was not much to see, but Etta's stomach lurched as she waited there, listening for the weird wailing that Kelly had heard.

There were no sounds and Etta had just about given up when the screen door screeched open. A bony old woman in a ratty print house dress and a torn, dark green sweater bumped through backwards as she wrestled with a battered wicker clothes basket. Etta stood still, watching as the old woman lugged the basket down the cement block steps and disappeared around the back. For a second Etta caught a glimpse of the old woman's haggard face surrounded by a neat gray bun fastened high in the back. The neat hair seemed out of place on the old woman, but it also made her look more human. Etta remembered the stories, though, and her imagination took over. She started to imagine what could have been in the laundry basket.

Etta went around the outside of the fence, looking for a way to peek at the old woman in the backyard. In back of the house she found a bank of locust trees that straggled branches over the fence. Etta didn't think about what she was doing; now she felt compelled. She dropped her books and grasped a low branch of the nearest tree and pulled herself up. She had barely begun to climb when she heard a weird off-tune singing coming from the yard. The voice was thin and wavering and she could not make out the words, but there was something about the voice that appealed to Etta Mae.

Etta slid down on her belly, grasping a branch that hung way out into the Varner yard, and began shinnying forward. She could barely make out the old woman through the leaves and she wanted to see her more closely. Besides, she felt an almost physical need now to find out what was in the basket. Etta stopped well out over the fence. She could see the old woman well from her vantage point, but still she could not see the basket. She lay very still so that she would not be detected as she watched. The old woman continued to sing as she bent over to pull something from the basket. A skirt.

Etta wanted to sputter her indignation as she watched the old woman hang up the wet skirt. Suddenly she felt foolish and yet angry, too, that she had believed Kelly Hogan's silly stories. Here she was hanging over some old woman's yard watching her hang up laundry. Slowly she began to inch her way backward.

"You came to see something, are you satisfied already?"

Etta jumped as she heard the old woman's voice, and lost her grip on the tree limb. She fell unceremoniously into the yard, her elbow striking painfully against the top of the fence.

Etta Mae looked up, pushing back her dark hair, and saw the old woman looking at her curiously through deep blue eyes.

The old woman held out a weathered hand and smiled. "Come, I will fix your arm and we will talk."

Etta felt trapped and stupid. Her face burned yet her stomach was light with fear. Her feet wanted her to run, but her legs seemed locked. She was standing in Witch Varner's yard. She ignored the hand, standing up on her own and dusting off her new school skirt that her mom had made.

"I'm fine. I'd just better be going. My brother is probably looking for me, and I left my books out back." Etta nodded at the line of locust trees behind the fence.

"Your elbow is cut, and I think that we need to talk."

Etta touched her elbow and her hand came away warm and sticky; she had cut it in the fall. She thought that she was in for a lecture if the old woman told her mother what she had been doing, but if she listened to the old woman and was lucky, her Mom would never need know.

The old woman turned around, picking up the basket, and started toward the house. "By the way, my name is Ruby. You may call me that or Mrs. Varner, but please don't call me Witch Varner or the neighbors will talk." The old woman gave a small laugh that made Etta's stomach turn guiltily. She drew in a deep breath and started after the retreating figure.

The porch was a wonderland of junk; everything from boxes of old newspapers to broken toys were stashed in the ancient cartons that were piled everywhere. Etta tried not to look as she passed them but she could not help herself.

The house was just as dark and old inside as out, but much neater. Mismatched dishes were neatly drying on the drain board and the room was cluttered, but well kept. Etta tried not to stare at the table which was covered with a dark cloth, and there were two black candles on it. She had gone to see a movie with her cousin, Alvin, once and there had been a witch in the movie who had a table decked out just like this one.

Ruby opened a cabinet door and pulled out an old cookie tin. "Sit over there." She indicated a chair at the table.

Etta chose the one closest the door and pulled it out so that she was sitting sideways and would be able to slip out of the door if necessary.

"You really shouldn't be spying, child." Ruby pulled open the tin with a grimace and sat it on the table. "Take off your sweater. What's your name?" She pulled a nicely snipped clean strip of sheet out of the tin and pried off the lid on a small can of foul smelling ointment. Beside that she sat a bottle of iodine and a small metal basin of warm, soapy water.

Etta gingerly pulled the sweater free of the wound. Already the woolly material had begun drying around the edge of the cut. "My name's Etta Mae Bradley. My family lives over on Cutshall Street."

Ruby carefully tended the cut, cleaning and rinsing it well before she let it dry. "I've seen you at the neighbor's place before. You friends with their little girl, Kelly?"

Etta nodded, trying not to wince as the old woman applied the iodine and the foul-smelling, green salve.

"What is that stuff, it stinks?" Etta could not help thinking that her mom could not help noticing the smell of that stuff.

"It's made out of herbs and pine tar. I make it myself, Etta Mae. It may not smell sweet, but it will keep that from getting infected and by morning it won't even hurt much." Ruby deftly tied the bit of sheet around the wound.

"There, that will do you well. Just keep the bandage on until morning and then you'd best wash it off before school."

Etta inspected the bandage and could see the ugly gray-green salve had already soaked through the cloth. "Thank you."

Etta slid off the chair and picked up her sweater. "I'm real sorry that I spied on you and all. You won't tell my Mom, will you?"

Ruby sat down at the table to replace the medicines in the cookie tin. She looked up briefly, laughter dancing in her eyes. "I won't tell your Mama if you promise to come visit me again."

Etta promised that she would, then thanked Ruby again before she slipped out the door. Quickly she retrieved her books and headed home. There would be trouble at the house when Mom found out that she had slipped away from Billy, and even more if Mom saw that she had ripped her good school sweater. She hoped that Ruby Varner was as good as her word and didn't tell what had happened.

The next day Etta found herself day dreaming about Ruby Varner. She was nothing but a nice old lady whom Kelly had lied about. She promised herself that the next time Kelly told scary stories about "Witch Varner" she would walk away.

Billy was waiting for her after school and Etta dared not run off from him again. Still, as they passed Main Street she felt a twinge and nearly dodged away from him despite the whooping she'd have gotten when she got home.

By the next day the desire to see Mrs. Varner was almost a physical need. Etta couldn't concentrate because Ruby's warbling voice drowned out the teacher. When Mrs. Jakes called on her, Etta was lost; she had been remembering the soft touch of Ruby's withered hands on her sore arm. At lunch she could not eat because everything smelled like the horrid, green salve, but even that was not all bad because with it came memories of Ruby's dark blue eyes. Etta had to see Ruby. She could just imagine the old woman looking for her at the gate after school let out.

At recess she found Billy and told him a lie. She said that she'd been bad and Mrs. Jakes was making her stay after school to pound erasers for punishment. Billy looked at her oddly, but he seemed to believe her. Etta would be able to visit Ruby for at least an hour without making her family suspicious.

When school let out she waited until Billy had disappeared, and then she took off running. The need to get to Ruby was strong and Etta Mae even refused to stop running when she got a stitch in her side.

Ruby was waiting at the gate, smiling and pushing the ancient gate back on rusted hinges. She beamed, making Etta feel very warm and important. "I knew you would come today."

Etta followed her into the old house and gasped in surprise at the beautiful tea set laid out.

Ruby chuckled and pulled out a chair for Etta. They had tea and funny tasting little cookies that made Etta feel wonderful. Then Ruby began teaching Etta the song that she had been singing the other day when Etta had spied on her. To Etta the words were just nonsense words, but Ruby insisted that they were very important. She smiled gently at Etta and patted her on the arm. "Just remember them in order, Etta Mae, for one day you will understand what a gift they are."

It was Ruby who called a quit to the afternoon. She walked Etta to the gate and gave her a small hug. "It's been a wonderful time, and I hope to see you again soon."

Etta promised that she'd come back. In fact, she was already thinking of ways to get back to Ruby.

As Ruby let Etta Mae out the rusted gate, she took her hand briefly. "Etta, listen to me." Her ancient eyes sought out Etta's lively brown ones earnestly. "Don't tell anyone that you come to see me."

Ruby smiled warmly, her eyes shining and taking the sting out of her message. "Other people would not understand and they would try to stop you. You wouldn't want that would you?"

Etta Mae shook her head solemnly. "I won't tell," Etta whispered.

Ruby gave her hand a little squeeze. "Good girl. Just remember to keep our secret and I will be able to teach you all kinds of wonderful things."

Etta found more and more ways to get to Ruby's after that day. It seemed that her need to be there increased with each visit. They ate those funny, little cookies, and Ruby told her stories or taught her songs or funny poems. Sometimes they even lit the candles on the table and Ruby said prayers. The prayers felt funny to Etta, not bad exactly, but like something she should not be doing. Still, they seemed to please Ruby greatly so she bowed her head over the black candles and muttered the nonsense words with Ruby.

Before long, Etta began looking forward to the ceremonies herself. One day Ruby told Etta that she now knew enough to lead the service herself. Etta carefully lit the candles and placed the smelly incense in the little pot of sand near the alter. She inhaled the thin trail of fragrant, blue smoke that wafted up. Etta loved the earthy scent of the incense. She pulled up the lacy black shawl that Ruby had made her for the ceremonies and began intoning in a solemn little voice the words that called to God. Etta had once thought it was funny that they never called God "God," but Ruby had explained that there were other names for God and other gods to worship. She explained that she worshipped differently because she did not worship the god Etta did in church.

Etta was lying more and more to make excuses to get away to Ruby's. Sometimes her conscious pricked her, but Ruby only laughed when she mentioned it. Ruby told her that the conscious was just a silly little voice, and Etta Mae should just tell it to go away if it bothered her. They hurt no one and nothing when they told their fibs so that they could have secret time.

Etta's mother was alarmed by the changes in her child. Etta had gone from an outgoing, curious child to an introverted, secretive one. She sensed that something was very wrong but Etta Mae refused to talk to her. All there was, was a terrible, nagging feeling that Etta was in danger.

Sometimes she would hear Etta singing strange nonsense words to herself, and she would see the girl carelessly rocking back and forth on her bed staring at the wall. Her lively brown eyes were vacant then, and it scared Mrs. Bradley so badly that she would shake Etta awake. Those awful, empty eyes would stay with her for days, haunting her dreams and warning her that Etta desperately needed help.

In desperation she and her husband turned to the school. Mrs. Jakes had seen a steady decline in Etta's grades. She had noticed that Etta had withdrawn from her friends, seeming to prefer sitting on the last swing at the far end of the playground, singing softly to herself. She did not have any answers, so Mr. and Mrs. Bradley turned to their pastor, but he did not know what to do. The general consensus was that Etta Mae was going through a stage. Mrs. Bradley was growing desperate because she knew deep in her heart that there was more to this withdrawal than that.

The other thing that bothered Mrs. Bradley was the fact that Etta Mae was disappearing for increasingly long periods of time. When they questioned her about it, she was vague, and more than once they had caught her lying. Etta took her punishments for the lies quietly enough, agreeing that it was wrong to lie, but when she needed an excuse for another absence she would offer them another lie.

The disappearances got so bad that Mrs. Bradley began walking to school to pick Etta up. Even then Etta sometimes took off running at some point and Mrs. Bradley lost her no matter how fast she ran to try to keep up. Other times, Etta would disappear from her room or the yard despite any precautions the family tried.

Etta never played with her friends anymore, calling them stupid and childish. Mrs. Bradley did have to agree that Etta was acting more and more like an adult. Sometimes it was hard to believe that her little girl was still only nine years old.

One afternoon Mrs. Bradley made arrangements with her husband and Billy to have them wait at various points along the short walk to their home. She would pick Etta Mae up, and if the child took off again they were to begin following her when she passed them. Perhaps Etta could outrun her mother, but it was nearly impossible that she could outrun all three of them.

She picked Etta up at the school and they started home. Mrs. Bradley tried to talk to Etta, but the child just shrugged off her questions and kept plodding along. At the corner of Mason and First Street Etta stood listlessly waiting for a break in traffic. Suddenly she darted out in front of an old sedan and took off running. Mrs. Bradley screamed as Etta darted into the street between two cars, but she couldn't follow her until the traffic cleared. Quickly she raced down the street after the retreating figure of her child. Ahead of her she saw Billy darting out from a store front and picking up the chase close behind his sister. Mrs. Bradley stopped and waited, watching her children getting smaller and smaller as they ran away. In the distance Mr. Bradley stepped out from the tree he had been leaning against, and took up the chase. That was all she could see. Etta swerved between two houses and she lost sight of them.

It seemed like an eternity to her until her family returned to the house. Mr. Bradley was carrying Etta who struggled frantically against him. Billy walked slowly behind his father.

"Where did she go?" Mrs. Bradley met them at the door and ushered them away from the prying stares of neighbors drawn out by Etta's screams.

Mr. Bradley grunted, dropping Etta Mae onto a couch and retaining her there as best he could. "You won't believe this, but you know that old woman Varner that lives down by the tracks? She went flying into that place like all the banshees of hell were after her. And when I knocked on the door and called for Etta to come out, the old woman came out instead. She was acting strange. She said Etta was no longer ours, and that I was to leave before she called the police. Well I offered to send Billy for them, then she got all stony quiet. Said she'd speak to Etta and send her back. She disappeared into that shanty of hers and a few minutes later Etta came out with her. Etta was holding onto her and crying. When I picked her up she began screaming that I was hurting her, that I was tearing her apart.

"Frankly, Ruth, I didn't know what to do. There was Etta screeching and fighting me, and that old woman glaring at me from those strange eyes of hers and smiling. I left in a hurry, but that old bird came after us as far as the gate and shouted after us: 'She's mine now, Mr. Bradley. You'll see! You'll see!'"

Mr. Bradley shuddered and looked at his little daughter who was laying, panting on the couch. "Something about the way she said it scared me, Ruth. It's hard to tell what she's been filling Etta's head with."

Mrs. Bradley bit back the fears that gripped her and sighed. "I guess we're lucky we know about it now. We'll put a stop to this nonsense."

She turned to Etta and took her hand gently. "Etta, Baby, I want you to tell me what Mrs. Varner has been telling you. Did she say we didn't love you? Did she say you were really hers?" Ruth Bradley had to concentrate to keep her voice from shaking.

Etta looked at her with hostile eyes and clamped her mouth shut.

Mr. Bradley stood behind his wife and looked at their girl. "Etta, we need to know what she's told you. She's an old woman, and she may be a little sick in the head and not understand that what she said to you was bad. We only want to help her and you to know the truth."

Etta's angry gaze shifted to him. "She told me that there are many gods and that her god is more powerful than yours. She taught me that her god is everywhere and that all I have to do is sing to reach him." The child's eyes lit with a strange light, and a crafty smile twisted her lips. In the same strange little voice that Ruth had heard before, Etta began to sing the strange words.

As Etta sang Mr. Bradley's hand squeezed into Ruth's shoulder, and she felt tears sting her eyes. What had been done to their little girl?

After that night the Bradleys redoubled their efforts to keep Etta away from Ruby Varner. Most of the time they were successful, but there were other times when the child just disappeared and they would always find her at the Varner house. Etta continued to change, to withdrawal from everyone around her except Ruby Varner.

It was late in November when Ruth began to understand exactly what Ruby Varner meant when she said that Etta was hers. That night Etta awakened at 3:37 a.m. screaming that Ruby was dead.

Ruth held her little girl and comforted her. For a few minutes it felt like the old Etta had returned to her. Her child allowed her to pick her up and cuddle her. While she held Etta, the girl looked at her with frightened, tear bruised eyes and whispered, "She said that she'd come to me when she's dead. She said that I'd be her power. She gave it to me." Etta shuddered and snuggled into her Mom's arms for a few more minutes.

Abruptly Etta pushed herself back from her mother's arms. The cold look in the child's eyes froze Mrs. Bradley's heart.

"I don't need you," Etta said, smiling. "Ruby is with me now that she's dead. I've inherited her power."

Ruth shook as she let her daughter go, but she tucked the blankets around Etta once more then went to her own bed. It wasn't true. It couldn't be! Old Ruby Varner could not be dead and using her little girl. Was this what the old woman had wanted all along? Ruth remembered all of the stories about Ruby Varner being a witch; at the time she hadn't believed them, but now she wasn't so sure.

In the morning Etta was better, but she had changed, too. There was a coldness there that hadn't existed before. Later that morning Ruth was not surprised to learn that Ruby Varner had been found dead by the mailman. In the next day's newspaper it said that Mrs. Varner had died at approximately 3:30 a.m. This time was fixed by the fact that she had knocked over her bedside clock and busted it when she had her lethal stroke.

Over the years Ruth would come to know that her daughter Etta was gone and Ruby Varner was somehow there, inside Etta, looking out. Etta grew violent and sullen. Time and again over her life, Etta was admitted to Psychiatric facilities only to be pronounced sane. In time, Etta grew to hate Ruth and began trying to kill her when she was in one of her fits.

Etta would be fine, acting normal for weeks at a time, and then for no reason she would begin railing against Ruth and threatening her. She attacked her mother many times, but through the intervention of others Etta never managed to murder her.

Ruth was not the only one attacked by Etta. Billy's wife, Karen, and one daughter were victims of her hateful rage. Once they took a terrible beating and then Etta left them screaming "I'm gonna kill her!" Karen knew that Etta meant that she would "kill" Ruth.

In a panic Karen ran red lights, wove through the traffic of the small city where Ruth now lived, and broke every speed law in the book. She left her children locked in her car and rushed into Ruth's house. Karen never paused to explain what had happened with Etta. One look at Karen told Ruth all she needed to know. She ran for the door followed by Karen and never paused for anything. She was now an old woman and the beatings that Etta gave her had taken their toll. Through the years Etta's attacks had gotten progressively worse.

As Karen opened the car door for Ruth to get in, she heard an impossible sound. Etta was screaming and charging at them from a little alley that ran along the side of Ruth's apartment. Karen slammed the door and dashed to her side, barely getting in before she started the car and took off, leaving black rubber marks where she peeled out.

Karen's mind reeled. She had been in the car when Etta had first attacked her. It was being in the car that had probably saved her life. While Etta had pummeled her, Karen had started the car and driven off. Etta had followed on foot. Karen could still see Etta's purse on the seat beside her. Etta had done the impossible; she had made it across a small city on foot, without any money, in nearly the same time a woman driving hell-bent had gotten across the city.

Later, when Bill, now a minister, found Etta she was locked in the bedroom of Ruth's apartment talking to someone. There were two distinct voices, voices that he had heard before. Etta seemed to be fighting or pleading with a man. The other voice was angry because Etta had not killed her mother. Etta whined and cried as the other voice berated her. Bill called Mental Health Services which came and forced the lock on the bedroom door to get to Etta.

Etta was quiet as she was taken away. After she left Bill stepped into the room looking for a radio, a television or something to explain the man's voice that had shouted at Etta. There was nothing in the room.

He knew what would happen, Etta would be observed for a few days, then released. No one would find anything wrong with her. It was always the same. The dark voices inside her retreated in the hospital, and allowed Etta to emerge there, alone. She would be sorry for the attempt on Ruth's life, and for the bruises and cuts she had inflicted on Karen and their daughter. But once she was out for a while, the voices would again gain control of her. They feared nothing, and no one had ever been able to break their control over Etta. Bill could not have said how he knew it, but he did know that that Fall, years ago, when Etta was nine years old, she had agreed to something she did not understand. And now Ruby Varner, and the dark man who spoke, held Etta hostage and probably would forever.

I have known the family of Etta Mae for most of my life. I would never have intimated that Etta was possessed if I had no personal knowledge of her and her medical status. She has been admitted to mental health facilities many times. She has been on various medicines and yet the doctors have no explanations for her case. It is not a case of multiple personalities. First of all, her own doctors have never diagnosed her as a multiple. Secondly, Etta Mae did not suffer any physical or sexual trauma. She has several real life siblings, all of whom agree that they had a normal family life.

Also, Etta Mae has fulfilled the criteria as set up by the Catholic church for possession. It is:

1) Knowledge of future events: From the time she predicted Ruby Varner's death on, she had future event knowledge.

2) Secret Knowledge: During these violent periods, Etta Mae would exhibit secret knowledge of people around her. She would tell intimate, embarrassing details of the lives of those she met...including the secret lives of strangers.

3) Superhuman feats of strength: Although Etta Mae is a very small woman, barely five feet tall, she has beaten men twice her size during a fit. She has destroyed things, and nearly ripped a car door completely from it's hinges.

4) Transports or floating: Etta Mae seems able to travel through space to get into place to attack people. She also will float above her bed or move things without physical effort when in these states.

5) Speaking in unknown languages: Aside from speaking in the strange sing-song language that Ruby taught her that one fall they spent together, Etta Mae has exhibited knowledge of ancient languages. Her brother, Bill, has taught ancient Greek as a college professor at a local Christian college. He is an expert on Biblical language and has recognized her speaking in ancient tongues. She has also answered herself, or the invisible persons she is conversing with, in ancient tongues. All of this despite the fact that Etta Mae quit high school, and has no knowledge of any language other than English when she is not in an altered state.

6) *Shows disgust or disdain for religious articles:* Etta Mae will attend her brother's Pentecostal church on occasion if there is a family wedding or other special event, however, she seems to show an active dislike of all formal Judeo-Christian religion which is contrary to her background. She dislikes church, and when in her fits can't abide anything religious including Bibles, Biblical books or papers, etc. She will even seek them out if they are hidden and try to destroy them while in a fit. Etta Mae even shows great anger when a Christian is near her during a fit. Perhaps that is why she attacks her mother so viciously.

With all of this said, it is still up to the reader to decide exactly what happened to Etta Mae to change that sweet little girl into a murderous woman her own family often fears. Her family believes that she is possessed, and that their prayers have gone unanswered because Etta Mae had accepted the demons willingly through Ruby's instruction. They also believe that one of the demons that possesses Etta Mae is that of Ruby Varner.

* For very obvious reasons the names of those involved have been changed to protect the family from persecution.

Those Evil Eyes
(The Williamsburg area, Blair County)

In the spring of 1979 my mother rented a nice farm house only about three miles from town. We were quite used to moving since we had done quite a lot of it since my father's death years before. It was as if Mom could not settle down after Dad's death. Still, we all liked the new house—that is except for the fact that my bedroom was painted hot pink. As a fifteen-year-old girl, I thought that hot pink was less than appropriate, but Mom promised to ask if we could change the bedroom's color after we had been in the house for a while.

The move had just begun when I first noticed that there was something wrong with my bedroom besides its hideous color. Every time I entered the room I felt watched from the one corner between the two large windows. The eyes that watched me were invisible, but I could almost feel them burning into me. They were malevolent, filled with hate. I knew that they did not want me in the room.

Through experience, I knew that my Mom would not listen to such nonsense as evil, invisible eyes that made me frightened. Besides, I tried to reason I was the only person who seemed to feel anything.

I was wrong about that. I had stepped into the closet to put some boxes on the top shelf when my aunt and uncle, who were helping with the move, brought up my dismantled bed. My aunt and uncle did not know that I was in the closet with the door nearly closed because it had swung shut behind me and I hadn't been able to stop it because my hands were full.

My aunt's voice seemed to shake and I couldn't help turning around and peeking out the door crack. She was standing in the middle of the room rubbing her upper arms and hugging herself.

"I don't know, John, " she was saying. "there's just something about this room. It's like you're watched. It gives me the creeps." She shuddered expressively and looked directly at the corner between the two windows. "I know it sounds crazy, but I'd swear that someone is glaring at us from that corner." She nodded toward the spot where I felt the evil eyes.

Uncle John stared at the corner thoughtfully for a few seconds, then he shocked me by saying, "It may not be as crazy an idea as you think. I feel it, too."

Aunt Betsey looked at him sharply. "Do you think we ought to tell Peggy?"

Uncle John could not suppress a laugh at that. "Peggy would never believe us. She's so strictly religious that if we told her anything like that she'd laugh us out of the house. Just don't mention it to any-one—especially the girls. There's no sense frightening them if they have to live here."

With that, they turned to go back to the truck for more boxes,

111

and I eased open the closet door. I could not help feeling the goose flesh rise on my arms. They had felt the eyes, too. It wasn't just my imagination.

During the next several weeks the feeling of being watched only got stronger. My mother worked a lot of twenty-four hour shifts, so quite often I'd get home from school and spend the entire night alone. My sister usually refused to stay home alone with me but she wouldn't say exactly why. Instead she'd stay with another aunt until Mom could go get her. This wasn't really an option for me, though, because someone had to go home and take care of our pets, two black-and-white kittens Mom had given us shortly after moving in.

The longer we stayed in the house, the more uncomfortable it became for me. The evil eyes seemed to burn into me whenever I went upstairs, so I made my trips up there as infrequent as possible. There was a small bathroom in the basement which I would use instead of going upstairs. I'd collect everything I'd need from my room when I first got home, and then I avoided the upstairs, sleeping on the couch, until Mom returned.

When Mom was home, the nights were horrible. Sleeping in that room was nearly impossible, but if I managed to sleep I'd have horrible nightmares that I could never recall, but I did remember that there were always birds, chickens I thought, on fire and screaming. I could smell the stench of burnt feathers and the horrible cries, but I never recalled how they caught fire or where I was in the dream.

The cats began avoiding my bedroom. They loved to be petted and played with elsewhere, but even if I took them in they would await their chance to escape and run away. They began sleeping in my sister's room, and so did I. When Mom was home I'd wait until she was sleeping, then sneak over to my sister's room to sleep on her floor. I felt safer there on the floor with the cats than in my own room with those horrible eyes constantly sending hatred at me. Whatever was in there wanted me out.

Once school was out I began reading all night long. I would fall asleep from sheer exhaustion around dawn but nothing would induce me to close my eyes before then.

Once I tried to tell my Mom about those eyes but she grew angry and told me that I was just imagining things. She warned me not to speak about it to my little sister because I'd just frighten her. I never brought it up again.

I had gotten so frightened by this time that I'd moved my bed over beside the doorway. There was no more than two feet between me and escape. I kept a chair propped against the door and used it as a stand because I had a horror of being shut up in that room.

One night I was dosing in my bed. The hall light was on, my Mom was downstairs, and my little sister was sleeping soundly. I was biding my time until Mom came up and I could sneak off to my sister's room to sleep. Suddenly I came full awake. The curtains in my room were billowing out strongly, as though a stiff wind was blowing through the room. I felt nothing but got up to shut the windows because it had been raining softly for hours. The storm must have been intensifying.

The windows were already shut! I stood staring at them and trying to comprehend what was really happening. Suddenly the chair blocking the door pitched over and skittered forward so that it was out of the doorway. Almost simultaneously the door slammed shut. I panicked. I was alone in the dark with those horrible burning eyes. I could not see them, but I could feel them radiating with hatred. I felt the curtains billow past me and I bolted for the door, tripping over the chair on the way. The door came open at my touch and I shot into the hall.

My Mom called up the stairs to find out what was going on. I told her that I'd bumped something over when I got up to use the bathroom. She cautioned me to be quieter and went back to her work.

I was nearly paralyzed with fear. My brain did not want to work. I couldn't go back into the bedroom because something was in there. Suddenly an idea came to me. I'd read somewhere that animals were sensitive to the occult. I'd get my cat and take him back to the room with me. He didn't like the room but he'd stay if I held him, then I'd know that everything was fine.

I found the cat curled up on my sister's bed. He began purring as soon as I picked him up. Slowly I worked my courage up to go back to that room. The cat's gentle purring gave me confidence and I stepped up to my shut door and pushed it open. Immediately the cat reacted. It screamed, bit my hand as I attempted to hold it and literally flew into the furthest hall wall. It hit the wall, slid down and, still staring at the place between the two windows, began making a terrible, mewling sound. It slunk back into my sister's room and hid beneath her bed.

I shut the door again and went to my sister's room. I fell asleep hours later laying on the floor of her room.

Not long after that night my Mom brought home a friend of hers,

113

Nan, who needed a place to stay while her home was being remodeled. She brought along with her a big, shaggy dog she called Bear. Mom told me that they were to have my room because it was larger and nicer than my sister's room.

Nan had lived a very colorful life. Her mother had been a witch, a practitioner of Wicca, and her stepmother had been an evangelist's daughter. She was well versed in both ways. She claimed to see auras around people, and often told odd tales about her childhood. Considering my Mom's strict religious life I thought that Nan was an odd friend for her to have made, but they were great friends.

The evening Nan arrived, Mom told me to take her and Bear up to see my room. Nan and I were laughing and joking as we went up the stairs. We all loved Nan and were excited that she would be staying with us.

Going down the hall toward my room, Nan suddenly got very quiet and serious-looking. I opened the door to my room and she literally gasped. Her face had gone white with fear and she made a small noise in the back of her throat. Her dog was growling and trying to pull from her grip. His hackles were up, and he seemed to be staring at that corner between the two windows.

Nan reached out and grabbed the door slamming it shut. "I can't sleep in there," she hissed. "Tell your mother I can't sleep there."

I was frightened, but I had to ask the question. "Why?"

She whirled and looked at me with incredulous eyes. "Why? Don't you feel the evil in there?" She pointed toward the closed door and her hand shook. "In there, in that corner between the windows, don't you feel eyes watching you? There's something in there!"

"Mom won't believe you," I warned her miserably. Quickly I told her everything. It was such a relief to have an adult that would listen to me.

When I had finished, Nan took my arm, propelling me back toward the stairs. "Your mom might not believe you, but she will listen to me."

Nan made me repeat everything for my mother who sat silent and grim-faced. Then Nan told her what she had felt there. Mom heard us out, but she was not swayed. She told Nan that she could have my sister's room if she chose, and that I could sleep on the couch if I felt better there, but she refused to believe that there were invisible eyes sending off hatred to anyone who entered the room.

During our brief stay two other people confirmed my feelings. My adult brother refused to go upstairs to use the bathroom unless I kept my bedroom door shut. The bathroom was in direct view from the corner of my room where the eyes were, and he claimed that they bothered him.

Also, a friend of mine came to sleep over because of a death in the family. I left her alone in my room, sleeping, to go unlock the doors for Mom early in the morning. Since she was sleeping, I stayed downstairs. Suddenly there was a thump and my friend was running down the stairs. She claimed that she woke up feeling someone watching her and that it had frightened her. She refused to stay for a second night.

During our whole tenure in the white house, my sister and I often smelled smoke and burning flesh. This was not surprising, since the barn far above the house had burned down taking with it the young cattle only a couple years before. I knew this smell because I had seen and smelled another barn burning down years earlier, and no one can forget the smell of living flesh burning once they have smelled it. Strangely though, the smell was strongest on the far side of the house away from the burnt-out barn. There, at times, it was almost overpowering.

Our last day in the white house was in late summer, barely three months after we had moved in. Mom had worked over night, and my sister had stayed home with me that night. It was just after dawn when I was startled awake by the sound of shotgun shots in my sister's room. I jumped up and ran in. She was sitting up in bed staring at her closet.

"It came from in there," she cried, pointing to the closet door.

I ran over and pulled it open. The closet was empty. There were only a few coat hangers and the belts to some dresses that she had outgrown.

Quickly I ran downstairs and out the door. I looked all around but there was no one about. We were alone I could see, for the fields had just been cut of hay offering me an unobstructed view of the surroundings. I ran around the outside of the house and checked the road for cars, but there was nothing.

My sister appeared at the door nearly crying. "I called Will and Mary," she said.

I knew what she meant. My mother's best friend was a preacher's wife named Mary. We had been instructed to call her and her husband if we ever had an emergency while Mom was working. They only lived about ten minutes away so I knew that they'd soon be there.

My sister and I sat downstairs in our nighties waiting for their arrival. When they got there we poured out the story of the gun shots and there being no one there. Rev. Will instructed Mary to stay with us while he checked things out.

Rev. Will went upstairs to look around. He was only gone for about ten minutes when he returned white-faced and frightened. Mary picked up on his state of agitation, too, but Rev. Will refused to answer any questions. Instead, he told Mary to help us find some clothes downstairs and then get us to the car. He went to the kitchen and called Mom at work.

We found some things to wear in the basement laundry room and quickly left the house. At Rev. Will and Mary's home we had breakfast and waited for Mom. Will did not join us. He had gone directly to his study and shut himself up in there.

When Mom came, she was closeted with Rev. Will for nearly an hour. She came out looking grim and frightened. Her eyes were red-rimmed from crying, but she would not tell us why. Instead she said that we were moving, and that until then we would not be left alone at the house anymore.

That night Mom found a house and within three days we were no longer living in the white house. We lost our deposit because we moved without notice and had to leave the oil in the barrel that Mom had filled for winter, but Mom didn't even seem to notice her losses.

The mystery of the house became slightly clearer to me years later when I was working for a local historical society. There I found records to indicate that there had once been a turkey farm where the white house was, and that one night all of the pens had gone up in flames taking the fowl with them. The pens had sat where we smelled burning flesh so strongly.

I do not know to this day what Rev. Will saw in the house, for he has maintained silence on that subject for nearly twenty years. My Mom, too, will not divulge the secret. She gets angry if she's pressed on the subject and says that Rev. Will saw something but that she has promised not to speak about it further. What lived in the white house that hated having people sharing its home? No one will ever know. Why was it that at least two times the animals housed on the farm had all burned to death in fires? No one knows why. I only know that whatever is in the white house won the battle, because we all left.

The story of the white house really did happen to my family ex-

actly as I've described it. I wish that I could tie up the loose ends that have been left, but real life is seldom as neat as fiction. I can only say that having slept in that room made me a believer that evil does exist. Living in that house also made my mother more liberal on her belief about evil spirits and ghosts. As for Rev. Will, he still refuses to discuss the subject. I have come to believe that whatever happened to him that morning was sufficient to frighten him into silence on that topic forever. That mystery he may take to his grave since the only other people who know what happened to him that morning are his wife and my mother, and neither of them are willing to tell the tale.

The Haunted Schellsburg House
(County TK)

Leah Thomas unhappily got into the car, beside her boyfriend Roger; her friends Melanie and Todd sat in the back. This afternoon would be the last time she could see Roger until he came back from Marine basic training. It was a terrible way to spend their last day, but the others insisted.

They'd always wanted to tour the old red-brick house that everyone said was haunted. On the way up, they talked about the story of the drunken man who sobered up, only to find his family dead by his own hand—and so he committed suicide. The house hadn't been lived in since the murders years ago. The porches sagged, rotted boards left gaps in the floors, and each step had to be tested carefully. The doors had been pried open by vandals who sprayed filthy messages on the walls.

Melanie thought the house was scary even in the daytime. But

117

the group walked through the house, to the stairs that led to the second floor. Roger flashed a light upstairs. It was rumored that the drunken father killed his children up there. The stairs opened onto a long, dusty hallway. They looked into each empty room, finding nothing but a dead raccoon. Leah refused stay any longer. Despite Melanie's taunt of "Where's your sense of adventure?", she insisted they leave.

Leah hurried outside and the rest reluctantly followed. At the walkway, Leah turned around to ask a question—and froze. In the doorway was a woman in a faded blue dress, her face twisted in fear. The woman turned and yelled "Hide, hide, he's coming!"

The others heard the commotion. They saw the woman scramble inside the house and soon heard a horrible screaming from inside. Then the woman in the blue dress appeared in the doorway and stumbled across the rotted porch. She tripped down the broken steps, fell, and disappeared at the precise moment the screaming stopped.

In unison the young people dashed for the car. No one spoke for a long while. Finally Melanie leaned forward and touched Leah's hand. "I'm sorry," she whispered.

Leah wondered if Melanie was apologizing for harassing her into coming or for what they had seen. Somehow it didn't matter. "I am, too," she whispered back and closed her eyes. It would be a long time before she would even admit that she had seen anything that day at the house outside of Schellsburg.

Outside of the small town of Schellsburg, on the maze of back roads that weave around the town, there is a large, abandoned red-brick house with a bad reputation. Many of the older local folks confirm that the house had a reputation for being haunted after the murders / suicide took place there. Unfortunately I could not find any other eyewitnesses.

The Phantom Feet
(Juniata, Blair County)

In the year 1889, Claire Mogel, then in her early teens, lived in a complex of row houses. (Row houses were often provided by companies to house employees cheaply, and to keep them close to their factory work. They also offered the added benefit of keeping employees in line since not only their jobs but their very homes were at stake if they lost their jobs.) Her family had lived in the house for only a few days when they began noticing something very peculiar about the master bedroom.

This bedroom was located at the head of the stairs, and could be looked directly into while climbing the stairs. As folks would go up the steps, they were treated to the sight of a pair of naked feet and ankles prancing on the far side of the bed. Nothing else, just feet and ankles in an eternal walk. When they'd enter the room for a better look, there would be nothing there, but from the stairs the feet would again be visible.

Her folks tried thinking of ways that the illusion of feet could be seen from the stairs, but nothing worked.

Finally, the naked feet unnerved the Mogel family so much that they decided to move. No one came around with tales of the place being haunted, and Claire's family didn't speak to the neighbors about their strange story either. They didn't want to be laughed at.

It was only years later that Claire finally had the answer to the puzzle of the phantom feet. She was reading an article in an area paper that said that skeletal remains of a pair of feet were found when workers were tearing down a condemned row of houses. The article gave the

119

address of the demolition, and Claire quickly realized that it was the house where she had once lived. The story went on to say that a murder had once been committed in the house. The police had never released the fact that the murdered woman had been found with both feet missing—cut off just above the ankles. At the time the police had speculated that the murderer had taken the feet as a grisly trophy of his crime. Now police felt that the murderer had been interrupted just as he began to dismember and hide his victim.

The skeletal feet were found under the floor boards in the master bedroom of the row house.

For Claire it answered a lot of questions, but it also raised others. Had the murder victim been trying to tell where her feet were buried? Or had something else been at work in that house? Claire never really knew, but she did know that she had seen those pacing feet many times herself.

Claire Mogel was my father's mother. She told the story to her children a few times, but I never was able to question her about it myself. Unfortunately, she died when my father was only seven years old. However, her older children remembered the story and passed it on down.

The Strange Case Of Fithian Minuit

(Chester County)

The London Tract Church Cemetery along White Clay Creek on Route 896 in Chester County has the dubious distinction of being associated with one of the strangest hauntings in Pennsylvania's history.

In the 1800s, a baby by the name of Fithian Minuit was born. Fithian was renowned throughout the area as being the fattest, ugliest baby anyone had ever seen. Young Fithian seemed born for only one purpose...and that was to eat. Stories of Fithian's prodigious appetite and of the types of things Fithian tried to ingest sprang up as the infant grew into a toddler.

When the famous surveying team of Charles Mason and Jeremiah Dixon (who surveyed what is now known as the Mason-Dixon Line) were in the area, young Fithian was taken along when he father went to see them. While his father spoke to the famous men, young Fithian was looking around the tent at the various gadgets. One thing that caught his eye was the gold watch chain worn by one of the two gentlemen.

The gentleman with the gold watch chain realized that the child was fascinated and called him over. Young Fithian hurried over to see the mysterious device. It was fascinating to the child to watch the hands twitch around the face, but more interesting by far was that wonderful ticking sound that it emitted. Young Fithian held the small watch to his ear in awe.

As the gentlemen continued to conduct their business, they forgot briefly about young Fithian who seemed so entertained by the small watch. Suddenly one of the gentlemen exclaimed in horror and lunged forward at Fithian. The men stood stunned over the child who was smiling up at them happily. Somehow Fithian had managed to get the watch off the chain and, as he did with everything, he ate it. Whether he swallowed the watch in surprise because the gentlemen had lunged at him is not known, but sure enough he had eaten the watch.

The doctors were at a loss as to what to do with the watch in the child's belly. They could hear that it still ticked when they placed a stethoscope against his belly, but how could they remove it? It seemed that young Fithian had suffered no ill effects from his unusual dining, so they decided to just wait and watch him.

Through the years Fithian continued to grow and the watch never passed through his body. Perhaps because of his having eaten the watch, or perhaps because he had been so fascinated by it, but for whatever reason, Fithian became a watchmaker as an adult. He liked to tell the story of having swallowed the watch as a child and dared folks to listen for the watch which he declared still ticked within him.

In time Fithian made a name for himself in the area as a great watchmaker. Throughout the rest of his life he continued to earn his reputation as a gifted watchmaker and he continued to tell his funny tale of eating a watch.

When Fithian was sixty years old he died, and until the very last he claimed that his internal watch had kept ticking.

At Fithian's funeral several people claimed to have heard a watch mysteriously ticking aloud. And from then until the present day, there are those who claim that if you stand at Fithian's tombstone and listen closely, you will hear a watch ticking from within the grave.

There is another story attached to the London Tract church yard which concerns a young boy named David who wandered from his family along the White Clay Creek. Throughout the day searchers hunted for the boy in the woods and fearfully walked along the creek.

Late in the afternoon the search party worked it's way toward the London Tract church. Near the church they found young David sitting quietly upon a large rock. It appeared that David had been there all day, and he readily admitted that he had been sitting there ever since shortly after he had disappeared.

The searchers were confused and angry with the boy. Why hadn't he ever thought to just get up and go home? The boy seemed dazed and said that he just couldn't have.

A while after this incident someone passing the church yard after dark happened to glance into it and saw a misty figure just sitting upon the same big rock where David had been found. Throughout the years this figure has been seen time and time again. Had this spirit taken over the boy, causing him to be dazed and confused when he was found? No one truly knows, but the rock now bears the child's name. Locals can point out to the tourist the large rock that they call "David Sat Rock."

The Ghost Ships Of Lake Erie
(Lake Erie, Erie County)

When a person mentions ghost ships, many people think of the legend of the Flying Dutchman or perhaps the mystery of the Mary Celeste. Others automatically think of the famous Bermuda Triangle, which has destroyed many ships throughout the centuries. Not many people know that in Pennsylvania we have a place where ghostly ships are said to sail endlessly through time. The stories of this body of water have somehow managed to stay out of the public light. These are the stories of Lake Erie.

Lake Erie have been notorious throughout the years for swallowing ships without a trace. The terrible winter storms have produced gales that have been more than many a doomed sailor could handle.

Throughout the 1800s Lake Erie was a major waterway traveled by hundreds of vessels. The lake was a link in the commerce trade which made it very important to many local sailors. Schooners, ferries, and cargo ships carried goods and people across every part of the lake. During this time there were several terrible nautical tragedies on the lake which are remembered because those poor sailors are doomed to eternally guide their ships across the lake's dark waters.

The schooner Radiant carried its usual cargo and ten-man crew when it left Toledo, Ohio one afternoon. Everything seemed fine when the ship sailed, but it never reached its destination. Other vessels were later dispatched to look for the Radiant but it had completely disappeared. Despite the fact that the lake was well traveled, no debris of the schooner was ever found.

Soon after the Radiant disappeared the nautical community was rocked when yet another ship simply disappeared. The Maumee Valley left Toleto, Ohio headed for Port Stanley, Ontario Canada but sailed into oblivion.

During the winter of 1860, terrible storms raged across Lake Erie and many sailors realized how dangerous travel across this waterway was. Still, few were prepared for what happened during one single night. That night two vessels, The Jersey City and the Dacotah, disappeared. No sign, even wreckage, was ever found of either of these vessels.

In December of 1909, the Bessemer No. 2 was a ferry that hauled railroad cars across the lake. Unknown to the Bessemer another ship, the Marquette, was also in the water. A terrible storm blew up which tossed the vessels about. When the storm was over, both ships were destroyed. This time many bodies were found. The captain's body had been savaged and bore slash wounds. Sailors later found a lifeboat in which the bodies of nine men had been frozen. This time there was much speculation about what had come out of the storm to destroy these two ships and their crews.

From time to time frightened sailors have come forward telling tales of seeing a schooner from another time or a vessel—that they knew should not have been there—sailing with them across the lake. Each time this happens they are surprised because the vessel is clearly from another time period, and they always comment upon how silently it moves along. They never spot any crew members, even when they hail the ships. Those who have seen such sights have left Lake Erie convinced that they have just seen one of the elusive ghost ships.

The General Wayne Inn
(Merion, Montgomery County

The General Wayne Inn, located at 625 Montgomery Avenue in Merion, PA, has long been renowned as the oldest working restaurant in the country. Started in 1704 by Robert Jones, it has served as a grocery store, a post office, and even a gas station briefly, but always the inn has served customers good food. The General Wayne Inn has also built up a reputation through the many years of it's service for something else. It is perhaps one of the most haunted houses in Pennsylvania and, at the General Wayne, the ghosts like to show themselves.

During the Revolutionary War, the inn saw a great deal of activity. It is located halfway between Philadelphia and Valley Forge on the main coach route, and it was a nearly mandatory stop for travelers. It became a central spot for spying operations for the patriots and, at one point, was taken over for three months by British soldiers and Hessian mercenaries. General George Washington stayed at the inn along with Marquis de Lafayette.

General Anthony Wayne used the inn at least twice, and the inn was renamed for his visit on February 9, 1795 when he celebrated his victory by holding a gala there. Men such as Captain Allen McLane, who fought as a spy and soldier for the American cause, frequented the inn. Many of the men who would sign our Declaration of Independence and many members of the Second Continental Congress stayed there with their families. Among the signers who stayed were George Ross, James Smith, John Wilson, and George Clymer, who was to have been hanged by the British for his treasonous patriotic duties.

Benjamin Franklin not only stayed at the inn, he opened the first post office in the territory and ran it himself from the inn. That room is now known as The Benjamin Franklin Room and it was a post office for 134 consecutive years.

Edgar Allen Poe began making trips to the Inn in 1839 and often came with his friend, Henry Beck Hirst. In 1843 he penned part of "The Raven" while at the inn. It is said that he preferred a back table in the Benjamin Franklin Room. He scratched his initials on one of the windows in the corner he favored.

With a history so filled with vibrant life, the General Wayne Inn seemed destined to be haunted—and of course it is. Approximately seventeen ghosts reside there.

The inn is presently run by Joseph Yoglanski and his family, who recently purchased it. I spoke to Mr. Yoglanski only a few weeks after he came to the General Wayne and he told me that already he knew that the building was haunted. He reported that he had been changing light bulbs in the chandeliers when he saw the bulbs he had just replaced unscrew themselves before his very eyes. And the chandeliers in the bar swing for no reason. He also told me that there is a man who has been repeatedly seen in the basement but he only appears from the knees up because he seems to be walking on the old floor (which was raised 150 years ago).

Mr. Yoglanski offers tours of the facility and has jokingly said to the tourists that they might see phenomena during the tour. Still, he was amazed when indeed unexplained events or even apparitions did appear during his tours.

Before Mr. Yoglanski, Barton Johnson owned and operated the inn for over 25 years, and during his tenure he witnessed much. He liked to tell of a mischievous spirit in the bar that blows on the backs of the women's necks on busy nights. The women at the bar obviously thought that the man behind them was responsible, and this led to some amusing confrontations. Mr. Johnson said that once the spirit started at one end of the bar, he would go down it, blowing on each woman's neck in turn. This happened so often that once it started, Mr. Johnson just stood back and watched the show.

The story surrounding this ghost is a bit amusing. It seems that in Colonial times there was a man who frequented the inn who constantly annoyed the female guests. He was so annoying that eventually he would end up in fights with other gentlemen. During one of those fights, the annoying man was killed. Since then his spirit has been said to continue the sport he enjoyed so much in life.

Edgar Allen Poe's troubled spirit is said to haunt the Benjamin Franklin Room. Poe's spirit has appeared wearing either a suit or a uniform that is presumably from his time as a cadet. He always looks the worse for wear and seems haggard.

There have been many sightings of the spirits in the basement by people over the years. There is a Hessian soldier who appears startled, as though trying to hide, near the wine cellar in the basement. He was first seen in 1848 when a local election was being held at the inn. A lady went down to the basement to get more ballots and came back reporting that she had just seen a soldier in a yellow and green uniform down there.

According to the inn's history this Hessian could have been one of several known to have died at the Inn. During the Revolutionary War, the British brought in Hessians—German mercenaries—who wore distinctive green uniforms with yellow lapels. There are several stories that could account for the Hessian's presence. It is known that at the end of the war a few of the Hessians who had been housed at the inn were left behind. Could this poor spirit be one of those men who waited, hiding, hoping in vain to be rescued?

There is also the historical account of the inn's owner during the Revolution who was a British sympathizer. He allowed a sick Hessian to be housed in his basement. The poor man was dying of pneumonia and was left behind when his regiment left for battle the morning after a bad storm. The innkeeper promised to care for the soldier, but he grew busy upstairs and never made it back to the basement that day to see to the soldier.

The poor man lay alone in the cold basement in great pain, moaning and crying out for help that never came. He died alone and uncomforted in that basement and was buried in the Quaker cemetery next door. People have often heard the man's moans and cries in the basement as he relives his ordeal.

Upstairs a Hessian soldier was said to have been murdered by several patriot sympathizers and his body is thought to be hidden in the walls of the basement. This spirit seems to have reached out through time to a man far away for help.

The man was Michael Benio, an Olyphant, PA resident. Mr. Benio, a general contractor, had terrible dreams about a man buried at the inn. Mr. Benio said that he witnessed the murder in his dreams time and time again. The dead Hessian was restless and wanted his body removed from the inn's walls and buried in sacred ground. The soldier desired that he be honored as a soldier, not left moldering away, hidden in the Inn's walls.

Those dreams became so persistent that Mr. Benio felt compelled to contact the then owner, Bart Johnson, in the beginning of 1978. Mr. Johnson was intrigued by the story and allowed Mr. Benio to visit the inn.

Mr. Benio did not know where the Hessian was buried, but his plan was simple. If the soldier had contacted him so many times with a request to be found, then surely the spirit would tell him where the body was once he got to the inn. So Mike Benio went to the inn and spent time alone in the basement, waiting for the ghost to contact him. When Mr. Benio targeted one wall, Mr. Johnson allowed that wall to be dug into. The dirt was sifted and human bone fragments were found. It became obvious that Mr. Benio's story had merit. Although no whole skeleton has ever been found, the bone fragments prove that at least one person was interred in the basement a long time ago.

Another man who seemed to have contact with the spirits of the

127

General Wayne Inn was Walt Bauer of Palmyra, New Jersey. Mr. Bauer was a truck driver severely injured when an eight-ton crane struck his head many years ago. Mr. Bauer fortunately survived, but found himself left with a new and disconcerting ability to see, contact and be contacted by the dead.

When Mr. Bauer toured the Inn several years ago, he made contact with the spirits of two Hessian soldiers he identified as Hans and Paul. Paul told of being a deserter from the military who had hidden in the Inn's basement. He told Bauer that he had been found and shot outside the inn, then his body was buried in the graveyard next door.

Bauer also spoke of the spirit of a barmaid from Colonial times who contacted him. She was said to have been raped and killed in one of the halls at the Inn. Her spirit has been seen both at the Inn and in the cemetery beside it.

Mr. Bauer also told about speaking to Edgar Allen Poe's spirit. Poe, he said, was standing by his own portrait which hangs at the Inn. He was making fun of it.

Poe told Mr. Bauer that he had become addicted to laudanum, a pain killer, during dental surgery and had often come to the Inn to procure the drug. There he would sit in his favorite corner and drink the drug dissolved in alcohol.

Mr. Bauer also spoke of seeing a little girl about whom he could tell little. He only knew that she had died there in a fire. Indeed, at least one tragic fire did occur in the Inn's history. Unfortunately, the report included no information about anyone being hurt or killed at that time.

One year, Mr. Johnson hosted a Christmas party at the Inn. The guests were all impressed with the beautiful atmosphere of the historic building. Many of the guests came up to thank Mr. Johnson for his hospitality, but one guest also complimented him on the unusual touch of history provided by the costumed gentleman who had mingled with the guests throughout the party. Mr. Johnson was puzzled. He had not arranged for a gentleman to attend in Revolutionary War period costume, and he had never seen such a gentleman during the evening. The guest was certain, however, that he had seen such a gentleman smiling and walking among the guests throughout the night.

According to an interview that aired on Unsolved Mysteries several years ago, Dave Rogers worked as a matre'd at the General Wayne Inn. One night as he passed a small cabinet in the corner of the kitchen by the swinging doors into the dining room, he saw the head of a man appear on top the cabinet. At first he continued into the room, but suddenly he stopped. "I saw a head!" he exclaimed to the other workers. "I saw a head!"

Another employee named Alice, who was interviewed for the same segment of Unsolved Mysteries, came face to face with the spirit of a man in a tri-cornered hat and official dress on the main stairs of the Inn. She stopped to look at the gentleman who seemed startled to see her, too. Instantly the man faded away.

One maintenance man hired by Mr. Johnson left the building in the middle of the night when he looked up to see a man standing in the corner dressed in an old-time uniform watching him.

There is a story at the Inn that a young British officer was taken there after he was wounded in battle. As he lay dying, he clutched at a locket he had. Despite the efforts of the doctor, the officer died. Once he was gone, the locket was taken from his hand and opened. Inside was a miniature painting of a young woman.

Several times throughout the years people have met a young officer in an old-fashioned British uniform who asked them if he could have his locket back. Before the astonished person could respond, he either moved on or faded away.

Mr. Johnson also liked to tell the story of a young parking lot attendant at the Inn who came inside to speak to a guest. He was very upset and excited. It seemed that the guest's new Cadellac had burst into sudden life as the attendant had walked by. The engine had started up, the lights came on, the wipers whipped back and forth and the horn sent out a long, continuous honk. The attendant tried to turn off the car, but found that it was locked. Mr. Johnson had to soothe the boy and let him know that at the General Wayne Inn, the employees needed to deal with the hauntings with a sense of humor.

Guy Sileo and another gentleman purchased the Inn from Mr. Johnson. Mr. Sileo had experienced the hauntings, too. He had trouble with radios that mysteriously lost their signal or which went off only to come on again after a few minutes. The music system in the Inn turned itself on. But most curiously he told of replacing a picture over one of the fireplaces with a floral wreath. Every few months he would find the wreath cast into the fireplace. It was as if the spirits did not like having the original picture replaced.

He also told of a psychic who once came to the Inn but seemed unable to sleep at night. One day the psychic dug some bones out from under the porch wall. After that the psychic said he could sleep there.

Many owners have noticed that the hauntings escalate when the building is remodeled.

Through the years many sensitive guests and psychics have come to experience the atmosphere of the General Wayne Inn. Other folks have come for the fine food and the atmosphere, but found themselves surrounded by the spirits of other times. It seems that the spirits at the General Wayne actively seek out the living.

There have been many happenings at the Inn which can't be explained. The racks of glasses will sometimes begin to shake and will continue for up to five minutes without anything vibrating them. The water in the bathrooms seems to turn itself on and off. Once Mr. Johnson came in to find that the cash register was filled with water, and several managers have reported that there is a certain crystal in the one chandelier which will vibrate by itself. Mr. Johnson told of coming into the dining room one morning to find that every napkin had been taken from the table and thrown on the floor.

Doors move by themselves, electrical equipment, such as the office adding machine, from time to time refuse to work properly, and many spirits have been sighted at the Inn.

Stories of the hauntings are legion. It seems that the spirits are alive and well, and living at the General Wayne.

George

Some of the stories in this book had to be researched, put back together piece by piece, separating the facts from the rumors, but other stories literally seemed to find their way to me. It was as if they wanted to be told and needed a person to give them voice. "George" is just such a story. I first met the family in-volved with the spirit they called George when I was working as a re-

searcher for a local historical society. One day a young woman simply walked in and struck up a conversation. She steadily worked her way around to telling me the story of her family's resident ghost since she had heard that I was interested in such stories. Before I knew what was happening I was visiting the home myself. There I was introduced to the specter that had haunted their home for over twenty years.

In the spring of 1982 I was doing research on the occult influences in the area where I grew up. It has always been my observation that where there are great forces of good, there are also great forces of evil. There had been stories circulating that a group of Satanists had moved into the area. There was some circumstantial evidence to support that claim in the form of mutilated animal bodies found in a couple secluded wooded spots by local farmers and hikers. The carcasses were of cats and dogs, some appeared skinned alive and others were so badly burned that the method chosen to kill them was not readily discernible.

During this time, I was asked to speak to a couple small groups about what might be happening. I have never been one to jump to conclusions, but I also believe that to ere on the side of caution is always safest. My credentials for speaking on this topic were a life-long interest in the supernatural in all forms, having written and researched the topic for several years, and a brief flirtation with the occult that ended when I realized that there was a subtle, powerful evil underlying what looked like Hollywood trappings.

During this time my name was on the byline of some articles about ghosts and hauntings that had appeared in the local papers and that was how a young woman I will call Isobel first heard of me. She walked into the office one afternoon and introduced herself. She was a petite brunette, no more than eighteen years old, who began to question me intensely upon what I thought about hauntings. Usually I keep my own beliefs about the concept of hauntings quiet, but I felt that she genuinely had a reason to ask her questions, so I answered her. I believe that anything is possible and nothing is certain. In other words, there is too much evidence to dismiss the idea but not enough to prove a case in a court of law.

Apparently Isobel was satisfied by my answer for she began to explain that she had been sent by her mother to ask me to come to their home for a visit. When I asked why her mother wanted to speak to me,

Isobel said she'd promised not to say anymore. Her mother wanted to explain everything to me in person.

I agreed to follow Isobel to her family home the next evening. Outside of her house she warned me that I must not mention anything about the supernatural to her father or while he was in the house. He was a staunch Catholic and refused to allow anything supernatural to be discussed in his presence. He'd been told that I was a friend of hers; that's how I would be introduced. I was not happy about the charade, but I had already committed myself to visit her mother. So I gave my promise hesitantly and she ushered me inside.

Isobel's parents, Sophia and Victor, were farmers. Her father ran a successful dairy operation of which he was rightly proud. We spoke for a while about farming and the price of milk. We chatted while we had coffee and at last Victor excused himself to begin the evening milking.

As soon as Victor shut the door, Sophia nodded to Isobel, who excused herself. Sophia sat down opposite me at the kitchen table and asked if she could look at my palms. I held out my hands which she studied in depth. She explained that palmistry had been a talent passed down through her family from mother to daughter for many generations, but that she feared her generation would be the last since Isobel was her only daughter and was not interested in the practice at all.

Eventually she released my hands and smiled. "You have an honest heart," she said. "I needed to know that I could trust you."

I smiled at her and assured her that I'd not tell her story unless she allowed me to.

Sophia nodded and sat back in her chair, taking a deep breath. "This house," she began, "is over two hundred years old. At least the back half of it is. The rest is a little over a hundred. When we first moved in, back in 1968, we lived in both halves. From the very first there was something about the house that felt odd. It didn't scare me, but I realized that there was something else sharing this space with us. There were cold spots on the stairs, in the hall leading to the front door, and the smell of smoke would be strong enough to wake us and send us looking for the fire.

"We have six children and soon the older ones were talking about the dancing ball of light that flew through the halls, bounced down the stairs and even knocked at the front door. At first I thought they were imagining things, then one evening I was bathing Isobel upstairs in the tub. She was only four years old so when someone knocked at the door I had to take her out of the tub until I answered it. There was no one there. I barely made it up the stairs again when I heard the pounding louder than before, so I turned around. This time when I answered the door there was this thing—a ball of bluish light pulsing and floating in the air nearly at eye level. I was shocked and it shot past me pulsing and literally flew through the hall, bouncing off the wall at the end of the hall and swiftly turned to bounce up the stairs.

"All I could think of was the children. My mind was spinning. Was this ball lightning, and if so, how would it effect the children if it hit any of them? I raced up the steps behind it, but at the top of the stairs it shrunk from about the size of a basketball to the size of a baseball and then just winked out. I turned all around, looking for it, and there it was again going back down the stairs. I had a distinct impression that this thing was mischievous. I didn't feel that it meant any harm.

"I tried a couple times to tell Victor about it, but he insisted that it was my imagination. When the children told him about it, he said that I'd filled their heads with nonsense, and when he saw it, he refused to speak about it.

We would often see the ball of light bouncing around the house; it seemed to appear particularly in the old section of the house. Especially in one of the bedrooms where it would often disappear. We found that we could not keep the mattresses on the beds in that room. We used to have old feather ticking mattresses, and every time we'd go in the room the feather ticking would be rolled up on the bed and tied with rope. The blankets and sheets would be on the floor in a pile. When we went to factory-made mattresses, they would be tossed off the beds as though it was frustrated by not being able to roll them up.

"We also had a problem with the closet in that room. There was a bare bulb in that closet that had a long pull chain and each time we'd enter the room we would find that light on. At first Victor blamed the children, but when he locked the room and still found the light on, he removed the bulb. Then one night we had some family stay over and we needed to use the bedroom. We went in to make the beds and there was the light burning in the closet as usual. You could see it underneath the door. Victor went over, yanked the door open complaining that I shouldn't have replaced the light, and suddenly he stopped dead. He backed away from the closet and I ran over. I looked in and there was a yellow ball of light hanging over and around the fixture, but no light bulb.

"After that we only used the room for storage. Victor would not admit that there was anything wrong with that room, but he kept it locked at all times and he always kept the key with him.

By this time we had lived in the house a couple years and our oldest boy, Charlie, was about seven. He had begun to want to use the matches to help us burn the garbage. He seemed to think that it was really grown up to be able to light a match.

"That's when this thing started to get dangerous. We would find burned matches everywhere. We always found wooden matches despite the fact that we only had the paper book type. We searched Charlie's room, we searched the house, and we even spanked Charlie for lying about having matches.

"Charlie kept insisting that he had nothing to do with it. We wanted to believe him, but maybe we also wanted to think that this was a normal problem—nothing to do with that ball of light.

"Finally the fires started. There were little fires all of the time. We'd smell smoke and wake up to find that someone had set a fire in the oven or the sink or in a waste basket. Then the fires appeared in the daytime. We'd all be outside and would come in to find fires everywhere. All of them were little, but they were frightening. How long until we missed one or one got out of hand?

"Charlie and the other kids went away to visit my parents that summer, and while they were gone the fires increased. One day we put out twenty-seven separate small fires. I was getting terrified.

"That's when there was a lull in the fires. Things appeared to go back to normal. We had been keeping the matches locked in a metal box which needed a key to be opened. We thought that we had this thing licked, but then the wooden matches began appearing on top of the box. We'd put them inside and in the morning they would all be laying burned, atop the box again.

"One evening we went out, when we came back everyone was tired so we checked the house and went to bed. That night we smelled smoke and got up. We rushed downstairs because the smell was so strong this time. Downstairs, the old kitchen was completely in flames. The whole bottom floor on the old side was burned. We've cleared it out now and made a porch there. The upstairs was saved and it's still as it once was—including that room where the mattresses stay rolled up.

"After the big fire this thing seemed satisfied. It didn't play with matches anymore, but it did seem to increase it's activity. We'd see it bolting along the halls or bouncing around the new kitchen that Victor was building. It almost seemed to be checking things out.

"That was when I first named it. One afternoon the door kept knocking. I must have answered it ten times before I got so frustrated that I started to yell at the thing. 'Just stop knocking you whatever you are,' I yelled. I was standing in the hall by the door and suddenly the ball of pulsing blue light flashed by me and I heard the words in my head, 'Call me George.'

"Victor was angry that I began calling it George, but by doing so it seemed contented. We saw less of it for a while, and frankly I was glad of that. I'd learned to live with George, but I didn't enjoy it. George was like having a mischievous, invisible child who was allowed to do whatever he wanted.

"Things went on as normally as they could for about two years, then George began acting up again. He would burn paper in the fireplace. We'd get up in the morning and find bundles of burned newspapers, paper bags, or other junk burned in the fireplace. The strange thing about this was that no one ever smelled any smoke from the fires. I have to admit that this scared me. If George could stop us from smelling the smoke, then would he set a fire one night that we would not wake up from?

"After we found several of these burned bundles in the fireplace Victor and I discussed it. I voiced my concerns about being burned up and Victor was very shaken by all of this. Suddenly two bundles of old newspaper fell from the ceiling followed by a small rain of wooden matches. I got the distinct impression that George had been listening and was telling us that he'd quit setting fires if they frightened us this much. I must have been right because there have never been any fires since.

"About ten years ago George began to act up again. He seemed almost bored, if that's possible. He began breaking knickknacks, spilling flower pots, and dropping the pictures off the walls. I know that it was him because he made sure of it. I'd get up to find all of the pictures removed from the walls and leaning against the wall on the floor below where they hung. I'd put them back up, go to the kitchen to start breakfast, and walk back into the living room for something only to find them all leaning against the wall again.

"Things went too far one day when he spilled all of my flower pots and threw the dirt across the rooms. I was furious. I began cleaning up and was scolding him out loud. I was telling him that he was a nuisance, that I was tired of cleaning up his messes, and that I wished he'd just leave us alone. Suddenly I felt a compulsion to turn around and look at the fireplace in the living room. As soon as I turned, a small Dresden figurine of a woman floated up in the air off of the mantle and then swung out over the floor where it was dropped. The little doll crashed onto the stones that make up the hearth and smashed into a million pieces.

"I was furious and I began screaming. I called George names and told it off. While I did that, I began to clean up the mess from my doll. That doll was very special to me because it was one of the few things I had from my own mother, and seeing it smashed and laying on the dust pan made me sad. I sat down looking at it and began to cry. I cried for a long time, then I dumped the pieces into the coal bucket to be taken out.

"About a week later the kids came in from playing in a storage shed all excited. They showed me what they had found. It was a Dresden doll identical to the one George had smashed. I took the figurine and turned it over. There, on the bottom, was a small chipped place where I had dropped the doll when I'd been dusting years before. I don't know how it did it, but I believe that George realized how much he had hurt me by smashing that figurine so he either fixed it or replaced it. I personally think that he fixed it somehow. I only know that it wasn't glued back together because there are no marks."

Here she paused to fill up her coffee cup. She turned back from the stove and looked me in the eye.

"Do you believe me?"

"I believe that your story could be true; I don't know why you'd tell me a lie. You have nothing to gain by it."

She shrugged. "Fair enough. Now I imagine you are wondering why it was so important to have you come visit aren't you?"

I admitted that I was curious about that.

Sophia sat back down and appeared to study the coffee in her cup for a few seconds. "It's because of those articles you did in the paper a few weeks back. You know, the ones about that cult that's supposed to have been in the area. Well, right about that time, a couple of our dogs disappeared. Victor found them, or at least what was left of them, up beyond the upper pasture in the woods. They were badly burned, but their metal tags were laying on the ground near them. Ever since then

George has been acting up. It's like he's worried or frightened. He pulls the blankets off our bed at night, he pounds on the walls, or whirls through the halls all night. I keep thinking that he's warning us or trying to protect us. What I'm afraid of, though, is that he'll start the fires again. Also, I suppose that I asked you here just because I needed to tell the whole story to someone else just once. It's been a lot to keep to myself. Victor won't even listen to me about it anymore."

I really didn't know what to tell her. I am a collector of ghost stories, not a parapsychologist. I explained it to her, and advised her to notify the police about the dogs. Other than that, all I could do was suggest that she contact someone who might be able to help her.

I did call her with some information she needed the next day. She told me that Victor refused to notify the police about the dead dogs. He was afraid that people would think that they might have had something to do with it. She also said that George seemed to have calmed down some. He hadn't bothered her sleep at all the night before.

It's been years since I spoke to Sophia, but recently I bumped into her. We spoke briefly about how things were. She told me that things had gone back to normal— well her home's version of normal— shortly after we had spoken. There had been no other gristly discoveries and that seemed to calm George down. In fact, she said that she rarely sees or hears George anymore. Perhaps they have grown so used to each other that merely co-existing suits him now. Or perhaps it is because all of her children are grown and married now. Maybe George doesn't play around so much because he misses her large brood. She confided that she often feels a coolness brush past her and then an acute sense of sadness, a loneliness that makes her pause. When this happens, she knows that George has gone by.

    *   Because Sophia's husband did not want her to tell anyone about their ghost, she asked that I not share their real names.*

Haunted Gettysburg

(Gettysburg, Adams County)

For the stories about the hauntings of Gettysburg, I am indebted to historian and writer Mark Nesbitt. Mr. Nesbitt has spent many years researching and writing about the tremendous battle of Gettysburg and about the hauntings of the battlefield, the town and the surrounding area. Mr. Nesbitt is a noted expert on both the history and the hauntings of Gettysburg and his books are well documented.

Mr. Nesbitt worked for several years as a park ranger for the Gettysburg National Military Park. While employed there, he learned that much of the area had a reputation for being haunted. Mr. Nesbitt became even more interested in the hauntings on the battle field and in the surrounding area after he witnessed some of the phenomena himself.

Before Mr. Nesbitt began his work to collect and collate the hauntings, much of the material was scattered in journals and various other sources and was nearly lost forever. He deserves to be given much credit for his efforts to save and pass on the haunting traditions and stories about one of this country's most historic areas.

There is perhaps no other town in the entire country which has effected more lives than that of the town of Gettysburg. Many people do not realize that there was a seven-week-long campaign being waged by the Confederates as they drove their forces into the Gettysburg area. The men waged war in countless little skirmishes and lesser battles along the way. The southern soldiers were in the Gettysburg area for weeks before the actual battle began. Interestingly, the Confederates left little in their wake to prove that they were in Pennsylvania. General Lee gave strict orders that his soldiers would not engage in looting, burning, or terrorizing the civilian population despite the ravages left behind by Sherman and others deep in the south.

The battle of Gettysburg during the Civil War was the most massive battle, and perhaps the most deadly and bloody single conflict of the entire war. The first three days of the month of July in 1863 saw more tragedy and suffering in that small town than any other before or since in the history of this nation. Gettysburg truly is an American tragedy, and it is very fitting that such a place would be haunted.

Much of the area where the actual fighting took place is now the Gettysburg National Military Park. The 3,865-acre park is filled with stories of hauntings that took place there. With areas named Devil's Den and Cemetery Ridge, how could it be otherwise?

Perhaps one of the least known of all the stories about the battle of Gettysburg is the story of Confederate Colonel Edward Cross. Col. Cross suffered for a week before the battle from recurring nightmares that he was about to die a horrible death while leading his men into battle on a wheat field. Since he was a commander during a war, he had every reason to believe that he could die in battle, but the further description of a wheat field seemed to stick with the colonel.

Col. Cross always wore the customary red handkerchief tied around his head, but on one particular day he felt so strongly that his doom had come that he tied a black handkerchief over his head instead.

As he passed his commander, Gen. Oates, the general cried out, "Cross, this is the last time you'll fight without a star."

The doomed colonel turned and replied, "This is my last battle."

Col. Cross was shot down and bled to death in a battle that took place in a large wheat field.

The area known as Devil's Den has been the site for recurrent hauntings. Major General Daniel Sickles of the Third Corps held the pile of rocks known as Devil's Den for a while. Union troops from Pennsylvania and New York along with other Federal troops fought deadly battles there those three days, but the group of men who will be eternally associated with that evil place are the men of Robertson's Brigade. Those Texans attacked the rocks trying to loose the Federal's grip on the high ground.

Stories about the Texan's fight have become legend. There is the story of Joe Smith of the 4th Texas, who tried to fight the intense heat of Pennsylvania in July by dipping his white handkerchief into Plum Run (later to be known forever as Bloody Run). Smith tied the cloth over his head, thereby making a perfect target for the enemy. Private Smith was shot in the head eleven times it was said.

The stories of ghostly sightings around Devil's Den have surfaced though the years. In one story a young woman who visited the park in the 1970s went to the National Park Service information center and wanted to know if there were any ghosts ever seen in Gettysburg. Officially the Park Service does not endorse the ghost stories, and the young woman was so informed. The officer could not help being curious, though, and asked the woman her reasons for such an inquiry.

The young woman told him that earlier that day she had been in the area known as the Devil's Den and was just about to take a photograph when she had a sense that she was not alone. She had lowered her camera to look around. She saw a man standing next to her who said, "What you're looking for is over there." The man pointed behind the woman. She whirled around to see what he was indicating, and when she looked back he was gone.

From time to time rangers are approached by bewildered tourists who have similar stories to tell.

One man brought a photo he had taken at Devil's Den back to the park. It was a photo of a man sitting on a rock. The left half of the photo was perfect but the right half seemed blurred. The man insisted that there had been no one sitting on those rocks when he had photographed the area.

In the summer of 1992 the movie Gettysburg was being filmed on the actual battlefield, and many of the actors, re-enactors and extras reported ghostly incidents on the battlefield. One such incident happened just after a scene at Devil's Den had been filmed. As the actors and extras relaxed for a few minutes, they heard the blast of two cannons firing and the sharp crack of musketry from across the woods on the slope of Big Round Top. The film crew knew that no one should have been in the area, and certainly they had no pyrotechnic experts setting off explosions there. Perhaps the spirits of the soldiers did not know that the battle being fought was just for show and they renewed their own timeless struggle.

Another time the actors were in the area of the Devil's Den to do some shooting and were relaxing between shots. They distinctly heard voices talking from near Big Round Top. Suddenly the shifting winds were filled with voices in song. The songs were ones known quite well during the Civil War era but little known today.

During the filming the actors and extras reported hearing

ghostly gunfire, seeing soldiers who faded into the mist, and cavalry men who rode by them on ghostly horses to join battles long ago fought.

Reenactors who periodically hold mock battles at Gettysburg have also witnessed phenomena. For the most part the reenactors are serious-minded men and women who pride themselves on their knowledge and the authenticity of the costumes and outfits they bring to the battles. One of the best known of these serious reenactors in a gentleman who has made it a passion in his life to know all there is to know about the battles, the customs, the costumes, the weapons, the tools, everything dealing with the time of the battle.

One evening in July of 1981, this man and a friend were resting on the slope of a hill between Devil's Den, Little Round Top and Houck's Ridge after a day of mock battle. The men were weary from the heat, their authentic uniforms were sour with sweat and their faces were smudged with dirt and gun powder. While they rested, a man appeared in the scrub brush just down the slope. He wore the uniform of a Union soldier and he began to slowly climb the hill in the last light of dusk.

When the man approached the two reenactors, he greeted them with a voice filled with a strong northern accent. "Hello, fellows. Mighty hot fight there today, wasn't it?"

The two men agreed even for July the heat had been especially bad that day.

The one reenactor, who was an expert on all things from the Civil War era, could not help studying this stranger's military kit. It was in good condition but he could have sworn that it was authentic. He was just about to comment upon the excellent quality of the kit reproduction when the stranger reached into his cartridge box and withdrew a couple rounds of ammunition.

"Here, take these. You boys may need 'em tomorrow." He gave them a meaningful look, then turned and began to make his way back down the hill.

The expert reenactor watched the dark figure as he worked his way through the brush on the hill. In his hands the expert held the cartridges he had been given. He glanced down at them, then stopped to study them more carefully. It could not be, but even to his trained eye the shells appeared authentic. These were not the blanks used by the reenactors for the mock battles; these shells had minnie balls inside them. The reenactors knew that such cartridges were forbidden on the battle field.

When the men looked down the hill to see where this man had gone, they found themselves staring at nothing but rock, brush and earth. The stranger who had given them such a deadly gift had vanished.

One of the bloodiest single events to occur during the three day battle was known as Pickett's Charge. Confederate General George Edward Pickett had been a graduate of West Point and had served in Mexico before leaving the Federal Army in 1861 to join the Confederate Army.

This gentleman from Richmond, Virginia must have felt great agitation as he fought against men who had once been comrades in arms. Still, Gen. Pickett knew his duty and on July 3, of 1863 he found himself leading his forces in a spearhead attack on Cemetery Ridge which was to break through the Union lines.

Pickett commanded 15,000 men as they entered that battle, but only 5,000 battered, wounded, weary men were left in his command at the end of the battle. He had failed in his attempt to break the enemy line, and Gen. Pickett would never again reach glory as a soldier.

During the 1992 filming of the mini-series, Gettysburg, the actors prepared to reenact Pickett's Charge. The day for the reenactment dawned hot and grew still hotter. The men in their uniforms were damp from sweat. The temperature reached nearly 90 degrees before noon. The actors began the mock battle over rolling, hilly terrain in the terrible heat, while sweating Union soldiers stood on Little Round Top gunning for Pickett's men easily.

Again and again the men in Pickett's mock charge surged over hills until they were swallowed up in a little valley which hid them from the film crews and their cameras. As soon as the men marched into the valley, they hit a wall of cold air. It was as cold as a freezer and later some of the men would say that they saw frosty plumes of breath as they breathed in that cold air. The actors paused, surprised by the sudden drop in temperature, and looked about for the cause. As they looked at each other, they suddenly knew without speaking that they were in a place they did not belong. Somehow they had stumbled into a world that was not their own.

The stories of the battle-related hauntings are numerous but there is one story of a reenactment that has always held special meaning for the park rangers who were working there when it happened.

Many years ago a group of foreign political figures came to see the battlefield. They received a special tour which included many little tidbits of history. One of the sights that they saw was the rocky area known as Little Round Top. From Little Round Top they had a view of nearly the entire battlefield scene and the men were impressed by the sights. As they stood on Little Round Top, they noticed a full regiment of men in Civil War dress moving along in the valley below them. The sight was awe-inspiring and the men assumed that this show had been arranged just for their trip.

The regiment marched through the valley, wheeled and maneuvered and moved on again as the delighted group watched. Obviously the rangers at the park had taken great pains to please their guests.

When the group returned to the park Headquarters, they thanked the rangers for the wonderful tour. The dignitaries made a point of especially mentioning the regiment that had entertained them from the valley below Little Round Top. They praised the rangers for their thoughtfulness.

The rangers, however, were confused. They had not arranged a demonstration for the dignitaries. There were no reenactors on the battlefields nor were any reenactments even scheduled. The bewildered rangers accepted the profuse thanks of the dignitaries and never told them that what they had seen was a ghostly replay.

Of course not all of the tragedies that happened in Gettysburg in 1863 were on the battlefield. There is the sad story of three young people whose lives were destined not to intersect.

Wesley Culp was born in Gettysburg but as a young man followed his employer to Shepardstown, Virginia. Wesley joined a local militia unit and when the Civil War began Wesley stayed with his unit to fight. This meant that young Wesley, like so many others, would be fighting friends and loved ones in this terrible war.

Eventually Wesley would end up under the command of "Stonewall" Jackson. Wesley fought with Gen. Jackson during Jackson's "Valley Campaign." They fought through Sharpsburg, Fredricksburg and onward until they reached Chancellorsville, where Jackson fell to friendly fire.

Wesley followed his commanders as they worked their way ever closer to his childhood home of Gettysburg. On the road there, they came upon a dying Union soldier named Jack Skelly. Wesley knew Skelly well for they had grown up together in Gettysburg. Skelly recognized his old friend and begged him to deliver a message to the girl he loved, Virginia Wade.

Wesley also knew Virginia well. She was nicknamed "Jennie" from childhood. Wesley took the letter that the dying Skelly pressed into his hand, and vowed that he would deliver the message if he could.

Outside Gettysburg, Wesley was killed in fighting before he could fulfill his promise. Ironically he died on ground that belonged to his own uncle. One of his commanders sent word to Wesley's family who still lived in the area and though they tried to find his body, officially it was not located. Stories of his sisters walking through the carnage of the battlefield looking for Wesley made some local families sympathetic to the Culp family's loss, but many others considered Wesley a traitor. There is a local tradition that claims that the Culp girls found their brother's body and buried him secretly in the basement of their uncle's home so that it would not be desecrated. Perhaps this rumor is true, for the Culp farmhouse has been reputedly haunted ever since. (Mr. Nesbitt tells the story of his encounter with a ghost at the Culp farm while he worked at the park. It seems that a male spirit still runs through the second floor of the old Culp house. A former park superintendent and his family lived there and heard the spirit themselves.)

During the three-day battle Jennie went to stay with her sister, Georgia McClellan, who had just given birth. The home her sister lived in was at the edge of town on Baltimore Road, and Jennie did not hide like most of the other townspeople. Jennie was greatly moved by the hungry soldiers who constantly streamed past her sister's home and was determined to do whatever she could for them. Early each morning Jennie rose and began baking bread to give to the passing soldiers despite the fact that her family was poor and could ill afford the loss of provisions. As the loaves came from the oven, she would hand them out to the men from both sides. Those who had received her simple gift spoke lovingly of her after her death.

One morning while Jennie was about her task of baking, a minnie ball passed through the outer door of the house and the inner door of the kitchen and found its mark in Jennie Wade's back. Jennie's death was an accident and Jennie was the only civilian killed during the three-day battle.

A small photograph of John Skelly was found in Jennie's apron pocket when her body was discovered. Her body was carried into the basement of her sister's home to await burial. Now the tragic triangle was complete. Three young people whose lives had held such potential had been destroyed by a fickle fate that deemed they should never again meet.

Today the home where Jennie died is a tourist attraction. Visitors pay their money to walk the boards where Jennie had once walked. Her story reaches out through time to touch generation after generation, but there is a spirit in the Jennie Wade house which often frightens visitors, too. Some visitors refuse to enter the basement area at all. They seem to sense something that makes them nervous or afraid. Others go down only to hurry out before the tour is complete.

There have been complaints by the staff of the house that the video tape system will not work in the haunted area. It functions perfectly well throughout the rest of the house, but records nothing in the basement.

A noted psychic visited the house where Jennie Wade had died, and she came away saying that the spirit in the basement of the house was that of Jennie's father. Mr. Wade had been a tailor who had gone to prison, and who had been sent to a mental institution after his release. Mr. Wade's condition forced his wife and children to live in very poor circumstances. According to this psychic, Mr. Wade is there to mourn his lost daughter whom he was too ill to mourn in life.

If anything noble can be said for this battle, it is that here men fought to the death for what they believed in. For three hellish days, freedom in its purest form was represented on that battlefield. Those men who died there left us a legacy which we should always cherish, and if the many folks who have seen the ghosts are to be believed, some of those long-ago dead are still fighting their battles eternally in Gettysburg.

Perhaps Mr. Nesbitt summed up Gettysburg best when he wrote in book I of his *Ghosts Of Gettysburg* series: "...as these stories will attest, something has been happening at Gettysburg since the battle, and a lot of people have seen things they cannot explain, but were certain enough they saw them to repeat them. Whether you believe all these witnesses to the unexplainable or not is part of the caveat. Nevertheless, here they are...."

I encourage the reader to learn more about the many hauntings in and around Gettysburg by reading Mr. Nesbitt's books. They are published by Thomas Publications, P.O. Box 3031, Gettysburg, PA 17325, and by visiting Gettysburg to see for themselves the place which history and the ghosts cannot forget.

The Giant Specter
(The Ormenia area, Blair County)

Dan and Rebecca Keene had only lived in the little shanty at the far end of the Ridge Road for a few months before hunting season began. Dan was not quite as interested in hunting as some of his relatives, but with five kids to feed he could use the meat.

The Ridge Road seemed like a good place to hunt. It was a long dirt road that connected two slightly larger country roads and served as a short-cut between the two for the few people willing to suffer the ruts in order to save a few minutes. It was covered with thick vegetation and trees sheltered the road itself, making it seem like twilight even during a bright afternoon. Dan chose the road because it was close to home yet was so far from civilization that he knew there'd be a good bit of game.

Dan got up early the morning after Thanksgiving to find that a light blanket of snow covered the ground and bits of frozen rain were being flung through the frigid air. It was a hunter's dream for the first day of buck season. The snow made tracking easier, and the cold wind could hide a scent if the hunter kept downwind of it. Dan bundled up after he fixed the kitchen fire and checked his gear. The 4.10 had been cleaned and sighted in a couple weeks earlier, so he shouldered the gun, took the canvas sack Rebecca had packed with food and an old coffee thermos, and headed out. He stopped outside to dig his red hat out of the pocket of the old coveralls he'd worn to work the day before, and pulled it securely over the back of his head.

Dan crunched through the frosty rind of snow and into the tree-shrouded lane that was the entrance to the ridge. The tree stand Dan had cobbled together in the woods during the summer was scant protection from the biting wind. He huddled in the perch, watching for movements or a flash of white.

It seemed that hours dragged by, but light was only freshening the sky when Dan pulled off a glove and opened the thermos of hot coffee. His hands were already stiff and he wished that he could quit, but there were five little mouths back at the shanty who would not understand why he had not gotten his buck.

The day wore on. By lunchtime Dan was convinced that he'd never get a deer if he stayed in the stand. He climbed stiffly down the boards he'd nailed to the tree as a ladder. He needed to warm up and perhaps scare up some game. But there was nothing out there. By now Dan had been out on the Ridge Road for several hours and had seen no game, and the ridge was preternaturally quiet. In the distance he heard shots from time to time, testimony that others were having better luck.

Finding nothing by dusk, Dan stepped onto the dirt track and turned toward home. He had a couple miles to walk, but it was already prematurely dark beneath the cover of the stark trees. Dan told himself that if he'd just stay on the path he'd be fine.

In the darkness ahead of him, something seemed to move. Dan strained his eyes to peer through the murkiness. There was someone ahead of him, someone abnormally tall. The person moved with a long jerky stride.

Dan picked up speed. It would be nice to talk to someone he thought. By the time Dan realized that he was not catching up to the figure, he was nearly running. No matter how fast he went, the distance between them remained the same. Winded, Dan gave up his chase, and merely watched the person swing along with long armed steps.

Dan saw the patch of road where the trees had been cut back slightly. On that stretch the darkness receded to a pale twilight. Now Dan would be able to see the man.

The giant man stepped into the light, seemingly oblivious of Dan's presence. Dan stopped on the dark road, gasping. He took refuge behind a clump of trees and peered in disbelief at the strange, horrible sight. The man going through the light was no man at all. It was a thing—a horrible caricature of a man. The creature stood at least a head taller than a man and was a ghastly gray color. It was completely naked and seemed to have no fur. The arms were disproportionately long, giving it a primate look.

The creature paused in the light for a second but it never turned around. Instead, it stepped off the road, moving through the stark trees

147

toward a sink hole. Dan followed slowly, fear warring with his need to know. He saw the creature scramble down the side into the pit.

Minutes ticked by after the creature disappeared into the hole. Dan waited, quelling the impulse to run. If he ran, it might come after him. It covered much more ground with its long strides than he could, so he'd be dead if it pursued him. Every one of Dan's senses seemed more acute as he strained for the slightest indication of what the creature was doing in the sink hole.

Finally, Dan could not stand the cold and the waiting anymore. He inched toward the hole and peered over the lip. The hole was empty. The gray specter had simply disappeared.

That was more than Dan could stand. Quickly and quietly, he made his way back to the dirt road, and started running. Somewhere along the line he dropped the canvas sack he'd been carrying. Runner's pains danced across his sides, but he never hesitated. At last he saw the shanty ahead and he didn't stop running until he reached the shack and had the door locked securely behind him.

He sat on the arm of a chair and shook. Tears ran unchecked down his cheeks. Rebecca was startled by the way he was acting. But he refused to talk about what had frightened him for several days. Rebecca stared at her hard-bitten husband shaking and crying like a frightened child. When she did pester him into telling, she wasn't sure that she believed him at first. Through the years, though, Rebecca changed her mind. Dan was absolutely adamant that the kids never wander the ridge—especially near dark. She often sat on the porch that faced the opening to the Ridge Road and watched it at dusk. Through the years she heard sounds, cries that were not quite animal and not quite human. She heard strange crashing sounds and caught glimpses of something moving in the dusk of night.

Years went by for Rebecca and Dan before any of their family would come face to face with the gray specter again. Their son, Dan Junior, was fourteen that summer.

D.J. had forgotten to feed the dogs his family kept across the road from the house along the opening of the Ridge Road. By the time his father discovered that the animals hadn't been cared for it was quite dark. Still, Dan insisted that his son get up and feed the dogs. They were raising a terrible fuss across the road.

Dan had installed a pole light near the dog boxes that bordered the ridge. The light lit the area nearly as well as daylight. Dan followed

D.J. as far as the porch.

"You make sure and water them well, too," he yelled across the road at the pens where D.J. was collecting feed pans.

D.J. grunted something back that Dan was not sure he wanted to hear, and thumped down the feed bucket. Dan turned around and went back into the house. He was watching a movie that he'd like to see the end of. But his heart was in his throat. It had been years since he'd thought of the gray specter he'd seen on the ridge, but suddenly the frightful memory loomed before him. He lunged out of his chair and threw open the door.

D.J. plowed into his father and grabbed hold of him.

"...it had red eyes..." D.J. was nearly hysterical. Dan pulled his son into the house and shut the door. It took a while for him and Rebecca to calm D.J. down. Nearly in tears, D.J. managed to tell his story.

D.J. had been feeding the dogs when he saw something moving near the edge of the woods behind the pole light. He had thought it might be a deer or something, so he stopped to watch it. Instead, he came face to face with a large, hairless creature that was humanoid, except for its gray skin and abnormally long arms. Its face looked like a skull over which gray skin was drawn. He saw no hair on it, but it had eyes that bore into him— red, glowing eyes that reflected the pole light. It merely stood looking at him while the dogs whined and pulled at their chains. The creature finally moved; turning back toward the woods and breaking the tableau. D.J. moved, too, dropping the feed bucket as he yelled and started running.

Rebecca and Dan exchanged frightened looks. They had heard stories over the years of people who entered the ridge and were simply gone. Dan and Rebecca had no way of knowing if the old timers tales were true, but they firmly believed them. After all, they had come face to face with the giant specter, too.

Like so many tales of folklore, there are no records to indicate what haunts a small stretch of road in central Pennsylvania known as the Ridge Road, but local memories are long and they say that the Ridge Road woods could get you killed. Over the years I've heard of eyewitness accounts of a "thing" that walks that little ridge, a thing folks at one end of the road swear is the cause of the deaths and disappearances of several people during hunting season over the past years. In recent years, no one has disappeared from the ridge, and no one has sighted the thing back there, but by now not many folks are brave enough or fool enough to wander that ridge after dark.

If this story had to stand on it's merits alone, it could be written off as the imaginings of one family, but there have been other gray specter sightings in the Appalachian Mountains over the years. Writer and ghosthunter Elliot O'Donnell related a similar tale in one of his books. This story entitled, THE GREY GHOST, relates a tale told to him in 1894 by an old minister. This story was about two young men who saw a horrible, gray monster in Grenberg Valley, on the Hudson River. O'Donnell described it this way, "It gleamed a horrible sinister grey. It had very long arms and legs and a peculiarly small and rotund head, and when it suddenly turned and looked at the two travelers it revealed a strange and startling countenance.

"The features were more or less human, but the expression in the big, deep sunken, light-green eyes was not. So frightful was it, so indescribably exultant and devilish, that Wren and Hall (two men who saw the creature) shrank back appalled, too petrified with fear to utter a sound..."

He described how it began to cry. "There was another pause, and then, apparently nearer, a yell of the most piercing intensity, the animal element in it seeming to strive for mastery with the human..."

Later O'Donnell described how eye witnesses saw the creature disappear into a sink hole behind an old abandoned house in the valley.

There have been other tales of strange, hairless creatures in the East. Some were reported as early as in colonial times when Native Americans warned whites to avoid the evil spirits in certain areas. When the scoffing whites invaded those areas, they'd been warned about, they received a horrible shock.

What are these monsters? That is a question I can not answer. They do not fit the description of Bigfoot, nor that of any animal indigenous to this planet. What is interesting to note is that despite the bitter cold of New England winters they are still seen. There is evidence that they either use or are drawn to sink holes which are large holes where the ground is constantly shifting, sinking. The natives called them evil spirits and said that they did enter the earth through the sink holes. Perhaps they were right, and these horrors, for horrible they are, are rising from the very bowels of the earth to walk among men.

* The names have been changed at the request of the family.

The Little Gray House
(Williamsburg, Blair County)

The first time Jeff Willard saw the FOR SALE sign in front of the little gray house, he knew that it was just the place he and his wife Becky had been looking for. He told her about the house that very night and within a week Jeff and Becky had viewed the house. It was perfect for their little family. There were three bedrooms, one for his small stepson, one for their new baby girl, Rachel, and a nice master bedroom. There was a small kitchen, a dining room, and a large living room. There was a long hallway which ran from the front door, through the house to the back and was bordered on one side by the stairwell.

Within two months Jeff and Becky were ready to move in. The first days in the house were hectic and it took them weeks to unpack. The house was living up to all of their expectations. It was nearly perfect, but slowly Jeff and Becky began to notice that things were moved in their absence. The ashtrays would be found on top of the china cabinet in the entry hall, the pillows would be tossed off the couch onto the floor. Jeff began feeling a cold breeze brush past him in the halls and in the kitchen. He wrote these things off to being in a new place, but Becky insisted that she wasn't the one moving the ash trays and knicknacks.

One evening Jeff got off work before Becky, and thought that he'd hurry home to start supper for her. At the gray house he got a start. The front door was standing wide open. Surely Becky had locked it when she had left for work that morning. Cautiously he stepped inside. He noticed immediately that the window on the hall landing was also open. Looking around, Jeff found that every window on the first floor had been pushed wide open. When he ascertained they hadn't been robbed, Jeff decided it was unforgivable for Becky to be so careless. They were going to have a serious talk when she got home. She had been very lucky

151

that nothing had been stolen.

Becky was livid that evening when Jeff accused her of leaving the house open all day. She insisted that she had not opened any windows, and she had double checked the front door to be sure that it was locked tight. There was no way she was to blame for this.

The next evening Jeff came home first to find the front door and the windows wide open again. This time he had been the last one to leave the house, and he knew for sure that he had given great care to locking up.

"There's something wrong with this place," Jeff told Becky that night in bed. "I think that we need to call in a contractor. Maybe the doors and windows are off plumb somehow and that's the reason for their always being open.

Becky argued that if that were the case then surely the door and windows would have acted up ever since the first day in the house, but things only seemed to get worse the longer they stayed in the place. She was inclined to believe that someone wanted them to move, that or someone was playing a terrible practical joke on them.

Jeff's contractor came and, after inspecting the house, declared it sound. Jeff had explained the problem to him but the contractor could not find any reason for the trouble they were having. He suggested that it might be best if Jeff had new locks and latches installed.

The cost of having the house outfitted with new locks and door latches was a bit steep for the young couple, but Jeff picked up some overtime at work and Becky sacrificed some things she had hoped to buy for the new house. They were both just glad that now, no matter who or what had been opening the door and windows, the problem had been fixed.

Becky pulled up before her little gray house and a gasp escaped her. The front door was standing wide open and the windows facing the street were open as well. Not only that, but it seemed that every electrical thing in the downstairs was on. She helped her children from the car quickly, and told her son to watch his sister while she checked the house out. Inside there was pandemonium. The lights were all blazing, the TV and radio were both blaring, and in the kitchen the electric stove burners were all cherry red. Becky felt a chill race through her as she stared at her home. There were knicknacks and throw pillows all over the living room floor. Someone had even upset the cushions on her couch and chair. In the kitchen she found broken dishes spilled from the cabinets, and the ceramic pot with a dried flower arrangement that she kept as a centerpiece on the kitchen table had been tossed to the floor and smashed into a million pieces.

Becky picked up the telephone with shaking fingers and dialed Jeff's job. She explained the situation to him and told him that she was afraid to bring the children into the house. He promised to get home soon.

As Becky turned to leave her home, a rush of cold air passed her and the front door slammed shut. The air had followed her from the kitchen, and she gave a cry when the door slammed shut, separating her from her children. She pulled open the front door and felt the cold air pressing against her again. She had the distinct impression that whatever was in her house was laughing at her. It was sending her and Jeff a message that new locks and door latches meant nothing to it.

When Jeff saw the mess in their home, he phoned the police. This had to stop. If he and Becky could not get this figured out, then maybe the police could solve the problem. A local officer came by to take photos of the mess and he made a detailed report, but the officer could offer no explanations. He asked a few questions, but Becky and Jeff were both aware that the officer seemed uncomfortable in the house.

After that incident the thing grew stronger. It was as if the longer they lived there the stronger it got. Becky and Jeff saw a black shape that looked like a silhouette or shadow slipping through the upstairs hall. Several times it slipped into their daughter's room and, in fear, they moved her crib into their room. Soon Jeff also set up a small cot for Doug because he began having horrible nightmares. The family was under siege.

One Saturday evening Becky fell asleep while laying on the couch in the living room. She was exhausted from staying up nights with Doug and his nightmares and trying to work during the day.

Becky woke as panic clutched her heart. She couldn't breath. Her lungs burned and there was a terrible, dizzy humming in her head. She tried to sit up, to push off the throw pillow that was on her face, but she couldn't move. Hard hands pushed the pillow even harder against her mouth and nose. Someone heavy was on top of her, holding her down and killing her.

Becky fought as best she could, thrashing and jerking beneath the weight. Her head felt light and she fought harder. If she gave in now, she would die, her mind screamed.

"Becky!" Jeff's scream cut through the horrible fog that was taking her over. The pillow eased up and then slid from her face. She sat up, gasping. Jeff was running toward her from the stairs, his face a mask of concern. She fell into his arms and cried. Shaking, she told him her story.

"Becky, we'd better get out of here," said Jeff. "What if I hadn't come down when I did, or what if this thing tries to hold a pillow over Doug or Rachel's face? We'd better put the place up for sale."

Becky sat, softly crying and shaking. Suddenly she felt Jeff's hand bite into her wrist.

"Look," Jeff hissed, pointing toward the heavy curtain that separated the kitchen doorway from the living room.

Becky looked up and saw that it was billowing inward at them as if a strong wind ran through the closed house. She could feel the cold as it brushed past her and headed up the stairs stirring the curtains as it passed.

Jeff's voice was taunt. "I'll get the kids. You go to the car. We're leaving tonight."

Jeff and Becky spent the night in a motel room, watching their children sleep. They were both frightened by what the future would bring and fearful for their finances.

In the morning both called off work to look for a new house to rent. Their money was tight so they ended up with a small two-bedroom apartment in a poor section of town. That was all that they could afford as long as they had to pay on the gray house.

Soon after they left, their realtor sold the gray house. The new owners stayed only a few months before the FOR SALE sign was once again staked in the front yard. Jeff and Becky watched the house closely. They felt guilty for selling a haunted house, but they grasped at the faint hope that the house would not act the same for the new owners. Now they knew that they had been wrong.

The house stayed on the market for a long time. No one else ever lived in the gray house. Years later it was bought by a neighbor who had the house torn down immediately and used the land to increase their yard. Becky and Jeff were both glad to see that the gray house was gone, but they sometimes wondered if the black shadow they had seen, the thing that moved on a cold wind, could be destroyed so easily. Becky doubted it when she remembered Doug's words the morning after they left the gray house for good.

He had climbed up into his mother's lap and hugged her. "I'm glad we're not going back," he had whispered, confidently. "I didn't like the black man. He kept coming in your room to watch you, Mommy. He scared me."

* *The name of the family involved has been changed.*

The Old Hag
(The Fay Mansions area, Blair County)

It was raining and cold as Terry Hammer got into his car at the factory where he worked in Altoona. It was 2 a.m. and he was beat. He had worked nearly a double shift that night.

The rain made the going slow and worse still, the monotony of the cold autumn rain and fogged wind shield, as he drove down Rt. 22, made driving both dangerous and tiring. The humming of the tires lulled him to sleep. For a brief second Terry's head drooped. Suddenly he jerked awake. The defroster had blown away the fog on the windshield and he saw clearly an old woman with long, silver-gray hair on the road in front of him. She was small, rotund and dressed in layers of ragged dresses. Her legs were obscured below the layers of cloth but he could see the rest of her plainly.

Terry jammed his foot against the brake but the old Ford Fairlane 500 slid around. The woman stood frozen in the swirling headlights. He tried to swerve, but it was too late. Now the car headed right for the woman. He braced himself for the sickening impact of the collision. The woman's face loomed before him.

The car passed through her without a jolt. Terry stopped the car

155

at the edge of the road and staggered out. He swore he'd hit her, in fact the skid marks passed right through her! But there she stood, looking back at him.

As Terry watched, she walked to the edge of the road and down the embankment. He followed after her, shouting for her to wait, but she disappeared into the fog-shrouded trees. Terry went back to the car, thoroughly soaked with the chilling rain, and sat there trying to get control of himself. Finally he started up the car and nosed it back onto the road. Now he was fully awake. By the time he reached the turn-off from Rt. 22 to Williamsburg, he had convinced himself that he'd been hallucinating.

With a sudden constriction of his heart, Terry blinked out of the windshield. There, before him on the rain-slicked road, illuminated in the blackness by his headlights, stood the woman once more. Before he could react, the car flashed through her once again. Panic gripped Terry as he stopped the car and jumped out. The woman looked at him briefly then turned away toward the Juniata River; she started over the slippery, wooded embankment toward the water. He ran forward to catch her, but she was gone. He looked down in the muddy earth where his headlights reached and saw the prints of two small, bare feet.

For a long time Terry searched in the cold darkness, but as the panic gripped him he made his way back to his car. He needed help. He headed for his folks' home. It was nearly dawn by the time he burst into the house, waking everyone up and babbling a crazy story about hitting some phantom woman twice. His father listened to the tale and saw the shape his son was in. Something was clearly wrong. If there was even one chance that Terry had hit some old woman, then she would need help.

Terry's father gathered some flashlights and ordered Terry to get into his car. Mr. Hammer told his two older sons, Andy and Jerry, to get in the car, too. On the way down the road, Mr. Hammer repeatedly questioned Terry about exactly where he had been when he thought he had hit the woman. Terry told them that it was at the Faye Mansions where the woman had appeared last. Mr. Hammer quickly decided to search that place first since it was closest.

Uncertain light streaked the sky as Mr. Hammer and the boys began their grim search. Using their flashlights, they searched through the dense undergrowth along the river. Jerry was the one who found the small, bare footprints that fit Terry's description. The tracks ran parallel to the river for a distance and then just stopped.

The area of road where the old woman was twice seen.

Next they followed Terry's directions to the place where he first sighted the woman. Here again they piled out and began a careful search. By now Mr. Hammer had become very quiet. He was remembering some stories he had heard a few years ago. Perhaps Terry was mistaken about what he had seen, or perhaps.... Mr. Hammer wasn't quite ready to admit the other possibility—even to himself.

At last there was nothing to do but to call off the search. Jerry wanted to call in the police but Mr. Hammer suggested that they just keep the night's events between themselves. For Terry the incident would have been over if it had not been for his oldest brother, Andy, who used the story of Terry's ghost woman to taunt him.

"Terry, you're seeing things." Andy laughed derisively. "I've driven that road a thousand times and I never saw anything. If you ask me, you dreamed her up."

At first, Terry took the teasing good-naturedly but eventually he'd had enough. "I don't care what you say, Andy," he finally said. "I saw that old woman. She was real, at least she seemed real until the car went through her."

It was about six months later that Andy found out that she was

157

not a dream. He was driving home from work after dark when he saw something in the middle of the road down by the Faye Mansions. At first it looked like a bundle of rags tossed in the road but, as his headlights picked it out, he realized that it was a small, plump old woman sitting cross-legged on the road as though waiting for someone. He braked, stopping just yards from her.

Andy was both excited and apprehensive as he peered through the rain-streaked windshield at her. His mind flashed back to Terry's ghost woman. He had described her in exactly the same terms. Andy could make out the straggly hair, the weathered face, the layers of ragged dresses. The woman watched him carefully, then slowly rose. Andy walked toward her but she moved away from him. Andy picked up his pace, but the woman maintained her distance. She entered a clump of trees on the river embankment.

"Wait," Andy cried, rushing forward. He was too late, the little old woman had disappeared into the darkness. He stood uncertainly at the edge of the river embankment for a long time trying to sort it out. At last he simply turned around, got back in his car, and drove home.

By the time Andy had pulled into the driveway of his parent's home, fear and shock were fighting confusion in his mind. He was a pragmatic man who did not believe in anything supernatural. But Andy found himself pounding on his parent's bedroom door. He couldn't simply go to sleep pretending that everything was all right.

Mr. Hammer listened closely to Andy's story. Terry asked questions and felt vindicated by Andy's shaken replies. He knew that there would be no more taunting about his imagination and wild ghost women. Oddly, Mr. Hammer didn't seem perturbed this time. He rubbed his chin when Andy finished his story and suggested that they go to bed.

"Aren't we going back to look for her again?" Andy asked, incredulously.

"There wouldn't be any use. It would probably be just like what happened to Terry. I suspect that that old woman is only seen when she wants to be." Mr. Hammer refused to speak further on the topic.

Nearly two years passed. Terry got a job in town working at the county's Children's Home. It was shift work where he'd have all sorts of odd hours. Still, Terry enjoyed the job, and he no longer had to drive that road between Faye Mansions and Williamsburg.

One night, while Terry was on duty at the home, he heard a noise in the downstairs. Arming himself with a heavy steel rod in case it was

an intruder, he went down the curving staircase that led into the downstairs hall. As he rounded the curve, there, near the foot of the stairs,
stood the same old woman he'd seen and hit with his car twice on that
lonely road two years earlier! Stunned, he stared into the crone's ancient face. She glared at him briefly, then turned and fled down the stairs
on bare feet.

It took him a moment to recover enough to give chase. He
heard the exit door shut at the bottom of the stairs and he swung
through it, expecting to see her only a few feet ahead of himself.
Instead, he burst through the doors into the empty night. Nothing
moved and no one stirred on the open grounds. Despite the fact that
there were no ready hiding places, Terry hunted over the entire
grounds before he returned to his post.

By now Terry was wondering why the old woman kept reap-
pearing to him. In the morning he filled out the report book, leaving out his late night encounter, but he could not help questioning
his male relief. Had anyone else ever seen an old woman fitting her
description on the premises?

When Bill, his relief, heard the question he was astonished. He'd
worked at the home for a couple years and had never seen or heard
anything out of the ordinary. For Terry this only deepened the mystery
surrounding the old woman. Who was she? Why did she seem to enjoy
showing herself to him? Over the following days Terry's story of the old
woman spread through the Children's Home grapevine.

One evening a teenage boy named Pat Rooney asked to speak to
Terry alone. Terry took Pat to the office. It was not unusual for a boy
who needed advice to ask for a private conference, but Terry really knew
little about Pat so he was slightly surprised that the boy had chosen him
to confide in.

"Mr. Hammer," the boy began. "I heard that you saw an old
woman on the stairs the other night?"

Terry felt uneasy. Now the kids were spreading the gossip. He
was both embarrassed and sort of sick over the whole thing. He should
never have mentioned it at all.

"I don't think that we should be talking about that, Pat," he
told the boy.

For a moment he thought that Pat would accept his answer, but
the boy stayed in his seat by the door. "Mr. Hammer, I think that the
woman you saw was my grandmother. My brother and I have heard the

159

story, and we've talked. It really sounds like it might have been her."

Terry stared at the boy in wonder. "Your grandmother? What would she have been doing here at that time of night? I mean, she was breaking in."

Pat ran a hand through his blond hair and sighed. "I know this is going to sound strange, but I think that she came to kidnap us. You see, once before we were taken away and she came after us. She kidnapped us then and took us somewhere far out in the woods where the welfare people would never find us. She was a mountain woman, so she hid us in some cave.

"We were really small back then so we stayed hidden in the cave for years. She would take us out to play and she would sometimes disappear for nearly a day to get food. She taught us to read and write in that cave; and she really took pretty good care of us.

"When were got older, though, we stopped listening to her. One day in early winter she told us to stay put while she went down for supplies. But it was so boring in that dark cave. We went out to play and that's when they found us. Some hunters caught us and took us off the mountain. We never saw Grandma again; she disappeared after we were found. When we heard your story about the old woman we just knew that it was Grandma."

Terry didn't know what to think. If Pat was right and this was the same woman, how could she have been hit twice and not hurt? How did she keep disappearing? "Pat, are you sure that your grandma's even still alive. I mean, you've been here for a long time."

"I don't know. No one's said anything about finding her, but she moved around in the mountains up along Route 22. If you really did see her, then I guess she is alive and trying to come back for us."

Terry didn't say anything. He had another idea. What if she wasn't alive, but was still coming back to claim her grandsons? He didn't know what to say so he tried to gloss over the whole situation.

Terry never really knew the truth of the situation, but he did have to wonder when a few years later some hunters, taking refuge from a storm in a cave above Route 22 near Faye Mansions, came upon the remains of an old woman dressed in layers of ragged dresses. The dead woman was later identified by some papers found in the cave. She was the grandmother of the two boys in the Children's Home. Furthermore, according to the coroner's report, she could well have been dead long before Terry had seen her for the first time that rainy night years ago.

As for Terry's father, he never would admit that he had thought the old woman was a ghost from the first, but he had heard the stories of the mountain woman and the kidnapped children. He merely said that he thought Terry's old woman and the mountain woman were connected. And to this day, Terry refuses to speculate much on who or what he saw. When he tells the story, he is reluctant to admit that he just might have driven his car through a ghost.

* *The last names have been changed in this story.*

Their Tiny Hands
(Cove Forge Village, Blair County)

This story came from a little village at the edge of Cove Forge outside of the town of Williamsburg, Pennsylvania, where I grew up. After I heard this story, I began asking around and found out that there had once been a small house in the same area that had reputedly been haunted for many years before it was torn down. No one either could or would tell me anything about who or what supposedly had haunted the house, but several neighbors confirmed that before it's destruction the house was often rented, but no one ever stayed there for long.

The village of Cove Forge was merely a loose cluster of houses with a highway running through it. It stood apart from the nearest town by only a couple miles but had retained its standing as a separate village for generations and probably always would.

When Nancy Masters was told that there was a small cottage

in the village for rent, she snapped it up. The cottage stood slightly apart from it's nearest neighbor. A small yard, with flowers growing in wild profusion, separated it from the woods, and a narrow strip of yard in front was bordered with high bushes protecting her privacy from the road. It was a lovely old structure of stone and wood outside, but completely updated within.

Nancy loved it on first sight, and she couldn't resist renting it. The cottage was rented for surprisingly little, and with its proximity to her new job it was very nearly perfect. The first few days were a flurry of shifting boxes to their proper rooms, and work. Nancy worked at a facility that treated troubled youths so she often pulled over-night duty. She did not get to actually spend a night in her new cottage for nearly a week.

Her first night there she unpacked the remaining boxes and finally put together her bed in the little master bedroom at the top of the stairs. She had been sleeping on her couch in the daytime because night shift wore her out so much she hadn't felt like wrestling with the big bed all by herself.

It was after midnight when she finally pulled clean sheets from the bathroom closet and made up the bed. She took a quick shower, allowing the warm water to sluice over her and relax her aching muscles. Finally, she toweled dry and pulled a clean nightgown over her head. She flipped on the light in her bedroom and made her way to the bed. She sat there for a few minutes, looking around. An undeniable sense of satisfaction warmed her as she looked at all of her possessions put neatly away in the beautiful, small room. She turned off her light and went to bed. The cool sheets soothed her skin as she fell into an exhausted sleep.

Suddenly Nancy woke up. Groggily she groped for the clock and brought it close to read its luminous dial: 3:54 a.m. Something awakened her, a sound—something—but now she heard nothing. She sighed, pulled the sheet closer, and started to go back to sleep.

There it was again. Startled, she sat up in the darkness and listened. A low moan reached her through the darkness. It sounded close. In fact, it sounded as though it were in bed with her.

She scrambled out of bed and groped for a light. Something fell over on her night stand but she finally managed to get a lamp on. There was nothing there. Nancy stood there in her clean pink nightie, staring at the room and waited. No sounds reached her and finally she managed to convince herself that she had imagined the moan.

She laughed at herself for being so stupid and decided to go back to bed, but first she had to go to the bathroom. As she turned away from the bedroom, the low moaning began again. It sounded like someone in pain. Nancy whirled around, staring wide eyed, but there was no one there. The moaning continued, low and pitiful.

She backed out of the room, shutting the door behind her. The lamp light seeped through the cracks around the door, and Nancy stood in the hall staring at the golden frame the lamp light made around the door, and listening to the slow, deep moaning from within. The longer she listened, the more she became convinced that it was a woman moaning. The sound of pain grated on her nerves, so she eased her way down the stairs. She huddled on her couch only half sleeping until the sun shone brightly in her front window and woke her at last.

Nancy made herself a cup of strong coffee and sat down at her little kitchen table sipping its bitter warmth as she tried to make sense of what had happened last night. Her mind tried different ideas and rejected each. It could not have been a neighbor's television that late at night. There were no other sounds that night, and she would have recognized a television show by the music that always played. Besides, she never even heard music or talking during the day from her neighbors. It was not a radio for the same reasons. At last her mind fixed upon an idea she could not completely dismiss. What if some young people were out in the bushes near the house having sex? She had been told that the cottage had been vacant for a long time, it would be a perfect place for young lovers to meet. Maybe it had not been moans of pain but of passion she had heard.

Nancy like the idea so much that she decided that it had to be lovers. She finally worked up enough courage to go back upstairs and cautiously push open her door. The room was just as she had left it. The light burned dully in the bright sun, the sheet was thrown back hastily, and her clock lay where it had fallen. She picked it up, then straightened the bed. She forced herself to open the closet and rummage for some clothes. The bedroom was quiet; there was nothing there to frighten her and she felt foolish.

This was Nancy's day off so she puttered around, rearranging things downstairs for most of the morning and, by the heat of the afternoon, she was exhausted. She forced herself to climb the stairs and lay down on her bed. She was going to take a nap in her room.

The room remained quiet and Nancy slept peacefully. When she awoke she was more convinced than ever that the moaning was either imagination or just kids in the bushes. After supper she decided to call a friend and went out to see a movie. It was quite late when she returned so she stumbled upstairs and quickly washed up. She pulled the pink nightie over her head and collapsed into bed. In seconds she was asleep.

Her eyes shot open in the dark. Petrified, she lay still, listening. There was the moaning, it came from her bed; it reached her from the pillow pressed to her ear. Her whole bed sounded with the cries of phantom pain. She lay there for what seemed an eternity listening to the painful cries, afraid to move while her flesh crawled with fear.

This time she did not waste time turning on lights or looking at clocks. In one desperate motion she flung off the sheet and ran for the door, slamming it behind herself. Standing in the hall she felt her heart beating painfully in her chest as the moaning continued growing in sound and intensity.

It's just kids, her mind hissed sharply. She stumbled down the stairs, grabbed a flashlight off the counter and ran to the door, flipping on the porch light as she went. The damp, cool air prickled on her skin, making her shiver. She flipped on the light and shined it into the darkness.

No sound of kids hurrying to dress or crash through the bushes reached her. There were only night sounds, katydids, tree frogs, and an owl. She breathed deeply of the cool air and forced herself to walk around toward the back yard.

"Look, whoever you are, I don't want to call the cops but I will. I live here now so just get going. Just go and everything will be fine." She played the light across the yard and into the woods where it was absorbed by the massive darkness. Suddenly this did not seem like such a good idea. She turned and hurried back into the house, slamming and locking the door with shaking fingers. Once she was back inside she felt better. She had let whoever was out there know that she was around and that she would call the cops if this continued.

Nancy did not sleep in the bedroom after that night. For nearly a week she rushed in the room before dark and gathered up whatever she thought she might need for the next day; closing the door tightly, she made a point of staying out of the upstairs. Once or twice, when she went to the bathroom, she could have sworn that she heard sounds—moaning, soft crying, and once even weak screams from the room—but bolted from the upstairs, always telling herself that it was just her imagination.

One evening her friend Jackie Gordon phoned to ask if Nancy would be free for a couple days during the next week. Jackie planned drive down for a visit, particularly since Nancy had called her old friend when she first rented the cottage and told her how beautiful and peaceful it was. Nancy could not renege on her offer but for several days she was faced with a dilemma. She could not let Jackie sleep in the bedroom, but she was afraid to sleep there herself. And how would Nancy explain keeping them both cramped together on the first floor when there was a perfectly nice bedroom upstairs?

When Jackie pulled up in her old battered red Mustang late on a Tuesday afternoon, Nancy was still not sure what to do or say. She couldn't imagine herself saying to Jackie, "We'll both have to sleep downstairs because my bedroom is haunted." Jack would laugh herself silly.

The afternoon and evening were spent catching up on mutual friends and with a tour of the cottage and the grounds. They went for a walk and had a late supper in the cool back yard at a small picnic table that some other tenant had left behind.

Jackie kept throwing hints that she was tired. The four-hour trip in the heat of late summer had wiped her out, and then there had been hours of talking and walking and getting reacquainted. Finally Nancy made up her mind. Jackie was a no-nonsense type of person, so she offered her the bedroom for the night. Perhaps, she rationalized, she had been alone too much and her imagination had gotten the best of her.

Guiltily, Nancy helped Jackie carry up her bags and showed her where everything was. With a heavy conscience she went back downstairs. Jackie settled in and Nancy pretended to do the same downstairs. Outside the living room window was a patch of yellow light on the ground from the upstairs bedroom light. When the light winked out, Nancy knew that Jackie was in bed. Time slipped by and eventually Nancy fell asleep.

Screams drove sleep from Nancy's mind. She bolted awake, listening to the horrified cries coming from upstairs. She jumped up and thudded up the stairs. She should never have allowed Jackie to sleep in that room. The screams were louder now and Nancy realized that they were actually words. "Their hands are burning me. Oh all their little hands! It burns, they're burning me...all their tiny hands." Over and over the voice cried out in terror and pain that tiny hands were burning. Nancy burst into the room, snapping on the light switch by the door.

Jackie was sitting up in bed, the sheet clutched in one hand, her eyes were bulging and strained, but she wasn't moving. She was not the one crying out in pain. She started from her trance of fear when Nancy stumbled into the room.

"Do you hear that? It's coming from the bed!" She shouted, jumping up and running into the hall.

Nancy followed her, slamming the door on the tortured screams—but they were loud enough now to fill the house and they could not escape them. Nancy went back downstairs with Jackie holding onto her shoulder. In the living room they huddled on the couch and waited for the screams to end. When they at last died out, they were replaced by those low moans that were now so familiar to Nancy.

Dawn streaked the room with gray light at last and the horrible noises were gone. Jackie reached across the couch and touched Nancy's hand. "Nancy," she whispered, "What was that?"

Nancy looked away. "I don't know. I've heard the moaning ever since the first night that I spent in the room, but the screams—those cries about the tiny burning hands—that was new. I've heard voices in there talking, at least I thought that I did, but I didn't want to really believe it."

Jackie's voice was low and angry when she answered. "You knew there was something in there and you still put me there to sleep?"

Nancy bit her lip and looked at her friend. "What was I supposed to do? Tell you that I have a ghost? You'd have laughed at me and said you wanted to sleep in the room anyway."

For a while they were both silent. Finally Jackie slid of the couch and stretched. "You know you're right. I would have laughed. I've never believed in..." She paused, looking toward the stairs, and stopped. "I don't blame you," she finally muttered and sat back down.

After that morning the visit was strained and awkward. Nancy slept on the floor and Jackie took the couch. Even so, they were awakened by the pitiful cries from the thing upstairs. It cried about the burning little hands and begged for help. It was impossible to sleep so they would both get up, turn on the lights, and wait for daylight to come before they fell back asleep.

Jackie cut short her visit. When she had loaded everything back into her old car, she got in and then looked out the open car window at Nancy. "Don't stay here anymore, Nancy, just get out. There's no place on earth worth all of this. Please just leave."

Nancy said that she would and then she waved Jackie off sadly. She did not like to think about night coming now that she was alone. She thought about calling her boss and asking if she could cut short her own vacation, but she knew that was not possible. Nancy could not go back into the little house she had once thought was so beautiful. Instead she sat on her front steps watching cars go by and listening to the normal summer sounds. Kids shouted and played. Somewhere off in the distance a tractor hummed, and more closely there was the whine of a lawn mower. The lady from across the road came out of her house, with clippers and heavy gloves, and fell to cutting the hedges that ringed her front yard. Suddenly Nancy had an idea.

"Hi!" Nancy called as she crossed the road. The older lady stopped clipping and smiled at her.

"Hi! I've been meaning to stop over and introduce myself but with the garden and all I've been so busy." The woman was friendly and chatty.

Nancy introduced herself and found out that the lady was Elizabeth Holtman. They chatted briefly about meaningless things. Finally Nancy got the courage to ask Mrs. Holtman if she knew anything about the history of the little cottage. She explained that she was a bit of a history buff and that it seemed quite old.

Mrs. Holtman shook her head. Though she and her family had moved there ten years ago, she'd never even heard anyone say anything about it. "The only thing I know," she confided, "is that it's often empty. Jerry, my husband, says that it's probably because it's hard to heat in the winter. I don't know. If you really are interested, though, I'll bet Bess Bates could tell you something. You really should talk to her." Mrs. Holtman pointed to another house kitty-corner down the road from the Holtman place and on the same side as Nancy's little cottage.

Nancy said she just might do that, then she chatted a few moments longer with Mrs. Holtman before she left. Back at her cottage Nancy wrapped up a couple sweet rolls left from the dozen she had bought before Jackie's visit and started out to the Bates house. At the door Nancy almost turned around. She was not a forward person, and this seemed almost too much to her, but if she went back she would have to sit alone in the cottage and wait for night and the screaming to begin. Finally she worked up enough courage to knock.

A pleasant-faced, little birdlike woman answered the door.

Nancy judged her to be in her eighties, though she moved remarkably well. She was petite, with cheery dark eyes in a classic face that had not lost its beauty with age. Her hair was cut in a short style and made a gray halo around her head. Instantly Nancy felt easier. Mrs. Bates offered Nancy a sweet smile and Nancy explained who she was and what she wanted. Mrs. Bates invited her right in.

"It's so nice to have a visitor," Mrs. Bates said, leading the way to the kitchen. "It gets kind of lonesome around here now that Dan's dead."

Nancy murmured understanding and explained that she lived alone, too.

Mrs. Bates poured out two cups of coffee and sat down. "So you moved into the old Arnold place. How do you like it?"

Nancy told her that it was pretty inside but that she wasn't sure how long she'd stay there. She had heard that it was hard to heat in the winter.

Bess Bates smiled. "I don't believe that it really is that hard to heat. Sometimes houses have other problems, hidden ones, though, that you can't see until you've lived there a while."

Nancy looked at her sharply. Could she know about the horrible tortured screaming that haunted her nights? Slowly she nodded her head.

Bess reached across the table and took Nancy's hand gently in her own. "You didn't come here, dear, because you wanted to know about heating the house, did you? Why don't you tell me what's really wrong. Sometimes it helps to tell someone."

Her voice was soft, comforting, and Nancy found her throat painfully constricted. With her free hand she swiped at tears that brimmed unbidden from her eyes. "I hear sounds in the house, a voice crying out in terrible pain. There's this awful moaning and then these cries. I can't stand them anymore. I don't really know why I came here today, I guess I was just afraid to stay there alone anymore." In desperation she squeezed Bess's hand tight. "Do you know why I'm hearing that? What happened there?"

Bess slowly withdrew her hand and drew a deep breath. "I've lived here for nearly sixty-two years, and in my time I've seen some things." She shook her head and paused, collecting her thoughts before she went on.

"Back in '32 a woman from town moved into that cottage. Her name was Jeanette Kramer and she had a bad reputation for running with men. She had been married once, to a man from the railroad, but she divorced him and took up with a fella who had a bad reputation, too. His name was Abbey Morgan and lots of folks claimed that he had connections to the mob. He had come up from Maryland and set up Janette in that cottage. He didn't spend all of his time with her because he was married and had a family back in Maryland, but every week or so a big black Chrysler would drive up late at night and stay parked there for a day or two.

"Anyway, I had heard all of the rumors, but I still felt kind of sorry for her, so once in a while I'd visit with her. Dan, my husband, didn't like it much, but I reasoned with him that it was our Christian duty not to turn our backs on her just because she sinned. I never went over when the black car was there, but I saw Morgan leaving a few times.

"She'd been living in the cottage for nearly three years before she ever brought up the topic of Morgan. She had met him almost ten years earlier, when she had been a waitress in a local road house, and they'd been together ever since. She said that her marriage had been a mistake, a way to pay back Morgan when he got married to some rich girl from Maryland. She regretted it from the start, but she'd stayed married for nearly five years before she got sick enough of it to leave her husband permanently. She told me that during the whole marriage she had carried on her affair with Morgan.

"I guess I looked kind of shocked because Jeanette's face grew pale. She leaned forward and said, 'Don't worry, Bess, I paid for my sins.' I thought she was gonna cry but she didn't. She just repeated, 'I paid for my sins in ways you'll never know.'

"After that I didn't go see her for a while. It wasn't because I judged her, but I didn't know what to say to her. But I could tell she was growing increasingly sad after Morgan's visits. The last time I saw the Chrysler, it was on a Saturday evening. There were lights burning in the cottage all that night, and the next morning, very early, the Chrysler pulled out fast like Morgan was in a hurry.

"I waited a day but when I went over no one answered the door. I don't know why, but I felt uneasy. I went back a couple more times, but there was never any answer. I started thinking that Morgan might have murdered her or something. The house was dark when we went over the last time—I asked my husband to come with me—but when Dan tried the door it wasn't locked. We went in and turned on a light. The place was a mess. The house had always been so neat, but now it was

169

torn to pieces. Furniture was upended and Jeanette's prized possession, a telephone, had been ripped from the wall.

"I was really scared now. I was sure that Morgan had killed her. Dan kept saying that we should go, he'd walk down to the post office and call the police. We had just turned to leave when we heard the moaning. It was loud and painful. My heart stopped for a second. Jeanette wasn't dead. Maybe we were in time to help her. It sounded like the moans came from the little bedroom so we went cautiously up the stairs. Dan flipped on the light and I gasped.

"Jeanette was laying on the bed and it was covered with blood. An old metal wash basin lay on the floor along with an unbent coat hanger. In my haste to reach Jeanette I bumped the basin with my foot and it flipped over revealing a perfectly formed little baby no bigger than my hand."

Bess held out a shaking small, wrinkled hand and a single tear slipped down her cheek. Nancy kept silent. Bess was not just telling the story, she was reliving it.

"The baby was horrible, pathetic, and I knew what Jeanette had done. She had been pregnant by Morgan and had aborted the baby. Jeanette was pale, she had lost too much blood and she was burning with fever. Dan went for help. He left me there with the pathetic child and Jeanette. Suddenly she screamed a horrid, wrenching cry and began beating her arms at the air, and pulling at something invisible that touched her. 'Their hands,' she cried. 'All their tiny hands are burning me.' She looked at me. 'Bessy, help me,' she cried. 'I can't stand it. All of my babies have come back for me.'

"I didn't know what to do. I went to the bathroom to wet a cloth to wipe her face. I spoke soothing words, and for a few minutes she seemed to come around. I held her and tried to calm her fears.

"She looked up once and there were tears in her eyes. 'Do you remember when I told you that I paid for my sins?' she asked. I nodded. 'This isn't the first time—there were six other babies. Morgan doesn't want kids. I killed them for him.'

"She fell into a daze after that, but then just before she died she began screaming about her babies' burning hands on her again. There was nothing that I could do. I held her and cried. I thought of her pretty eyes clouded with fear, and of the seven pretty babies that she would never smile on. In my heart I hated Morgan for what he had done. I never knew real hate until that moment. Jeanette grew still in my arms and I finally let go. By the time Dan had found someone with a phone and got help there, she was dead."

Bess's eyes cleared; she reached for a tissue to wipe a few tears away. She smiled sadly at Nancy. "I can't forget the sound of Jeanette's voice crying out about their tiny hands burning her. You've heard it too, haven't you?"

Nancy nodded her head. She was almost afraid to speak.

"I thought so. Others have come and gone over the years. I've heard stories and once I went to visit someone I knew who rented the place and I heard those cries myself. I don't think Jeanette could hurt you, but I understand why you couldn't live with those pathetic cries. Jeanette paid more for her sins than she should have."

Bess looked out the window behind Nancy for a moment. "Sometimes I wonder about God and justice. You know, Morgan lived to be an old man. Had seventeen grandchildren, I heard, and was considered quite a family man down in Maryland. Too bad he didn't care as much for Jeanette and those seven little babes of hers."

There was nothing for Nancy to say. She finished her coffee and left Bess's house. It was twilight by that time, and as she walked toward the little cottage she had conflicting emotions. She no longer feared Jeanette but the terrible cries would be even worse now that she knew who made them and why. She could not stay there where Jeanette Kramer relived her final terrible moments, where she saw and felt the tiny hands of her unborn babies burning into her skin. They should have come for Abbey Morgan, Nancy thought, but perhaps his justice was to be meted out elsewhere.

Nancy moved out that night. She packed a bag and rented a room at a local bed and breakfast until she could find another place. She only entered the cottage once more, on the day when she packed to move. That night, before darkness fell, she climbed the stairs to the little bedroom for the last time, and stood in the middle of the vacant room. She closed her eyes and said a prayer for Jeanette, and then she spoke aloud to the air—to Janette's spirit.

"Find peace, Jeanette Kramer. Find peace. You have been dead for a long time."

A couple years after Nancy moved out, the owners tore down the cottage and sold the grounds. When Nancy saw the house being torn down, she stopped for a few minutes to watch. She wondered if Jeanette would now find peace or if she'd haunt whatever building would go up there. After a few minutes Nancy put the car in gear and drove off, leaving behind a piece of herself with Jeanette Kramer and her tragic babies.

* *The last names of those involved have been changed at their request.*

The Black Horse Of Seven Mile Stretch
(Reel's Corner, Somerset County)

This haunting was said to take place approximately half a mile north of Reel's Corner, on the old state road in Somerset county, near Buckstown in the area known as the Seven Mile Stretch. In the accounts I found the doctor's name and the horse's name were not mentioned, so I have given them names to make the story clearer. Mr. Jacob Lambert, however, was a real person. His name is listed in all historical accounts of this event.

1700s

Doctor Nathaniel Martin spent a great deal of his time on the road. Being a doctor was not a lucrative profession, but he enjoyed it. He was still a young man and he had hoped to set up a practice in the west—maybe as far west as Ohio—when he had started this trip. He had taken only the few possessions he thought he'd need and was riding his most valued possession, a large black horse. He was quite proud of the beast, which moved with grace. The stallion was strong and when he ran at a gallop his hooves sounded like thunder on the dirt road; that was how the beast had gotten the name of Thunder.

It was a cold night and darkness was rapidly approaching; Dr. Martin knew that he'd have to find a place to rest and bed his horse soon. Snow and ice made the traveling more hazardous after dark. As Martin, astride Thunder, rounded a precarious curve in the road, two black clad figures jumped from the hillside onto the road. One dashed at Thunder, grabbing for his bridle, while the other fired a rapid shot that hit Martin in the torso. Fast upon the shot the gunman swung at Martin, knocking him from his mount and breaking his leg. Thunder reared, screaming shrilly, and dashed forward riderless. Behind him a gun blasted again.

On the road, the body of Dr. Martin was being picked clean of whatever valuables he had possessed. The two bandits dragged the body to the edge of the embankment and pushed it over. They slid down after it and quickly broke enough brush to cover the body well enough so that a casual observer would not immediately see it. It was really too bad that they had lost the horse, they thought, but the brute seemed ill-trained and difficult anyhow. They did not need the trouble.

Thunder ran on in the growing darkness, breath plumed from his nostrils as darkness brought the colder temperatures back. He ran until he came to something that seemed familiar and the horse stopped in the door yard of the Lambert farm.

Jacob Lambert was more than surprised to see the riderless horse galloping up the road toward his house. Lambert ran out into the cold and caught at the horse. The beast was slick with sweat and there was a dark spot of blood on the horse's side. Lambert knew that something bad had happened to make the horse abandon its rider.

Lambert tied the horse, ran into the house for his coat, and then came back out. At first he thought of saddling another horse, but there was something about the beast's fidgeting and snorting that made Lambert decide that time could not be wasted. He took a chance that he would be able to control the beast and mounted Thunder.

The horse responded immediately by turning and running back the way it had come. Lambert gave the animal its head and prayed he could hold on. Thunder seemed to gallop faster than any other horse Lambert ever rode. He clung to the beast, waiting for the fall that seemed imminent. Somehow Thunder did not fall on the icy, snow-covered road, though. He sped on as though Hell hounds were after him.

Lambert realized that the horse was heading back the way it had just come. He began watching the snowy ground for signs of the rider. They were at Reel's Corner on a narrow curve where the road snaked around the side of a hill and the berm dropped sharply into the woods when he first saw signs of a struggle.

Lambert dismounted and looked around. It was a cold, clear night with a large pale moon that shown with near daylight brilliance. In the moonlight he stumbled around calling for the rider. Had the horse stumbled and thrown its rider? he wondered. A frozen trail of red in the snow made him stop. Blood? He followed it to the edge of the embankment and looked down. There in the pale reflected moonlight a huddled bunch of cloth lay half way down the hill hidden clumsily by some brush. Lambert froze for a moment, just staring at the dark bundle and looking for any signs of life. He stumble-slid down to the man and turned him over. Martin lay frozen and quite dead. Vacant eyes seemed to stare into his own. A gun shot had chewed up Martin's chest and the side of his face. One leg was twisted at a macabre angle.

Lambert rigged a crude rope to the body and with the help of the horse pulled him back up the slippery bank. With a heavy heart Lambert worked the stiff body onto the horse's back. Thunder carried the body of his master back to town. Lambert walked beside them feeling a pain that was deeper than the biting cold that gnawed at his fingers and toes. He did not enjoy his trip with the dead man.

The town constable took charge of the body and the next morning he rode out after whoever had robbed and murdered Martin. Eventually the two robbers were caught and found guilty. One of the robbers was executed and it was said this man was the first person to be executed in the history of Somerset county. Although Lambert took good care of Dr. Martin's horse, the horse ran off whenever it could; he often found it standing on the road where Dr. Martin had been murdered. Then one day, when Jacob was searching for the horse again, he caught fleeting glimpses of it before it vanished, never to be seen again.

Eventually Jacob Lambert built a hotel near the place where Dr. Martin was murdered. Lambert had been deeply affected by the death of the doctor and by the black horse. He chose to name his hotel The Black Horse in commemoration of the tragedy he'd been part of. In front of the hotel he erected a nearly lifesize sign of a black horse. The hotel became a favorite wagon stand for teamsters and travelers between Stoystown and Bedford.

174

Over the years many local residents and wayfarers alike came to Jacob Lambert's hotel and tavern, shaken by having witnessed a large black horse running in front of them. The horse ran like the wind until it hit a certain spot on the road—where it just vanished!

Lambert would offer the frightened witness some fortification and would then tell them the story of the young doctor he had found murdered and about the black horse the doctor had ridden. Lambert knew that the horse always vanished in just the spot where the young doctor had died so long ago. Even in death the black horse had been compelled to continue returning to the spot where it had lost its beloved master.

The Ghost Hounds
(Cornwall Furnace, Lebanon County)

In 1740 Peter Grubb began building what would be a great iron smelting furnace near the city of Lebanon, Pennsylvania. By 1742 it was complete and Grubb became a very wealthy man. Unfortunately, Grubb was also a drinker and a braggart who could fall into black rages when he was drunk.

By the autumn of 1750, Grubb, wanting to impress his city friends from Philadelphia, bragged about the abilities of his excellent pack of hunting dogs. He insisted that his Philadelphia friends come join him on a hunt. It was a cool, brisk evening a few weeks later when his friends took Grubb up on his invitation. After a meal at which the wines flowed prodigiously, the hunters mounted their horses and the pack was loosed.

175

Perhaps Grubb was too drunk to give proper commands, or perhaps there simply was no game scurrying about that night, but it soon became obvious to everyone that highly trained or not, the dogs were failing abysmally. Grubb tried beating the beasts back into shape, but they still failed to scare up any game for the hunters. By the time Grubb got back to his home he was deeply embarrassed by the dogs failure, and he was sinking into a black rage.

His friends, seeing how furious Grubb was, tried to counsel him to let it go. Even excellent dogs sometimes had a bad night. But Grubb would not stop his brooding. All through the night Grubb drank more and more and the black rage took him over completely.

By the early morning hours, he was uncontrollable. Grubb ordered his iron furnace master to build the fires up to their most intense heat, and then he led the pack of hunting dogs to the furnace. Against the horrified protests of the others, Grubb threw the dogs, howling in fear and pain, one by one into the immense heat of the iron furnace.

Perhaps Grubb felt remorse when he roused from his drunken rage. Or perhaps he was only ashamed of his actions because of the whispers and stares that forever after followed him wherever he went both in Philadelphia and in his hometown of Lebanon.

In time Grubb regretted his horrendously evil act for other reasons. It was said that from the night of their deaths until the night that Peter Grubb died, the pack of hounds haunted him. It didn't matter if Grubb was awake or if he was trying to sleep.

In fact, there are those who claim to still hear the horrific howls of the dogs being tossed into the iron furnace's inferno. They say that in the early morning hours, in the dead of every autumn, Peter Grubb must relive his terrible deed throughout eternity.

The Inn Philadelphia
(Philadelphia, Montgomery County)

L ocated at 251-253 South Camac Street in Philadelphia is The INN Philadelphia, known for its award-winning cuisine, its intimate atmosphere, and...its ghosts!

The INN Philadelphia dates back to 1822. The atmosphere that co-owner George Lutz and his partner of 14 years have created is both relaxing and luxurious. As you enter the INN, you will find yourself wondering if you've entered a private home. From the sofas and wing-back chairs that decorate the parlor area to the two fireplaces crackling merrily, you feel right at home. The sweeping curve of the stairs will lead you to the dining rooms; or if you'd rather stop first at the bar, with its soft music coming from the parlor grand piano and it's crackling fire, you will find it equally enjoyable.

Upstairs there are three dining rooms. The first is the Franklin Room named, of course, for Benjamin Franklin. This room boasts a rare hand-painted print of Benjamin Franklin at the court of France, which dates back to 1853. There are two original fireplaces, brass chandeliers and a two-story cathedral ceiling, which adds a sense of drama to the comfortable room.

Next is the Green Room. This room features original red-heart pine flooring, oriental carpet, brass wall sconces, and Federal style window treatments.

Yet another treat awaits the visitor if they opt for the more modern environment of the Gallery Dining Room. Here the owners meld modern style with the romance of a bygone era to create a thoroughly enjoyable dining atmosphere.

When diners come to the INN Philadelphia it is for the cuisine and for the atmosphere so painstakingly maintained by both staff and owners. But many have found much else at the INN Philadelphia—they have found hauntings.

When George Lutz and his partner first purchased the INN, they were complete skeptics about hauntings. Mr. Lutz's first experience was approximately three weeks before the opening of the INN. George was in the basement, reviewing alarm codes over the telephone with the alarm installer, when he heard loud footsteps and the sound of dragging overhead. At first he ignored it because he was busy, but slowly he realized that he should have been alone in the INN. He realized that the crew had already left for the weekend and whoever was upstairs must be an intruder. He quickly told the installer about the person walking on the floor above him, but declined the installer's offer to phone the police for him. Mr. Lutz instead phoned his business partner and asked him to come over while he checked out the building.

George Lutz found no one in the building, so he waited for his partner to arrive. As soon as his partner came in, they began a second check of the building but still found no one. During the next couple weeks George Lutz forgot about the noises that he had heard from the basement. He was after all busy setting up for the opening.

About 7:30 a.m. on August 3rd, a six-man work crew at the INN sat down to their coffee break. As the workers sipped their coffee, they heard muffled voices in the second floor hall, then a loud bang. The workers rushed up the stairs to investigate the loud noise and found that a print hanging on the wall had been thrown violently against an opposite wall. The freshly painted wall where the picture had struck it was gouged out from the force of the picture's flight.

After that incident Mr. Lutz began hearing other stories from the employees. One mentioned sightings of something that the morning prep-crew had encountered. These incidents became so numerous and so unnerving that the prep-crew refused to leave their first-floor kitchen area. The prep-crew also repeatedly heard muffled voices and footsteps in the hallway of the floor above them.

One night in October of 1995, the bartender and the manager were closing down the INN as they always did. The bartender finished up and told the manager that he was going upstairs to the Gallery Dining Room to change into his street clothes. The bartender entered the Gallery Dining Room, closing the door behind himself, and paused— for

178

he had suddenly heard the Ladies' Room door open and close. He quickly decided that someone must have hidden in the Ladies' Room to wait until the INN had closed. Now that person must have assumed that the INN was empty and had come out of hiding.

Swiftly the bartender back-tracked down the stairs and went for the manager. Together they went straight back up the stairs. They first entered the Franklin Room and there they stopped suddenly. They watched in fear as two of the ceiling chandeliers were swinging in opposite directions.

"What the hell is going on?" the bartender gasped.

As suddenly as they had started, the chandeliers paused, then they began rotating in the opposite direction.

All thought of intruders or hidden guests fled from the men's minds. Together they rushed downstairs once more. The downstairs was suddenly filled with the blare of the stereo system turned on full blast. Stunned, the manager groped for an explanation. He had turned off the system himself only fifteen minutes earlier.

The men gathered their courage and quickly turned the system back off. Together they locked up quickly, set the alarm and left.

In the morning the manager called Mr. Lutz and reported what had happened the previous night. Mr. Lutz admitted that the story his manager related "rattled" him. He made a point of finding the bartender as soon as he came on duty and questioning him. The bartender related the exact same story as the manager had. Mr. Lutz knew the bartender and the manager were not friends so there was little chance that they had been playing a trick. In fact, both men seemed very disturbed by the events they had witnessed.

As the incidents grew, Mr. Lutz thought again of his experience in the basement that night when he had heard footsteps and something dragging across the floor above his head. Even as a skeptic, he could hardly insist that all of his employees and the work crews that he had hired had been imagining things when he had heard something himself.

One evening a couple named Nancy and Bob came in for dinner. They were seated in the Green Room and served appetizers. After the server left, Nancy whispered to Bob that the waiter had pulled her hair. Bob was surprised because he had seen nothing. Surely she had been mistaken or else she had gotten her hair caught on something else which had made it seem that the server had given her hair a small tug.

As the meal progressed, Nancy insisted that someone had pulled her hair a couple more times. Again Bob assured her that it could not have been the server, but he was beginning to have his doubts. Was someone playing a trick on them?

Suddenly Nancy's head snapped back sharply as though someone had yanked her hair hard and she exclaimed. This time there was no doubt that something had happened, but just what had it been? Nancy was sitting very near the wall and Bob wondered if there might not be a rough spot on the wall where her hair was snagging. Quickly they examined the wall but it offered up only a smooth, finished surface.

Bob summoned the server and demanded to know what was going on. He explained what had happened to his wife and accused the server of playing a practical joke. The server vehemently denied the accusation, but he was not very surprised, after all, this had happened before. He calmed the patrons and summoned Mr. Lutz.

George Lutz knew as soon as he saw the angry, frustrated expressions of his customers that something was very wrong. He and his partner pride themselves on catering to their customers desires and in creating a very pleasurable dining atmosphere. George listened as the server and his customers explained the night's incidents, then sighed. This was not the first time that customers had complained of having their hair pulled while dining at the INN.

Quietly he explained that the INN seemed to be haunted and that one of the manifestations that the ghost took was pulling hair occasionally. He tried as best he could to soothe the feelings of his valued customers. A hair-pulling ghost made for strained customer relations sometimes.

During the two and a half years that Mr. Lutz and his partner have owned and operated the INN Philadelphia, they have had many other occurrences.

One Sunday in April of 1996, eight people were gathered in the Inn's bar to await the opening of the upstairs rooms for Sunday Brunch. While the customers passed a few minutes waiting at the bar, Mr. Lutz spotted a married couple who were old friends. George and his friends struck up a conversation while standing near the doorway. George was facing the entry hall and his friends were looking inward toward the bar as they spoke. Suddenly, George said, his friend's face changed expression and he seemed startled.

Quickly George turned to see what had upset his friend. At the bar a sudden confusion of voices was breaking out. Startled customers all seemed to be staring intently at the corner between the piano and the wall at the end of the bar. The customers were demanding of each other if they had just seen the same thing.

Quickly George learned of the situation. While he had been visiting with his friends, the customers had heard footsteps coming from the coat-check room and a transparent figure came out of the coat room! The figure walked between the customers and the piano, disappearing at the far end of the bar before the astonished eyes of the entire group.

There have been several times when customers have seemed uncomfortable dining at the INN Philadelphia. In particular, George remembered one lady who came up and asked him if there was anything strange going on at the INN. George admitted that things did occur from time to time. The woman smiled and told him that she was sensitive to those things and had picked up that the INN Philadelphia is haunted.

One couple abruptly ordered their bill tallied in the middle of their dinner and they prepared hastily to leave. Mr. Lutz inquired, as he accommodated them, if they were leaving because of the service or the food. The couple quickly assured him that neither were the case, but that the lady was very sensitive to the spirit world and was disturbed by the people in the "shadows" that she saw moving about in the dining room. Since then the couple have refused to eat inside the INN Philadelphia, but they often return to dine in the Secret Garden, the outside dining area which is open from spring until the fall.

Through the past couple years George has been approached several times by people who are sensitive to the supernatural. He has, from them, pieced together a partial list of just who haunts the INN Philadelphia. People have seen a little girl between the ages of seven and nine inside the INN. Others speak of seeing another child in what are often described as "period clothes." Others talk of a group of men and women in their 30s or 40s, in clothes from the mid-1800s, moving about inside the building. After each sighting they are described as being translucent, yet seeming to have substance.

The spirits which haunt the INN Philadelphia seem more mischievous than malicious. Mr. Lutz and the staff have reported that plates are sometimes sent flying from a shelf to smash against the opposite wall. This is about as destructive as the spirits have been and, although it is unnerving to have dishes sent crashing by invisible hands, it is something that the present owners can live with.

Mr. Lutz admits that through the past couple years his attitude about the spirits has changed considerably. In fact, he has found himself unconsciously acknowledging them.

One night the INN Philadelphia was rented to a party of 110 people. The group had a popular pianist flown in from New Orleans to entertain them. As Mr. Lutz listened to the superb playing of the lady from New Orleans, he found himself thinking aloud, "They aren't going to like this." He realized that he was referring to the spirits not liking the loud, fast music that was presently filling the restaurant and was surprised at himself.

Mr. Lutz was correct. The spirits were upset by the boisterous music that blared though their home. That evening as the party progressed, Mr. Lutz and the staff noticed that items were mysteriously moved from their accustomed places. After the party the chef and an assistant were cleaning the kitchen when they saw three plates lift themselves from their place on the shelf and launch themselves at the wall with enough force to smash them. And, Mr. Lutz said, throughout the entire weekend the spirits made their displeasure known through various little incidents.

George Lutz is a compassionate man and he began thinking that perhaps it would be better if he arranged a seance where the spirits could be put to rest. He had heard that ghosts were souls that had not gone on into the light of the afterworld and he hoped to relieve the spirits of their earthly turmoil. Accordingly, George, made inquiries with two paranormal groups in the area and was surprised by what they had to say. Each, independent of the other, asserted that it could be dangerous to try and remove the spirits. Both groups felt that contacting them might confuse them or might even empower them with the ability to turn hostile.

George Lutz decided that he would consult his staff before he made his decision about the seance. After all, he had planned for the seance to follow a dinner where they could have made a great deal of money from tips. To a person, each staff member gave him an emphatic "No!" As long as the ghosts did not turn hostile, then they could deal with whatever walked the INN Philadelphia. This convinced George that his staff truly believed the restaurant is haunted and they felt that they should leave well enough alone.

According to George Lutz the incidents of hauntings are sporadic. From the end of 1996 into 1997, there have been almost no incidents.

These lulls have happened before, however, and Mr. Lutz is prepared to again have to explain to surprised customers that the INN Philadelphia is haunted.

I'll leave the reader with Mr. Lutz's own words from a letter that he wrote me to clarify the events at The INN Philadelphia:

"The recountings above are accurate and truthful in that I have no reason to disbelieve these credible people. Although as a skeptic I do, on occasion, sense something. It's a feeling of being not alone or that someone is watching. So often science discounts ancient remedies only to find that, indeed, there is merit in them."

Because of the hauntings at the INN Philadelphia Mr. Lutz began to look into the history of the building. He found that the people who occupied the building as far back as the 1970's had known that the building was haunted. They related similar experiences and reported that they had suffered minor damage at the mischievous hands of whoever haunts the building.

I recommend that anyone visiting Philadelphia stop for at least one meal at The INN Philadelphia. Perhaps your dining will be enlivened by a spirit making it's presence known, or at least you will have enjoyed an award winning meal.

The Jean Bonnet
(The Schellsburg area, Bedford County)

O n Rt. 30 West, between Bedford and Schellsburg, is the Jean Bonnet, a large brown fieldstone and wood structure, which has fed and housed travelers since 1762. It has low ceilings criss-

The Jean Bonnet Tavern

crossed by blackened oak beams that were hand hewn. There is a large fireplace in the restaurant that still works. Huge kettles sit on the mantle where once food was prepared. There are glass-enclosed candles at each table, and rough stone walls that offer the diner a feel for what it must have been like when George Washington and his troops had stayed there during the Revolutionary War. The entire building is steeped in history, and it has the feel of a place where much has happened, but for many of those who work or have stayed there, the Jean Bonnet is famous for hosting several ghosts.

The inn and tavern was purchased by Mark and Lynn Baer in 1983, and they have run it ever since. The Baers are skeptics who admit that they have never had any strange experiences in the building, but Lynn graciously agreed to allow me to speak with several employees who told me of experiences they and others had witnessed.

Perhaps one of the oldest ghosts that haunts the building is the spirit of a young woman who died there during the Revolutionary War. It is said that her fiancé was a scout for General Washington, and that the young scout had arranged for her to meet him at the Jean Bonnet.

She arrived there and, when he didn't come immediately, she rented a room. As the days turned into weeks, she became increasingly anxious. Every time she'd hear a horse enter the yard below, she'd run from her room to a front window on the second floor and look out, hoping to see her lover. After several months of anxious waiting and countless trips to the window only to be disappointed, the young woman grew ill. What she died from is not clear, but local legend claims that she died from a broken heart. At length she passed away not knowing that her lover had died for the cause of freedom.

There is no record of when exactly she began to haunt the building, but since shortly after her death people have heard her footsteps as she rushes by. They feel a cold breeze pass them in the hall. They hear the rustling of crinolines and petticoats as she hurries on her eternal vigil to the front windows.

Several employees of the Jean Bonnet have experienced this phenomena throughout the years, but it is when guests who know nothing of the building's history come forward with stories that even the employees seem impressed.

Several years ago a husband and wife stayed at the inn for the night and came away with a strange story to tell which they wrote down in the Jean Bonnet's guest book. The gentleman in question is a retired no-nonsense military officer. During their stay, the gentleman was walking down the hall toward his room when he felt a distinct rush of cold air and heard the crinkle of material rustling as if someone in stiff skirts had just rushed past him. The retired officer was very much surprised since he saw no one and could find nothing else to explain his experience in the hall. He and his wife later spoke to employees at the Jean Bonnet who told him of the waiting woman and assured him that his experience is fairly common.

There is also the ghost of a horse thief who took refuge in the Jean Bonnet when he was being chased by some local Indians. In those days the upstairs was used for what they called "open court," and court was in session on the day the horse thief came running in screaming that he was being chased by Indians.

They protected him from the Indians until one of them recognized the man as a horse thief who was wanted by the law. Since the court was still in session, the man was tried and convicted on the spot. His sentence was swift and deadly. He was ordered hanged until dead, and they strung him up right in the courtroom area.

Through the years many folks have seen a man in rough clothes from early America walk past them or they catch a glimpse of the man. Others have reported that he has been seen sitting at tables both in what had been the courtroom area and downstairs where the restaurant now is.

There are rumors that two other men were hung downstairs and that their ghosts still reside at the Jean Bonnet, but I could not find any corroboration for the hanging of the second two.

A hostess named Barb, who has worked at the Jean Bonnet for nearly ten years, tells the story of a priest, who is also a college professor, who had a rather disturbing dinner at the restaurant. The man reproached his waitress because he had seen "a young lad" come through the dining area struggling to carry a heavy bucket. The priest was outraged that such a young child would be expected to do such heavy work. The waitress had no idea what the priest was talking about, but he was very insistent.

The waitress was forced to bring over the hostess and then the management to assure the gentleman that there were no children laboring at the Jean Bonnet. Still, the priest was not satisfied. He had clearly seen a boy, and he would not tolerate being lied to. The management finally sent back to the kitchen and asked the dishwasher, a high school boy, to come out. The priest took one look at the young man and declared that this definitely was not the boy he had seen. The child had been much younger and dressed in shabby clothes. No one knows who this child ghost might have been, but it is very conceivable that a young bond boy from another era is still haunting the Jean Bonnet as he struggles with his heavy chores.

Barb said that a couple years ago a married couple stayed at the Jean Bonnet and after only one night there they had a strange story to tell. It seemed that in the middle of the night the husband had been awakened by the shower running in their bathroom. The man sleepily assumed that for some reason his wife was showering at that odd hour .

His wife was awakened by the shower and she also assumed that something must have happened to cause her husband to get up and shower in the middle of the night. This was most unusual, but she drifted back to sleep while she waited to ask him why he was showering so late.

In the morning they were surprised to find out that neither of them had been in the bathroom showering the night before. The bathroom had no entrance except through their bedroom, and their door had been locked. How could anyone have been using their shower? Puzzled, they brought up this enigma to the management who was forced to admit that this had happened before. Not only had other guests heard the shower running when no one could have been in the bathroom, but they have also reported hearing the commodes flush and hearing the sink faucets turn on and off.

Barb also spoke about a waitress who was alone in the restaurant before opening time. The waitress heard a woman walking about behind her in what sounded like high-heeled shoes. The waitress looked around but found herself very much alone, except for the spirit that went clicking through the place on heels.

Barb confided that one of the young men who bused tables curently seems to be having trouble with the ghosts. Only days before, the young man had called her into the back section of the dining room to see a table that he had set up. One of the saucers had been moved by an unseen hand. He has also complained that something picks up the cloth napkins, which are especially folded for each place setting, and tosses them about.

Once a female customer was struck by the appearance of a man in a flannel shirt who was sitting by himself at a very large table. The man never moved but just sat at the table for some minutes. Finally the woman looked away to summon the waitress so that she could ask about the curious man. When the lady looked back, the man had simply disappeared. There was no way he could have left the room without passing by her table.

The waitresses in the restaurant have told many stories about customers seeing ghosts. A waitress named Shirley told me that she had a customer once who claimed to see a young lady in colonial dress standing by one of the first tables in the dining area. Could she be the spirit in high-heels?

Shirley passed on another story about a waitress whose job was to close one night and lock up the restaurant before she left. This waitress was doing a "turn-around," which meant that she would also be the first person opening up the restaurant the next morning. When she came in, she was surprised to find that the dryer in the kitchen was running. The waitress knew that the dryer had not been on when she left the night before, and besides it had a timer which should have shut it off long ago. She also knew that no one should have been in that section since the previous night She was further stumped when she opened the dryer and found that it was empty. Why a spirit had been playing with the electric dryer she never knew.

187

The area of the Jean Bonnet where the tavern is and where the ghostly woman still looks for her lost lover.

The most unusual incident that Shirley knew about was the story of a couple who had stayed at the tavern a few years ago. The couple had a young baby with them and they had left the baby asleep in its crib in their locked room. The mother had taken a baby monitor with her into the bar area where they were dining because it was very close to their room. She had left a bottle on the porch where it was cold, and thought that as soon as the baby awoke she'd have the bottle ready.

As the couple ate, they began to hear a noise like the baby cooing and sucking on something. They got up and hurried back to their locked room. There they found the baby was happily drinking its bottle, but who could have given it to the child? No human could have entered the locked room without the couple having heard them on the monitor!

Another waitress who had witnessed several incidents is a lady known as B.J. B.J. says that she often feels that someone has passed just behind her, but when she looks no one is there.

The incident that struck B.J. as the most inexplicable was that of a young family she had served only the summer before. The couple had several children, including a five-year-old boy. Throughout the meal, the boy had pestered for desert but, as B.J. finally brought it, he suddenly grew wide-eyed and burst into frightened tears. He kept staring at the wall beside an air conditioner. His father asked him what was wrong, and the child said that "eyes were in the wall watching him." The longer the child stared at the wall, the more frightened he became. At last the parents were forced to take him outside to calm him down. The little boy never had a chance to eat the desert he had wanted so much. B.J. said that no one else saw eyes in the wall, but the child was thoroughly frightened and convinced of what he had seen.

Throughout the years since the Baers purchased the Jean Bonnet, there have been many such incidents. The ghosts do not seem evil or bent upon harming the living. They just go about their business, and every once in a while they are seen or heard as they wander through this building that has long been their home.

I first became interested in the hauntings at the Jean Bonnet when a friend of mine, Lori H., worked there.

One evening at a party she approached me and said that she had to tell me something because I was the only person who might believe her. She related the following story:

A few nights earlier she had been waitressing at the Jean Bonnet when a woman came in and asked for a table for two in the back. The woman said that her husband would be joining her in a while and would Lori direct the man to the back if he asked her?

Lori took the woman to a small back table and got her some coffee. While the woman waited, Lori went back from time to time and freshened her coffee.

It was a very busy evening and Lori could not get back to the woman for about twenty minutes. As soon as she had a chance, she went back again to freshen the woman's coffee. When the woman saw Lori, she grew agitated.

"I don't think you're very funny," she said to Lori in a huffy voice.

Lori was surprised by the woman's change of temperament. Was she that angry because Lori hadn't freshened her coffee earlier?

"I'm sorry," Lori said. "I came back as soon as I could."

"That's not what I'm talking about," the woman informed her. "I'm talking about that man you sent back."

Lori was nonplused. She had sent no one back to this woman's table, and told her so.

"Don't be ridiculous," the woman snapped. "You sent a man back

a bit ago. He was dressed in rough clothes like some from the 1700s and he just sat in that chair. I was looking around and when I looked back there he was. I turned away to find you and tell you about him, but when I turned back he was gone. Now I don't think you're very funny. I don't like having tricks played on me, and I have half a mind to complain to the management."

Lori insisted that she had not been playing a trick, but she remembered the ghost of a man from colonial times whom others had seen and knew that this ghost must have been the one who had been sitting with the woman.

Lori was so rattled by her story that she announced she was looking for another job. Shortly after we spoke she quit working at the Jean Bonnet.

The Death Of Lily
(The Roaring Spring area, Blair County)

When they moved into the big blue gingerbread house, Hazel and Winston Martin thought that it was perfect. It was a house large enough to accommodate their seven sons and one daughter. The boys ranged in age from fifteen to six months old. Their only girl, Lily, was six years old with raven hair, cornflower eyes, and a precocious smile that endeared her to everyone, especially her mother, Hazel.

Lily was a bright and open child unafraid of anyone or anything. In fact, it was a great surprise to Hazel when she realized that her daughter was frightened of the little room at the end of the upper hall where they had put Lily's bed. Hazel and Winston had papered the room in pink cabbage rose paper, and Hazel had made fine curtains of eyelet lace to cover the one narrow deep-welled window.

The first week that they were in their new house, Lily had complained of bad dreams and then of seeing a man standing over her bed. She ran crying into her parent's room nearly every night. Both Winston and Hazel took turns at night holding the terrified child in the cabbage rose bedroom, but they never saw the bad man that had terrified Lily.

Hazel was inclined to move Lily but Winston refused. They had spent too much money decorating the little room. And besides he argued, it was way too small for the boys who shared the two biggest bedrooms.

Hazel gave up temporarily and continued putting Lily to sleep in the little bedroom every night. She left lamps on, sat with Lily, and even tried praying each night, but still a terrified and sobbing Lily would run to her parents' bed in the middle of the night.

If Hazel had her way she would have just shut up the little room, but Winston was growing stubborn on the issue. "Lily has to get over these fantasies," he'd roar when she'd bring up the issue. "She's just doing it because you baby her so much." He'd stomp from the room, cutting off all discussions.

One evening Winston came home in what was, even for him, an unusually foul mood. Hazel knew as she tucked Lily in that night, that Winston would brook no foolishness. He had already been yelling about Lily's fantasies.

"You stay put tonight, Lily," she counseled the child.

Lily wrapped her arms around her Mommy's neck. "I can't help it. I don't like the bad man. I think that he wants to hurt me, Mommy." Her little voice and haunted eyes almost made Hazel relent and stand up to Winston, but then she heard him slamming around downstairs and her courage failed.

"Honey, daddy is in a bad mood and he doesn't want you to keep coming over every night. Just try to stay in your own bed this once."

Lily looked at her with serious eyes. "I could sleep on the floor beside you, then he'd never know."

Hazel shook her head. "You'd best not. Just try, okay?"

Lily nodded and rolled over. Hazel sat in the rocking chair beside Lily's bed and waited for her child to go to sleep. She could hear Winston still thumping around downstairs and the boys getting ready for bed rather boisterously in the other rooms. She had already tucked Nat, her baby, into the cradle at the foot of her bed, and she prayed that he'd stay asleep all night.

Finally she heard the slow even breathing she had been waiting for coming from Lily. Still, Hazel sat in her chair slowly rocking.

There was something different about tonight. Perhaps it was Lily's words, "I think he wants to hurt me, Mommy," or just her own growing fears about Lily's changing behavior, but Hazel again almost gathered up the child, blankets and all, and took her to the boy's one room. Later she often wondered what had stopped her, but she knew that it was the fact that Winston had come upstairs just then.

"It's time for bed." He looked at his only girl child. "She's fine. You coddle her too much, woman. She's afraid of her shadow anymore, and it's your fault."

Hazel bit back an angry retort and glanced at her daughter. "Be quiet, you'll wake her."

She got up and followed her husband into the hall. She had promised Lily that she would not shut the door, and she made a point of blocking it open with a little wooden wedge.

"What are you doing that for?" Winston's eyes were sharp and angry.

"I promised I'd keep it open."

"Oh, you did? Well, too bad!" Winston went back and toed the wedge away from the door. He gave it a sharp kick and it skittered away into the darkness of the little room. "She gets everything her way. She'll just have to learn that life isn't always going to go her way. I should have done this the first night she came screaming into our room."

He reached up above the door and took the key from its hook.

Hazel hurried back making a grab for the key, but Winston was faster. He shut the door and turned the key in the lock.

"Stop that!" Hazel struggled with him for the key. "You unlock that door. She won't be able to get out of there if she gets scared."

"That's the idea. If we'd have made her face her fears in the first place, none of this would have happened. She might cry for a while, might even scream, but when she's done being mad she'll just go back to sleep. You'll see."

He tucked the key in his pocket and patted it. "This stays with me."

Hazel couldn't tell if she was more angry or frightened by the way Winston was acting. In the back of her mind Lily's voice played over and over, "I think he wants to hurt me, Mommy... I think he wants to hurt me..."

She went to bed but she couldn't sleep. Hazel lay awake listening to Winston's snores and waiting for the little cry and the pattering of tiny feet that told her Lily was awake. Finally it came in the wee hours of the morning.

Hazel heard the thud of feet hitting the floor in Lily's room, then Lily's struggling to open the door. Hazel inched carefully out of bed, thinking that if she could reach the chair where Winston's pants lay she could get the key and free her child.

She had begun to think that she'd make it when Winston's hand clamped down on her wrist painfully. "Leave her."

Lily was wailing, crying for her Mommy, shouting for help and struggling against the unyielding knob. Hazel begged Winston to relent. The screams continued from the little room, tearing at Hazel's heart and soul. She had to get Lily out. The child was growing more and more crazed by the second. Lily had ceased to scream intelligible words. Now she was keening long shrieks and beating at the door with little fists.

Hazel fought with all of her strength. Winston let go of her suddenly and she tumbled backward off of the bed. She hit the floor with a painful thud that woke Nat who added his wails to Lily's. Hazel's mind was filled with Lily and she scrambled off the floor and dove for the chair with the pants, but it was too late, Winston already had them. His hand was clamped tightly around the key, and he held it aloft, out of her reach.

"Give it to me," she hissed, clawing at him. He pushed her away.

"She's got to face her fears."

"She'll go mad!" Hazel shot back.

Suddenly the screams stopped. All she could hear now was Nat's thin, plaintive wails.

Winston looked at her in triumph. "I told you." He looked like a man who had waited all of his life to be proven right. "She's just spoiled."

Hazel subsided, picking up Nat and clucking at him distractedly. "Now unlock the door and check on her, please, Winston?"

She jiggled Nat to quiet him, but gave up and uncovered one beast to feed him.

"I'm going back to sleep." Winston flopped down in the bed still holding the key. He lifted his pillow, dropped the key inside the case, then lay back, tucking the pillow securely beneath his head. "It won't do her any harm to find out that she's not the only person in this family. I'll unlock the door in the morning.

Hazel sat on the edge of the bed rocking Nat, crooning to him lowly as he nursed, and praying that Lily was all right. By the time she replaced Nat in his cradle, Winston was snoring soundly. She slipped from the room and padded down the hall to the little bedroom. She put her ear to the door, listening for signs that Lily was awake. She heard nothing. In frustration she knocked gently. "Lily, Lily, are you okay?"

Hazel's whisper was loud to her own ears. She glanced up the hall half expecting Winston to come charging out, angry at her for disobeying. There was nothing. She pressed her ear against the door again, but there was no sound.

There was nothing to do but wait. Winston would not give up the key until morning so Hazel slipped back into her room. She couldn't sleep, worry gnawed at her like a dog chewing her heart and mind. When she thought that the darkness would never end, the first gray rays of dawn lit the bedroom. She rolled out of bed and deliberately knocked over the heavy Bible that sat on her night stand.

Winston sat up. "What's that?"

"Nothing," Hazel whispered loudly. "I just bumped something. It's morning, better get up."

Winston shifted, making no effort to get up.

Hazel frowned at him in the early half light. "Well if you're gonna stay in bed a while, give me the key to Lily's room. I want to check on her before I go downstairs."

Winston tossed it in Hazel's direction. Careful not to show Winston how frightened she was, she slipped from the room. She put the key in the lock, calling out to Lily to wake up. For one fearful second she thought that Winston had tricked her with the wrong key. The key finally engaged and she felt the lock give way. She pushed the door open not really knowing what to expect. Her eyes searched the bed, but the child was not there. The bed clothes lay in a tangle and Lily's pillow was on the floor. Where was she?

Hazel picked the pillow up automatically as she advanced into the room. Behind the headboard of the bed lay something white. It took Hazel's mind a second to register what it was. The screams tore at Hazel's throat as she threw her weight against the bed, making it skitter outward away from the wall. Lily lay there in a little bundle of cold flesh, arms drawn up over her head, and her body pushed into a little fetal bundle against the wall.

Hazel screamed and screamed. She tried to pick Lily up but she was stiff and awkward. She never heard Winston enter, still pulling on his pants, or the boys excited, frightened voices at the door. All she saw was Lily. Every sensation was focused on the child. She tried to force the arms down to see her daughter's face, and then she cried. Loud wracking sobs shook her, and she fought Winston's hands as they tried to take Lily from her. Her child's face was hideous. The eyes, so blue and alive yesterday, bulged in horror. Her lips, lips that had kissed Mommy good night, were pulled back in a silent scream. The little hands, hands that had touched her yesterday, Hazel thought wildly, had turned into little bird claws trying to defend herself against...what?

"I think the man wants to hurt me, Mommy." Lily's voice whispered in Hazel's mind.

Winston finally wrested the child from her, and arms pulled her from the room. She fought to stay, to protect her child, but it was too late. She should have protected Lily last night.

"I think the man wants to hurt me, Mommy."

The doctor was called and he gave her something to drink to make her sleep. Before Hazel drifted off, she heard voices in the hall. Winston and the doctor were talking outside the door.

"What happened to my daughter?" Winston's voice sounded hollow, shaken. Hazel allowed herself a moment's bitter satisfaction at that.

"I don't really know, but if I were guessing I'd say it looks like she died of fright."

Hazel closed her eyes and saw once again her little girl's face ruined with fear. She knew that she would be seeing that haunted little face for the rest of her life.

Shortly after the child's death the family left the house. No one knows what became of Winston, Hazel, or the boys after that. I, however, would not be surprised if there was the specter of a frightened little girl with dark hair and cornflower eyes who joined the haunting of the little bedroom at the end of the hall.

I found my first references to this story in journal entries recorded in the 1800s. The woman only referred to the family as her neighbors. She gave her address as The Cove and as far as I can tell the family involved lived on the main road into the small town of Roaring Springs.

* Since no names were used in the journal entries I gave the family names in order to tell the story more clearly.

London Bridge Is Falling Down
(Cove Forge Village, Blair County)

This story has come to me from multiple sources, but I am tell-ing it with specific emphasis on two eyewitness accounts which I found to be most reliable. One was a woman who had agreed to watch the house for the owners in exchange for the use of a small cabin in back of the main house. The other is a Catholic priest who was visiting the caretaker.

In the early 1800s, Samuel, Daniel, and John Royer came to central Pennsylvania to settle. Each of them built large houses outside of the town of Williamsburg where the three brothers made their fortunes in the iron ore industry. And each of the brothers left the legacy of a haunted house. Samuel Royer's home was destroyed in a fire years ago, and though I've heard rumors that it was haunted, I can find no definite tales to relate. Daniel Royer's story is told elsewhere in this book, so it is John Royer's home which we are now going to visit.

In the early 1930s, John Royer's descendants were still living in the house he built near the Cove Forge where he had amassed his fortune. The house remained in the family all of those years, and now Jacob Royer and his wife Sarah were living there alone, having raised their children. They had the help of two servants and a housekeeper who also served as the cook.

Even as a young man Jacob had not been very tolerant of chil-dren, and he was less than pleased when Sarah had agreed to take in their seven-year-old granddaughter, Dorothy, after the child's parents were killed in an automobile accident. He had warned Sarah that he would not tolerate the child disturbing his day with noisy prattle and play. In fact, he even warned the rest of the family not to expect him to play doting granddaddy.

Sarah was secretly pleased to have Dorothy's company. She had been happy when none of the other relatives had volunteered to take on the small child. Her days had been lonely for a long time. Moving about the place fearful that she'd disturb Jacob had been trying, but now she'd have Dorothy to share her love with. She hoped that in time Jacob would come to share her joy at having Dorothy.

Jacob was true to his word. From the day Dorothy first stepped into the Cove Forge house he was polite, formal, and very strict. The child was not allowed to play downstairs, make noise, disturb adults, or speak and sing unless given permission.

It was all too much for a lively seven-year-old. She hated the isolation of being confined to the second floor while her grandfather insisted that Grandma Sarah stayed on the ground floor with him. She hated the way she had to request permission to speak and often forgot that she had to ask. In fact, Dorothy spent a great deal of time in trouble for various infractions ranging from singing to skipping in the downstairs hall.

At first Jacob used a variety of punishments to keep Dorothy in line, but he soon realized that what the child feared most was to be alone. It was not surprising that she craved the attention of her grandma and the servants who doted upon her. She chafed at confinement to her room, but even there she would make the best of it and play or sing to her dolls.

Jacob devised a plan to punish Dorothy so that she'd remember all of the new rules in her life. He ordered that an attic room be opened and instructed that a cot, a small table and one chair were to be taken to that room. The room itself was an uninviting place with bare unfinished walls, dormer windows where Jacob allowed no curtains to hang, and no pictures were to adorn the walls.

Sarah thought Jacob's plan to make Dorothy stay in the attic room was horrible. She pleaded to at least be allowed to fix up the room. The only small victory she won from Jacob was that she could outfit the bed with comforters, pretty blankets, pillows and a dust ruffle. Sarah comforted herself with the fact that Dorothy would only have to use the room when she was bad.

She ordered the servants to watch out for the child. Indeed, the whole household tried to protect Dorothy from her grandfather, but Jacob seemed determined to punish the child. For the least infraction of his rules Jacob would banish her to the attic. He would light two candles each evening and walk the child to the attic room. The old man would leave one candle on the table and shut the child in. He'd make his way back to the more populated part of the house with the remaining candle.

Over the weeks that followed, Dorothy spent increasing amounts of time in the barren room. She was allowed no toys, but her grandmother, with the help of the servants, hid a doll under the dust ruffles of the bed. Dorothy would take the doll out, open the dormer windows and sit there rocking it and quietly singing London Bridge Is Falling Down. She spent hours just rocking and crooning that song to her doll. When she'd hear her grandfather's tread on the attic stairs, she'd dash over to the bed and hide the doll. She'd then race back to the window and sit there singing until her Grandfather left.

Sarah quickly realized that keeping Dorothy was a selfish thing to do. Dorothy needed to be with other children, she needed to laugh and play without fear of punishment and, most of all, she needed to get away from Jacob and that awful room. With a heavy heart, Sarah began writing to relatives asking if any of them could take the child. Within weeks the reply that Sarah both hoped for and feared came. Some distant cousins said that they'd take Dorothy. They had children of their own and would love to adopt the little girl.

Sarah went to Jacob with her letter. He was overjoyed with the news. He made the arrangements and quickly packed Dorothy off.

For months Sarah wrote to her grandchild and received replies, but then the letters suddenly stopped. Anxiously she began writing to the cousins who were in the process of adopting the child. Why had Dorothy quit writing? Was something wrong? For a long time Sarah waited for their reply, and then it came. The letter said that Dorothy had been ill and had passed away. The cousins begged forgiveness for not replying sooner, but they had been prostrated with grief for the child that they had grown to love.

Sarah's heart was broken. First her child had died in the accident, and now she had lost her precious Dorothy. It was too much to bear. She collapsed with grief. While she was grieving, Jacob ordered that all traces of Dorothy be cleared away. He ordered that the attic room be dismantled and the room aired out.

It was hard for the maid to go into the attic room to finally tear it apart. She and the other servants had loved the child and had hated that room passionately. Still, she had to do her job so she began pulling sheets and blankets from the bed and stacking them in a neat pile on the table. As she did, the little doll they had smuggled in fell out of the dust ruffle and hit the floor. The maid stared at it, feeling tears well up in her throat for the child. Suddenly the doll was swept up from the floor and it floated to the window. As the maid watched in horrified fascination, the window opened and the doll began to rock slowly back and forth as the voice of Dorothy sang London Bridge Is Falling Down.

In the years that followed every member of the house witnessed the floating doll which Sarah insisted be kept in the room, and heard the voice of Dorothy singing out her little song.

Interestingly, when old Jacob died he apparently joined the haunting. Soon after his death, people said they'd see two flickering lights floating up the stairs into the attic. Shortly after that, one would return to the steps where it would blink out. The other flickered in the little attic room where Dorothy once lived. Then the window would open and Dorothy could be heard to sing.

The house sat empty for years before it was bought by a wealthy out-of-state man who restored it. During the restoration he asked a friend of his, Nancy, who worked near the house, to keep an eye on it for him. In return, he offered her the small cottage behind the house in lieu of payment for house-sitting.

One night Nancy came home from a meeting with a friend of hers, a Catholic priest named Father Tim. When they pulled into her driveway, she noticed that there was a flickering light in the attic of the big house. She was not a local so she had never heard of the haunting. She immediately thought that a tramp had broken in and accidentally set a fire. She knew that the house had once been a flop for transients; the owners had run several off during the renovations. And the house was not yet equipped with electricity.

Quickly she told the Father Tim to call the fire department. But he insisted that first he would check it out for her. He took the keys she gave him, a fire extinguisher, and a small pocket flashlight. He went through the place looking for tramps, checking each floor, room by room, as he moved upward. There was no one in the house. In the darkness he made it to the small attic room where they had first seen the flame.

While Nancy waited for her friend, she circled the house and came back to stand below the window where the light still glowed. It

199

was a cool, clear night and the moon was nearly full so she had a good view of the attic window. As she watched, the window swung open and a little girl's voice began singing London Bridge softly into the evening air. From inside the house she heard Father Tim's voice and then a thump followed by someone stumbling down the stairs.

Within seconds Father Tim came stumbling out of the front door. He swore that no one was in the house, and that there was no fire. There was just that attic room, eerily lit by some unseen force, and while he had stood there the window opened by itself and he had heard a child begin singing London Bridge.

During the next few days, Nancy told her story several times before a co-worker finally told her the story of Dorothy and her grandfather. It explained a lot. Nancy now understood why she had not felt frightened listening to the child, just very sad.

In an interesting sidebar, a gentleman from out-of-state came to Pennsylvania to do research on his family tree. He sought out the Cove Forge house and spoke with the employees of the owner. He said that as a child his grandmother told him a story about a young cousin named Dorothy who lost her parents in a car accident. The little girl briefly lived with his grandmother's family before dying of a childhood disease. After the child's death, her ghost had gone back to her grandparent's home to haunt the attic where she had so often stayed. The little girl ghost would open a window in the attic room and would sing, "London Bridge is falling down" over and over again....

The Lost Hunter
(Huntingdon Mountain, Huntingdon County)

Hunting is a large part of rural life for most of the folks I know. It is no surprise then that many tales have been centered around the rites of hunting and hunters who have died for their sport. A local hunter, a very religious man, told me of a mountain in Central Pennsylvania between Cove Forge and Huntingdon that is haunted by the ghost of a hunter shot there long ago. He did not remember the names of those involved so I have given them names for the sake of telling the story clearly.

Only during buck hunting season does this man's spirit wander the mountaintop where he died. People driving across that steep mountain during buck season have reportedly seen the man as he reenacts his last desperate moments before he was shot by a false friend.

Lost! The word echoed in Al Everett's mind as he stumbled through the late twilight of dusk. He tried not to think about it, but he knew that it was true. He had passed that same clump of mountain laurel twice before. He was merely going around in circles in the darkness and snow.

Night descended cold and black, settling the matter for Al. He would be forced to stay the night on Huntingdon Mountain. If he was lucky, his wife Alma would already be calling the police to report him missing.

Al looked for somewhere to rest and cursed himself for being so short sighted as to have not packed a flashlight or even a book of matches. There was little ground cover, just ancient trees that he was too old and too cold to climb. So he took refuge under a thick clump of laurel. It was warmer there, out of the bitter wind, but he was still frightened that he'd freeze.

Time dragged by. He tried to forget his rumbling stomach so he concentrated on Alma. He conjured up her beautiful and perfectly proportioned face with dark almond-shaped eyes. Her long dark hair smelled of apples. Surely by now she'd have notified the police.

He cringed, thinking of how stupid he had thought other hunters were who got lost during buck season. Now he'd be a laughing stock, but even that wasn't as bad as the cold and damp that bit into his back where it was exposed to the wind.

It was nearly light when he roused, cramped and stiff to start out. He hoped that searchers were on the mountain looking for him.

When her husband failed to return from his hunting trip, Alma Everett got increasingly worried. By dark she was on the phone to his friends, but no one had seen him. Her mind whispered a multitude of horrible possibilities, but Alma tried to hold on. Al had never been one to worry her unnecessarily. Perhaps it was only that his truck would not start, or that he had shot a massive buck late in the day and was even now wrestling it through the trees.

By 10 p.m. Alma was truly scared. She picked up the phone once more and dialed Al's best friend, Jerry Barker. Al and Jerry had tramped Huntingdon Mountain together since they were boys. If anyone could find Al, it was Jerry.

Jerry came right over once she explained the situation, but Alma did not want him there. She begged him to begin looking for Al, so Jerry took Al's heavy duty flashlight and set off. He told her not to call the police yet, but she did anyway. They promised to get search parties out on the mountain if Al hadn't come home by dawn.

Dawn came, but Al was still missing. Alma was beside herself with worry. She was ten years Al's junior and all she could think about was Al's heart, or if he'd been shot or... There were too many bad thoughts. She was comforted, though, by the idea of Jerry tramping the mountain calling for Al, and of all the groups the police had called out to look for him.

Al eased his way through the weak light and strained his ears to hear any sounds of the road that should have been nearby. There was nothing. He did hear gunshots in the distance, but he couldn't see any other hunters.

It was nearly noon when he heard the sound of a honking horn. Al crashed through the brush in that direction. The road had to be that way. Al broke through the brush at the edge of the road and nearly cried. He had found the road, he would be safe. He took stock of his surroundings and realized that he had wandered further in the darkness than he had thought. His truck was at least three miles down the road, pulled off in a thicket of young trees.

Al had been walking for well over half an hour along the edge of the road back toward his truck when he saw a familiar face coming toward him in the distance. It was Jerry. Alma must have called Jerry for help. Good old Jerry wouldn't make him suffer too much embarrassment over getting lost.

They were only about a hundred yards apart when Jerry stopped the truck and got out. He had a rifle slung over his shoulder. Jerry quickly brought it up to his shoulder as though sighting. Now Al felt the pit of his stomach drop. What was Jerry doing? Had he seen a buck behind him? Jerry knew better than to shoot past a person at a target. Al half turned to look, but the road was deserted. With sudden clarity, he realized, "He's gonna shoot me!"

Al launched himself sideways but he was too late. A bullet tore into his hip, shattering the bone and making movement impossible. He dropped short in the gravel road. Suddenly Jerry was standing over him with the rifle pointed at his skull. Al looked upward but the mask of Jerry's face bore little resemblance to his childhood friend.

"Why?" he whispered, but he never heard the answer. The rifle's report echoed through the hills and Al was dead.

Jerry might have gotten away with it, if Alma hadn't called the police to look for Al. The woods were filled with searchers, and one group stood back among the trees in horror,watching Jerry pull the trigger the final time to snuff out Al's life.

When the police arrested Jerry, he said that he had killed Al so that he'd have a chance at Alma. It seemed that for years Jerry had been in love with his best friend's wife but had never had the courage to act until that day. He planned to blame Al's death on a hunting accident.

A year passed after the murder. Early on the second day of buck season a group of hunters were driving over the Huntingdon Mountain road when a man in hunter's colors suddenly appeared before them. He was in his mid-fifties and he looked tired and cold. They swerved the truck to avoid him and slowed to a crawl, but the man did not move.

As they watched, another middle-aged man suddenly appeared in the distance. He raised his gun and shot. The driver of the truck hit the brakes as the wounded man lurched to the left and hit the gravel at the road's edge. The shooter came running and pointed his gun at the wounded hunter. One of the men in the truck tried to get out and help, but an older man pressed him back in his seat. "Stay put. That's old Al Everett and Jerry Barker out there. They're both beyond our help now."

When the shooter pulled the trigger for the second time, both men suddenly vanished. The men in the truck were left staring at nothing but gravel. A preternatural hush fell over the group and the driver slowly eased the truck back onto the road. The older man waited a while to tell his companions the story of Al Everett. He needed the time to calm down.

Over the years many motorists driving the Huntingdon Mountain road have reported witnessing the murder of Al Everett by Jerry Barker. Barker had committed suicide in prison before he could be brought to trial, so both men's spirits seemed drawn back to where betrayal had ruined both of their lives.

Sometimes a few years will go by before anyone will claim to have seen the murder. But in time Al Everett and Jerry Barker will again—and perhaps forever—be stalker and stalked, betrayer and betrayed, on that lonely mountain road where hunters no longer walk, and where one lost hunter changed the lives of several people long ago.

"Mad" Anthony Wayne
(Erie, Erie County and Elk County)

G eneral Anthony Wayne left an indelible mark upon the state of Pennsylvania during the Revolutionary War. Stories of "Mad" Anthony Wayne's military exploits filled many an evening in the local taverns from Philadelphia to Lake Erie. Wayne's triumphs over the British secured his place in history, but Wayne seems to have decided that he is not ready to leave this world yet.

In 1796 Anthony Wayne was stationed at Fort Presque Isle (which is now the city of Erie), when he fell ill with a fever. Despite the doctor's best efforts, "Mad" Anthony died. After his death, he was buried nearby at the post.

Thirteen years later his family, located in Philadelphia, wanted his body back. They sent his son, Col. Isaac Wayne, to retrieve his father's body. Isaac was expecting that after being so long in the grave, his father's body would have decayed to the point where it would be only bones. So he took along only a small case that he could carry cinched to his horse's back; the small case would be used to carry the remains. However, upon exhuming the body, Isaac Wayne found that his father's corpse was still virtually intact.

Isaac decided upon the unprecedented course of boiling the flesh from his father's bones. What else was he to do? he reasoned. The family had expected only bones, so he had not been prepared to move an entire casket nearly the length of the state. He had to reduce the body to a form which he could carry back on horseback. He procured a large cauldron and had his father's body boiled until the meat and sinew separated from the bones. The skin and clothing were reburied in Erie.

Isaac took the bones and placed them in the case, then he began his journey back to Philadelphia. Apparently this entire proceeding affected Isaac more than anticipated. As a result, he had done a poor job of packing his father's bones. In Highland Township, Elk County, Isaac rode his horse over steep, coarse hills that jostled his pack greatly. Isaac did not realize that, because he had packed the case badly, the jostling caused the case to come open. As he rode through the area, some bones dropped out. By the time he noticed the open case and realized that he had lost some of his father's bones, he was nearly home. He had only a vague idea of where he might have lost them.

The stories began soon after Isaac's trip. Startled travelers told of hearing the thunder of hoof beats along the track Isaac had traveled. People said that they spotted a man on horseback—a man that fit the description of Mad Anthony Wayne. He was riding the route taken by his son and looking himself for his lost bones. When approached, this man just faded away. Of course, eventually these stories of the haunting of the track in Elk County by "Mad" Anthony Wayne reached the ears of his family.

Through the years those who lived in the area noticed that "Mad" Anthony seems to ride out to look for his bones more often around New Year's and also around the time of his birthday. Is he determined that another year should not pass by without his body being reunited?

What the Wayne family did about "Mad" Anthony's unrest is not known, but the story has remained until this day. In fact, the relics left by Wayne and his son are on display at the Erie Historical Museum at 356 W. 6th Street, in Erie, PA. There people will find, among other things, the very cauldron which was used to separate Wayne from his bones. Visitors are welcome to visit the museum as well as both of "Mad" Anthony's graves. There is one grave in Erie at First Street And Ash Street, and a second grave in Philadelphia at St. David's Episcopal Church.

The Innocent Hand
(Jim Thorpe, Carbon County)

During the heyday of the coal-mining era in Pennsylvania, no name struck dread in the mine owner's heart like that of the Molly Maguires. The Molly Maguires were a secret society formed in 1862 in response to the terrible wages and working conditions in the anthracite mines of both Pennsylvania and West Virginia. The Molly Maguires took their name from a secret anti-landlord group that had sprung up in Ireland in the 1840s. The mostly Irish-American miners used any means possible to frighten mine owners, superintendents, mine bosses, police officers and judges into improving conditions and pay. The secret society intimidated, threatened, and murdered anyone necessary to see that conditions changed. They also formed several successful strikes and created the mine workers' union.

By 1874 the mine owners had had enough. They were terrified of the "Mollies" and were seeing their profits shrink by giving in to the demands for above-poverty wages and decent, safe working conditions. In response to the "Mollies" they hired Allan Pinkerton (of the Pinkerton Detective Agency). Pinkerton had made a name for himself during the Civil War by working for the Union cause. Now Pinkerton began working for another cause, that of busting the budding labor union movement in the United States.

Pinkerton and his men infiltrated the Molly Maguires, searching for evidence that they could use in the courts to convict the members of the secret society. Pinkerton and his agents were very successful and by 1875 they had gathered enough evidence to convict several Molly Maguires of murder. By 1878 the Molly Maguires were officially crushed, but the idea of laborers banding together to demand better working conditions and fair pay had permeated the psyche of the American worker.

Pinkerton would find employment working for other companies that were trying to break unions by any means necessary.

Tom Fischer heard about the Molly Maguires before the infamous gang came to the Carbon County, Pennsylvania mine where Fischer worked. Mining was all that he knew how to do and was the only thing that most of the men he knew could do. Tom would have been the first to admit that mining was dangerous and deadly. Mine bosses and owners skimped on timber for reinforcing mine shafts and on buying decent equipment. Mines caved in, and the black dust from the anthracite (coal) deposits hardened the lungs. Worse yet, most of the mine bosses skimmed off their meager wages, forcing the men to work twelve- and fifteen-hour shifts just to provide the staples that their families needed. But even with all of that, Tom stayed away from the Molly Maguires who were murdering mine bosses and mine owners to get the needed improvements. They terrorized the mining companies so that they would provide decent protection and offer better wages.

Tom heard the rumbling in the mining camp as the Molly Maguires began infiltrating his mine. He needed no part of the grief that they brought with them. Some owners merely shut down mines, punishing workers even if they rejected the Molly Maguires. Others hired thugs and paid stoolies to turn on fellow workers. Perhaps the thing that Tom found most frightening was that owners sometimes bought off law enforcement officials who then persecuted and prosecuted suspected members mercilessly.

There had been rumors for days that something big was going down at Tom's mine, but he had no idea that it would be so awful. Morgan Powell had not been a well-loved man—most mine bosses weren't—but Tom still was shocked when the rumor reached him that Morgan was about to die.

Tom did what was probably the easiest thing: he just didn't get involved. He knew that speaking out could get his own family hurt. And so Tom was not surprised when the news came that Morgan Powell had died at the hands of the Molly Maguires.

"It's over," Tom thought. The Molly Maguires had done what they had come for, they had terrorized the local mine owners and now the mine

owners would make some changes. Tom was not prepared when the local sheriff arrested him, along with nineteen other men, for the murder of Morgan Powell. The sheriff claimed there was proof that Tom Fischer was a member of the Molly Maguires and had participated in the brutal slaying of his own mine boss.

What followed was a kangaroo court, where the prisoners were convicted and sentenced to death on the flimsiest of evidence. Throughout the proceedings Tom maintained his innocence, but not one of the other nineteen spoke a word either on his behalf or to condemn him. After the trial, Tom was held in the Jim Thorpe Jail, in cell No. 8, to await his hanging.

On the night before the hangings, one of the Molly Maguires, who would also hang in the morning, went to the sheriff and told him that Fischer was not the man they sought. He confessed that Fischer was not part of the gang and had not taken part in the murder of Morgan Powell.

The sheriff was shocked. In less than twenty-four hours he was scheduled to begin the hangings. Could it be that Tom Fischer had been telling the truth all along? Was it possible that in their zeal to quell the murderous rage of the Molly Maguires his officers had framed an innocent man?

Quickly the sheriff got in touch with Governor John F. Hartranft. There was no earthly reason for the Molly Maguire member to lie, he'd be dead in the morning anyhow. Should they put off the execution of Tom Fischer until the matter could be looked into further? Governor Hartranft was not impressed by this midnight confession. He ordered that Tom Fischer should hang as scheduled.

When Tom learned that his last bid for freedom and justice had failed, he placed his hand on the wall of prison cell No. 8, declared his innocence, and said, "My mark will stay here as long as the jail stands." This, he said, was to mark the cell where an innocent man was kept before being murdered by the law.

Tom Fischer died by hanging the following morning. If the sheriff or Governor Hartranft ever felt remorse for the hanging of a man who was in all probability innocent, it will never be known. But the hand print that Tom Fischer left in cell No. 8 of the Jim Thorpe Jail in 1878 can still be seen today. It seems that Tom Fischer will never give up protesting his innocence—even from his grave.

Since this story is based upon historical fact, and none of its participants are still alive, the real names of those involved have been used. There are some historians who claim that only ten Molly Maguires were ever executed for their crimes, but local historical documents from Carbon County, Pennsylvania will prove that in 1878 nineteen men were hung by the neck until dead for murdering their mine boss, and one, Tom Fischer, still protesting his innocence, was among them.

The Night Mary Died
(Blair County)

It was a warm summer night with a nearly full moon. Sixteen-year-old Terry Bookhammer would have truly enjoyed being out late that night if he had been walking home under any other circumstances. He knew that at home his father would be sleeping fitfully on the couch—if he even slept at all. For several months Terry's stepmother, his father's second wife, Mary, had been dying of cancer. Her death was a slow and painful one. Terry grieved for his father, but he also grieved for himself because he loved Mary. She had been a positive influence on his life, marrying his father when Terry was nine years old. She won over Terry and his two brothers with her gentle love. Now it was very hard, nearly as hard as when their mother had died, to watch Mary suffering so.

As Terry walked, he watched the scenery. The entire journey was along a wooded road until he turned at a certain farm. There the road ran right beside the farmer's house and then alongside ploughed fields. Rows of crooked wooden fence posts would mark his route for almost the entire rest of his walk.

Terry walked by the farmer's house as quietly as he could. He didn't want to disturb the big dog that lived there. He heard the lowing of the cattle in the field beside the house, and the hum of the bulk tank from the milk house as he passed. He saw a couple barn cats who stared at him curiously as he passed by, as if to question who had interrupted their night life.

At the stop sign below the house, he turned left and started past the newly mown hay fields. The fragrance of the cut hay was sweet and pungent and Terry rather enjoyed it. He paused to look across the fields and enjoy the little breeze that had just sprung up. He was only a couple miles from home now, so he could dally a bit if he chose to. In fact, his father was not even expecting him that night. His father thought that he was staying with Mary's mother, but at the last moment Terry had decided to walk home instead. He hated leaving his father alone every night when Mary was so ill.

Terry turned his head abruptly. Something was moving in the field along the fence row. At first his brain didn't seem capable of registering what his eyes told him he was seeing. He just stared.

"Mary?" His voice was nearly a whisper of surprise.

Coming along the fence row toward him was his stepmother, Mary. She was dressed in a green nightgown which billowed softly behind her as the night air played with it. A hundred questions burst in his mind at once. How could she be there? What was she doing? Had she suddenly gotten better? She looked just as she had before the cancer had begun to ravage her body.

Mary stopped about six posts away from Terry and just stood there staring at him. Why had she just stopped? Terry walked toward her, but she walked away. He tried to catch up to her but Mary seemed to just fade backward as he moved toward her. Without making any apparent effort she seemed to keep six fence posts between them. He picked up his pace, at last breaking into a run, but still Mary kept moving backward and they remained six posts apart.

Finally Terry slowed to a walk once more. So did Mary, who watched him with a soft look of love on her face.

Suddenly Terry felt a wave of sadness wash across him and he knew why Mary had come. She had never been able to have any children of her own, so she had poured her love into her stepsons, and the one child who had benefited from that love the most was little Terry. He was a gentle child with a big heart; he was easily hurt and he had been damaged irreparably by the loss of his mother. Mary had loved that wounded child as her own. She had given him back a measure of security and that was why she had come. She had come to tell him of her death and that he shouldn't grieve too much for she still existed. She had come to watch over her stepson once more. And she had come to say good-bye to her dear little Terry.

There was no fear in Terry as he watched his stepmother looking at him. He felt only sadness and a rush of love that lasted as he walked through the summer night. Mary maintained her distance and preceded him along the fence row until he entered a wooded area once more.

As suddenly as she had appeared, she left him. She had prepared her stepson for her death and she had said good-bye.

At the house he found his father sitting on the swing on the front porch in the darkness. As Terry came down the steps toward the porch, his father rose.

"Terry," his father began, the pain was evident in his voice.

Terry stood still in the darkness. "I know, Pop. Mary's dead."

For a while Terry and his father sat silently on the dark porch. Only later did Mr. Bookhammer remember that Terry had known of Mary's death before he had been told. Terry would eventually confide his story of Mary's last visit to his father and a few other people.

Mary's last visit did not stop the pain of loosing his stepmother, but it did help him to accept that loss. He felt special, and he knew that Mary had truly loved him so much that even after death she had reached out to him.

Terry's father would eventually remarry and from that marriage there would be two little girls. I am one of those two girls. My brother told me this story many years ago after our father died. It gave me hope that I'd see our dad once more.

I can only say that I am very glad that Mary was so kind to my brother Terry because he is truly a gentle soul easily hurt in this world. Those who know Terry well know that he is a rare creature, a man with only love and compassion for those he meets, and I will always be grateful to Mary Lee Bookhammer for loving him when he needed it so much as a child, and for making her final effort to reach him even after her death. From her I learned that love does survive even death.

The Memory Plate
(Acosta, Somerset County)

The reader should know that a memory plate was a small commemorative plate placed at the foot of a casket during the viewing and funeral service of people in Central Pennsylvania many years ago. the plate often contained a bit of gilt edging, a Biblical picture and perhaps a Bible verse. The plates were given to the next of kin after the funeral service as a memorial to the deceased.

Using a clever trick, Helen had married at the age of four teen. She hid a slip of paper with the number "16" printed on it in her one shoe. She didn't want to lie to the preacher, so when she was asked if she was over sixteen she said yes knowing that she had misled a preacher, but technically had not lied. By the time she was seventeen, Helen had a daughter, Jacqueline, and a baby boy, Johnny. Life was not easy for her. Her husband Chet was not a very hard worker, nor was he the loving husband that he had promised to be. Life was more difficult than Helen had ever expected, but she did not allow her personal pains to interfere with her natural inclination to be outgoing and helpful to others.

Helen and Chet rented a small cottage at the bottom of Town's Hill, near the north edge of the town where they had grown up. Helen's father worked in the electricity plant and was well known in the town. Chet worked in a local factory, taking whatever shifts he could get. Usually Helen spent her time at home caring for her two small children and taking in other people's laundry for money.

By the time Helen turned twenty she had grown into an important part of local life. Despite her youth, others relied on her for help in bad times, and shook their heads sadly at Chet's ill treatment of the gentle woman. It was, therefore, not surprising when Helen answered the frantic pounding on her door one day and saw Red Brennen standing there looking shaken and frustrated. The Brennens lived at the top of Town's Hill; Helen had been to their home a couple years back to midwife the youngest Brennen child. Since then she had passed pleasantries with Carol, Red's wife, but beyond that she had not spoken to them much.

Wiping her hands on an old apron Helen ushered in Red and tried to calm him down. Red stood just inside the kitchen door, his flaming red hair wind tossed and his manner frantic.

"Helen, I hate to bother you, but Carol's taken a bad turn and I need to get the doctor. Could you go sit with her for a while? The kids are all in school except for Billy, our youngest, and I can't leave him alone with Carol."

Helen agreed and quickly scribbled a note to Chet. She gathered up her kids and Red carried their bag up the hill. He deposited everything on his front porch, then raced back down the hill for the doctor.

Helen found Carol laying on her bed in the largest bedroom. The room was cluttered and baskets of unwashed clothes were pushed into a corner. Billy was playing with a wooden car on the floor beside the bed. He was dressed in worn clothes that smelled a bit dirty, his little face was unwashed, and his hair badly needed combing.

"Carol," Helen called softly, as she entered the room. "Red asked me to stay with you until the doctor arrives."

Carol opened her eyes briefly and smiled. "That was nice of you, Helen. I hate to impose, but I just can't seem to be able to..." Her voice trailed off into a grimace of pain as Carol tried to pull herself up to a sitting position on the bed.

"Don't you bother getting up for me." Helen patted Carol's shoulder and was appalled to see that her skin was stretched over bone. And her skin had the pallid, papery look of someone who had not seen the sun for a very long time. "You go back to sleep. I'll just let Billy play with Jacqueline so that you can rest."

Carol flashed a wane smile at Helen and then allowed herself to drift off. Helen bustled about locating clean clothes for Billy and washing him up. She sent him to play with Jacqueline in the living room as she began cleaning. There was a pile of dirty dishes in the sink. The floor gritted beneath her shoes and the table had been lost beneath a clutter of dishes and clothes. Helen worked fast, sparing glances for the children and running back the hall every once in a while to check on Carol.

By the time Red returned with Dr. Gilbert, Helen had cleaned the dishes, the counters and table, and was swishing a broom deftly about the kitchen floor. Red sent her a silent "thank you" with his eyes. Dr. Gilbert went directly to the sick room, it seemed an eternity until he returned. Helen worked feverishly while she waited. She had always been one to work off worry and so she continued cleaning until the living room took on the same shine as the kitchen. Red sat holding Billy and watching the hallway for Dr. Gilbert's return.

When Dr. Gilbert came back his face was grim, and he motioned for Red and Helen to follow him onto the porch. Helen wiped her hands, told Jacqueline to watch the boys, and followed Red out the door.

"Red, I'm afraid that there's nothing I can do but try to help with her pain." The doctor rubbed his chin absently. "She's been sick a long time. It won't be long now until she'll be gone." He eyed Helen. "It might be best if there was a woman here to look after things some. It'd be hard if one of the children were here alone when it happens."

Helen nodded, already thinking of what argument she'd use to persuade Chet that she should be allowed to help the neighbors. Chet could be stubborn and hard if his comforts were jeopardized. "I'll talk to Chet and do the best I can to be here when Red's not."

Red didn't seem to hear her. All of his attention had been focused upon the doctor. "How long's she got?" Red's voice came out in a strangled whisper and Helen felt her throat constrict.

"It's hard to say, but not more than a few days, I'm afraid." Dr. Gilbert opened his bag and rooted around in it for a few seconds. "You give her one of these as often as she needs for the pain. He pressed the pill bottle into Red's hand. "I've got to go now."

Red reached into his pocket to dig out his wallet, but the doctor caught his arm. "No need of that. I couldn't do anything for her."

After that Helen spent the next week and a half split between her chores at home and caring for Carol. Red worked trick shifts, so she relieved him to let him rest and she tried to help Carrie, the oldest child, who was only twelve, with the cleaning and cooking burdens. Even with the extra work, Helen was saddened when Red stopped late one afternoon to tell her that she wouldn't be needed to sit with Carol anymore.

Carol had died earlier that day. Helen's heart went out to the widower and his three children.

Several weeks went by after Carol's funeral, but Helen just couldn't seem to find the time to go up the hill for a visit. She had heard that Carrie was managing fairly well, and that elderly Mrs. Talbot had been staying with the children while Red worked. Chet was happy for Helen's undivided attention and gave her a half-hearted okay to occasionally help Red when necessary.

Late one afternoon heavy pounding at the door brought Helen up from the basement of her little house where she had been doing washing. She peeked out the curtains before she opened the door and was surprised to see Red standing there.

"Red, what can I do for you?" Helen asked, opening the door.

"Helen, Mrs. Talbot can't sit with the kids; she's feeling poorly. I've got to go to work and I hate to ask you but I've asked everyone else and ..." He shrugged, looking highly uncomfortable.

Helen bit her lip, trying to think of what she should do. She did have Chet's half-hearted approval. "Give me a few minutes and I'll go set with the kids, Red." She wiped her hands on the apron she wore and untied it.

"Thanks, Helen, I'll never be able to repay you for all of your help. I'll go back up the hill and tell Carrie to expect you soon."

Helen left a note for Chet, grabbed up her two children, and said a small prayer that Chet wouldn't be mad about the wash she'd left soaking in the basement. Red met her halfway down the hill and carried Johnny while she struggled with Jacqueline and her sewing basket. She'd taken the sewing to appease Chet if he got difficult about her leaving her own work to help others.

Red didn't stay long; he was already late for work. Helen noted that place looked much better than expected. She found Carrie, a little redhead who favored her father, peeling potatoes in the kitchen. "What's for supper?" she asked, settling Johnny on the floor to play with some blocks.

"I'm frying potatoes and there's some of Mama's canned meat left, so I figured we'd eat that." Carrie pushed back curly locks that were escaping from her careless pony tail. Helen could not help feeling sorry for the little girl. A great burden had been dumped upon her shoulders and she felt that Carrie would not ever know what a joy childhood could have been.

"Where's the boys?" Helen peered out of the window into the narrow strip of dried grass that served as yard, alley, and parking lot for the neighborhood cars.

"Jess is over at the Markels, and Billy's playing on the back porch. He don't like to stay in the house anymore, and he won't play alone in his room."

Helen settled herself at the table and pulled the potato pan over so that she could begin peeling into it, too. "Well, I suppose that it will take him a while to adjust to the loss of your Mom. He is so little and he was here with her when she passed away. I guess he'll just need some time."

Carrie looked at her curiously. "It's not that. Helen, do you believe in ghosts?

Helen stopped peeling for a second. This was a delicate question. "I believe in the Holy Ghost, but I don't believe in ghosts per say...at least I don't think I do. There are a lot of things in God's world that can't be explained. Why?"

Carrie began slicing the potatoes into a pan of cold water. "I was just wondering," she muttered.

Helen busied herself with washing and cooking. After supper she helped the older children with their homework and made sure everyone got their baths. Chet came up the hill and took Johnny and Jacqueline home with him. He was a little upset about Helen's helping Red out once again, but he didn't make an issue of it in front of Red's children.

Helen shushed everyone off to their beds. Billy fussed a little, but Carrie quieted him with a promise that he could let the light on until he fell asleep. Helen tucked the two boys in bed, then went to Carrie's room.

"Everyone's in bed." She sat on the edge of Carrie's bed. "You gonna stay up and read for a while?"

Carrie shook her head. "I'm kinda tired. I might light this candle here for a while and just look at the stars."

Helen patted Carrie's hand. "If you get lonely, you just come on out. I'm going to be sewing in the living room."

Helen poured herself a cup of coffee, took her sewing box to the living room, and settled into the chair next to the room's only lamp. She was looking forward to a quiet evening alone with her sewing. At home Chet would be growling about something, and she would have been chasing after him. She was darning a pair of Chet's socks when the lights began to flicker. They blinked twice and then they winked out.

"Darn," Helen muttered, laying her sewing aside. She looked out of the window and could see lights twinkling across the town. "Must be the fuses," she said aloud, getting up and trying to maintain her bearings. She nearly made it to the hall before she tripped on the upturned edge of a throw rug.

Helen called out for Carrie but the girl didn't answer. She doubted if she could find the fuse box by herself in the dark, so she felt her way down the hall. Carrie's was the last room. Helen knocked on the door lightly but the only sound that came to her through the door sounded suspiciously like a whimper. Helen pushed the door open and stopped. Carrie was sitting on her bed with her back pressed against the headboard. She was staring at the floor, her eyes shining with fear in the uncertain moonlight.

Helen followed Carrie's gaze to the floor. She froze, watching as a gauzy mist seeped upward from the scarred linoleum.

"It happens every night since Mama was buried." Carrie never shifted her gaze as she spoke. "I think it has something to do with her, but I don't like it anyway."

Helen pulled her eyes from the shifting mist to Carrie. "Come here!" Helen was surprised by how steady her own voice was. She darted past the mist that had begun forming into the loose shape of a woman and grabbed Carrie by the arm, dragging her sideways off of the bed, toward the doorway.

The mist hovered over the bed for a few seconds, then began moving slowly. As it passed her, Helen felt a trail of cold dankness brush her skin and she shivered. Behind her Carrie pressed her face into Helen's back to avoid the rush of cold air.

Helen followed the mist down the hall to the boys' room. It floated through the door and she hurriedly opened it. The mist washed over Billy's sleeping form. He shifted restlessly in his sleep, then subsided.

Carrie crept up beside Helen and took hold of her arm. "It won't hurt you, but it scares me. It's so cold." She leaned against Helen.

The misty figure moved to the next bed, hovered there briefly, then moved back toward the doorway. Helen backed up, not wanting to feel that coldness again. The mist faded into the master bedroom door and Helen followed. On top of the dresser, visible through the mist, was a beautifully ornate brush and comb set that had clearly belonged to the now dead Carol.

The mist enveloped the dresser and then faded into it. The lights flickered on briefly, and Carrie stepped up beside her again nearly causing Helen to scream. Never in her life had Helen been so frightened. Fear seemed to constrict her chest, her skin prickled with sensitivity, and the hair at the nape of her neck seemed to take on a life of it's own, sending chills down her back.

"It'll happen again," Carrie whispered.

Helen turned around, frightened that the misty form might rise up behind her and touch her. Carrie pointed to her open door where the moonlight lit the stretch of linoleum at the foot of the bed. There, in the moonlight, the mist was again pulling upward from the floor to hover over Carrie's bed as it began its rounds once more, pausing over each child's bed before moving to the master bedroom where it faded into the dresser. When it had gone the second time, the lights flickered and returned.

"It's over now," Carrie sighed.

"Does this happen every night?" Helen could not think clearly. She turned on the bedroom lights, flooding the hallway with brightness.

Carrie nodded. "Ever since the night Mama was buried. That's why I didn't want to go to sleep, and that's why Billy fussed for a light. He saw it once and refused to sleep in his room for days."

"And that's why your father couldn't find a sitter, right?" Helen added.

Carrie looked at her sheepishly. "Mrs. Talbot refuses to come anymore," she confirmed.

Helen was rapidly getting over her fear; now she was getting mad. She was angry at Red for setting her up in this situation.

As though reading her mind, Carrie added, "Dad doesn't want to admit that there is anything to this. He says he never sees it, but he has to. It think he's afraid to admit that it's Mama."

Helen patted her on the arm. "Don't worry about it. Come on, I doubt that we'll get much sleep tonight, but I suppose we should try to get some rest. I'll speak with your Dad when he gets home."

Carrie and Helen gathered blankets, and Helen insisted that they find two candles just in case the mist returned, and they camped out together on the couch. Soon Carrie drifted off and Helen had to admire her constitution. It would be a long time until Helen allowed herself the luxury of sleep.

As dawn crept into the sky and reddening it with promise, Helen roused herself and made a pot of coffee. She deliberately left the blankets laying around the living room. Red was going to know that something strange had gone on there last night.

She waited in the kitchen, nursing a cup of coffee. At last she heard Red's footsteps on the porch and the rattle of the keys being used. Red took one look at the living room, with its disarray of blankets and Carrie still sleeping on the couch, and went directly to the kitchen.

"Had a little excitement here last night," Helen said by way of greeting.

Red dumped his lunch box on the counter and sat down in a rickety old chair by the back door. "Suppose I shoulda told you, Helen, but I was desperate. Mrs. Talbot has been spreading rumors all over the neighborhood, and I can't get anyone to sit with the kids anymore."

"You should have told me. That was nearly enough to scare a body to death last night. You'd better try to do something about it."

He shrugged helplessly. "What can I do? I don't have the money to move and I can't just walk up to the Reverend Holtzer and say, 'Pardon me, pastor, but we have this misty ghost that might be Carol, and I need you to get rid of her.'"

Helen felt sorry for Red and his dilemma. "I suppose that the best thing to do is look at this logically. Let me ask you a question, what's in that dresser in your room where the mist disappears?"

Red shrugged. "Not much, now. It was Carol's dresser, but I packed up her clothes and gave them to the mission collection a few weeks ago. There's a few of my old clothes, a couple boxes of things of Carol's that I wanted to keep for the kids, and the memory plate from her casket."

Helen sipped her coffee absently as her mind worked. A memory plate was a small plaque that was placed at the foot of the casket with a Bible verse or a special saying on it. "Red, why don't you take those things of Carol's out of the dresser and store them somewhere else? See if that helps. Maybe she's coming back to where her things are."

Red promised to move the things, and Helen helped him pack them up and take them to the attic before she left. A few days went by and then one evening Red came to call. He seemed slightly uncomfortable as he sat at the table sipping coffee and chatting with Chet. Finally he put his cup down and turned to Helen.

"Helen, do you remember what you said about getting rid of Carol's things ?"

Helen nodded.

"Well, I've packed up everything of Carol's from the room and I'm storing it at my folks home now. But the mist is still there."

Helen sat down at the table beside Chet and rubbed her chapped hands absently against her apron. "I've been thinking about this, Red, and I've got a feeling that it's the plate that's holding Carol up there." She glanced at Chet self-consciously, but he didn't seem inclined to make fun of her. "It's just my opinion, but I think I'd take that plate and bury it with Carol. I can't explain it, but I've been praying about it, and I think that burying the plate is the answer."

Red accepted Helen's suggestion and went home to get the plate. He took it to Carol's grave that night and buried it, saying a prayer.

After that, the mist was never seen again.

"Do You Hear The Music?"
(Hollidaysburg, Blair County)

Throughout this book are many stories from my family's collection. These are stories I've known and loved for many years. This story has always been special to me because of the gentle way that God ushered my great-grandmother home. My grandmother Helen and grandfather Chet witnessed the angel's visit and told this story with great love.

When Rachel Richardson realized that she'd never recover from her illness, she also had to admit that she needed help. The only one of the children willing to help her by giving up their own home and moving in with her was her son, Chet. Chet had a wife and several children. The children Rachel thought she could tolerate, but she disliked her daughter-in-law, Helen.

For Helen, the idea of giving up her own home was less than pleasant; but she was a strong woman who believed in duty so she buckled down to the task. With few tears she watched her possessions carted off and sold. There would be little room at Mother Richardson's home for extra furniture.

Helen also knew that the move was nearly as hard on her mother-in-law. Rachel had never really approved of her and it must have humbled the old woman to find herself dependent upon her unwelcome daughter-in-law. Still, Helen tried to make the best of the situation by reminding herself about God's love and charity in the bad moments. After the move there really was not much time to think about her situation. With six children, a husband, a large garden, and a dying mother-in-law there was little time for rest, let alone introspection.

Mother Richardson had lost the use of her legs and was dying by degrees as gangrene and bed sores slowly destroyed her flaccid body. She had been forced to re-evaluate Helen. Not only did the girl care for her and the children, but she kept a clean home, raised a garden large enough to feed the family through the winter months, and even helped Chet with his work. Helen was always patient and sympathetic with Rachel's demands. Helen bathed, clothed, and cared for her without complaint. In fact, it was Helen's display of Christian love that moved Rachel to seek a closer relationship with God herself.

As the gangrene grew worse and the pain got to the point where the medication could not hold it back, Helen saw death in the old woman's eyes. Helen could also see an almost unbearable tiredness. Mother Richardson simply wished that the pain would end.

The last day of Rachel's life was a bad one for Helen. The kids were inside fussing and making extra messes. Chet was being sulky and she was late with Mother Richardson's dinner. Finally she'd had enough.

"You'll just have to take the tray up to your mother yourself," she exploded at Chet. "I've got to wash sheets yet. She's dirtied three sets already today."

Chet picked up the tray with its carefully laid out dinner of ham, green beans, and potatoes, buttered bread, coffee with real cream, and a small jar of blackberry jam, his mother's favorite, and headed upstairs. He hated going into the sick room. He hated seeing his mother, an iron-willed big woman who had ruled his father mercilessly, laying in her bed

221

like a ruined doll. Worst of all, he hated the smell of gangrene. He pushed the door open, then pasted a false smile on his face.

"Good...." Chet stopped as he saw that his mother was asleep. She had been only marginally pretty in her youth and now age and sickness had ruined the last of that. He put down the tray and carefully covered it with her napkin. He would come back later to see if she had eaten. The pain medication made her sleep and she had told him that she felt blessed when the sleep came and she was no longer conscious of the pain.

Chet crept from the room and left the door open so that if his mother needed anything she could just call out. He thought about calling the doctor but decided against it. The doctor had already told them that it was only a matter of time until she died. In fact, every day could be the last, although the doctor had told Chet and Helen in private that a weaker-willed person would be dead already. Chet knew that it sounded cold, but he wished that it could all just end.

Chet joined Helen and the kids for dinner. Helen and he passed a now familiar look. It was one of sympathy and grim acceptance. They tried to keep the worst of it from the kids, but it was impossible to protect them. Helen started Barb and Peggy, the two oldest girls, on the dishes, then went upstairs to gather the soiled sheets.

"You'd better check on your mother, Chet," she called from the landing.

Behind her she heard Chet mutter something, and she sighed. He'd never know how bone tired she was of all of this. The gangrenous smell clung to the upstairs like a blanket, and she held her breath unconsciously until it hurt her lungs. When this was over, she promised herself, she would burn the mattress in that sick room and throw open every window in the house until fresh air had removed that stench.

Helen's back throbbed and her legs ached from the constant trips up and down the stairs. She was not being unkind, but she hoped that it would soon be over. The pain she had seen Rachel suffer was inhuman, and Helen prayed that God would take her mother-in-law home.

Somewhere behind her she heard Chet's heavy tread. She looked up from her laundry basket. "What are you doing?"

He shrugged. "I thought I'd take the gun down to the barn with me. I saw coon tracks around the hen house this morning."

They were interrupted by the thin voice of Mother Richardson. "Chet, Chet, come here."

Chet stiffened at the sound. "I'm coming, Mother."

Helen went back to sorting sheets while Chet went to his mother's room. She was laying in the bed in almost exactly the same position as before, except that now she was gazing with rapt attention at the large wardrobe in the corner. She glanced briefly at her son standing in the doorway and a smile tugged at her lips.

"Do you hear it, Chet? It's the sweetest music I ever heard. Do you hear the music?" Her face was wreathed in a smile. Chet was not sure that he had ever seen her smile so beautifully.

"I don't hear anything." His mother must be hallucinating. The doctor hadn't warned them about that.

"Look!" With a great effort she raised one arm and pointed to the wardrobe.

"Mama," Chet began, taking her hand.

"Look!" She shook her arm. She was so agitated that Chet turned to look.

Breath stuck in his throat. His eyes could barely take in what he saw. There on the wardrobe sat an angel. It was white, so bright that he had to squint to keep the glare from hurting his eyes.

Just then Helen passed the doorway with her basket heaped with sheets. Chet had to get her to see this. He needed conformation that he was really seeing this.

"Helen, come here." His voice cracked.

Helen heard the tremor in Chet's voice. *It's happened*, her mind flashed. *Mother Richardson has died*. She dropped the basket and entered the room. Mother Richardson was not dead. Both Chet and his mother were staring at the wardrobe in the corner.

Helen froze. Mother Richardson was muttering something about the music, the sweet music, but Helen wasn't paying much attention. Before her was an angel. He smiled sweetly and stretched out his hand toward the bed. Helen watched, amazed. He nodded at them and then he just seemed to fade upward. Her ears caught what might have been a faint strand of music but she couldn't be sure.

"Chet," she breathed at last. "I can't believe..."

She looked at her husband, but he was staring at his mother. She was laying back in the old bed still smiling sweetly, her eyes stared upward vacantly. She was dead.

"The angel came for her." Chet touched his mother's hand. It was still warm. Helen came over and put her arm around him.

"She's gone home now. Chet, don't grieve." She gently closed her mother-in-law's eyes and then she led Chet into the hall.

God had granted a miracle and confirmed his answer to her prayers. Helen would never doubt or wonder about death or Heaven again. She knew that God simply sent an angel to take home his children, and they were led of by the hand and accompanied by sweet music.

The New Hope Hauntings
(New Hope, Bucks County)

The small town of New Hope in Bucks County, PA has the distinction of being one of the most haunted towns in Pennsylvania. In fact, Adele Gamble of Ghost Tours in New Hope makes part of her living by telling the stories of the hauntings. Adele walks through the town of New Hope with her tour groups, telling stories that range from tales about a phantom hitchhiker to the more historical story of Aaron Burr's spirit, which is seen at a local inn. Burr is said to stare about with sightless eyes and has startled more than one person through the years.

But Adele's brushes with the supernatural are not just through her stories. She has personally witnessed hauntings around New Hope herself. She tells a wonderful story about staying at one of the three local inns upon the hill overlooking New Hope. Years ago she discovered for herself that not all of the guests of the inn were living.

Back then, Adele worked with author Adi-Kent Thomas Jeffrey. Jeffrey wrote books about the hauntings in New Hope and throughout the Delaware Valley area. She and Adele were also friends who enjoyed working on the annual murder mystery weekends that were held at a local inn.

This particular weekend was in the fall of the year, and on that Friday night after the "murder" had taken place, some of the participants decided to go out for drinks. None of them knew that Adele was part of Ghost Tours or that she was helping stage the mystery for them. To the guests she was one of the party.

Adele decided after the group went out for the evening that she would go up to her room and rest. She had noticed earlier that the room had sense of masculinity about it. She felt that she hadn't been wanted in there. Adele had an a strong impression that this room had once been a "man's room." Something about it reminded her of a place where gentlemen of another era had once gathered after dinner for coffee and port and a bit of good conversation while they smoked their fine cigars. To Adele there was definitely something that did not want her in the room but she was not troubled by it. Old houses do have personalities of their own, and many people often get a "feeling" when they enter them. But ghosts were actually the last thing on Adele's mind that night.

Adele retired to her first floor room at the foot of the stairs for the night after she was sure that the mystery weekend guests were all back. As she lay in bed, she heard footsteps coming down the main stairs by her door. At first she thought that it was just one of the guests, but after ten minutes no one had returned to go back up the stairs.

While Adele was laying there trying to figure out why one of the guests was wandering the inn in the middle of the night, she again heard heavy footsteps descending the stairs. Quickly she dashed out of bed, threw open her door and stepped out at the bottom of the steps in the foyer area.

Immediately she encountered a drop in temperature. A large, misty figure of a man stood on the stairs before her. The man paused in his descent and looked at her. To Adele the man appeared to be a see-through image, and she stared back at him and waited for something to happen. The man simply looked at her for a few seconds before he faded away before her surprised eyes.

The first thing Adele noticed after the man disappeared was that the air at the bottom of the stairs had warmed up once more.

She went back into her room and sat on the bed. Adele looked at the clock on the night stand and saw that it was about 2 a.m. She was very excited by her sighting but there was no one she could tell. Instead she sat up the rest of the night waiting for the guests to stir so that she could find out more about the ghost she had seen.

In the morning she told Adi-Kent Thomas Jeffrey, who had started Ghost Tours. Adi-Kent told Adele to write down her encounter so that they could examine it more closely later. Now they were too busy with the mystery weekend to work on the haunting.

When the group decided to go out for lunch, Adele had to stay behind and plant the "clues" for the guests to later find during the mystery weekend. The innkeeper accompanied Adele on her mission. They entered each room of the inn and planted "clues." By the time they were done, Adele knew that she and the innkeeper were the only ones in the building. Now that she was done, she could rest. Last night's activities had caught up to her and she was exhausted.

The innkeeper told Adele that he was going to have to leave for a little while. He said that he was going out the back door and would lock it behind himself. This meant that Adele would be alone in the inn and she decided to grab a pillow and take a nap on the couch in the living room. There she was sure she could catch a couple hours sleep since no one would be back before the innkeeper was to return a little after 3 p.m.

Just as Adele was drifting off to sleep on the couch, a noise caught her attention and roused her. Adele sat up as she heard the noise a second time. Someone had just opened and closed the back door. Had the innkeeper returned early for some reason?

Adele called out, "Harvey, is that you?"

Silence.

Suddenly Adele felt an overpowering conviction that the same misty figure she had seen the night before was just now opening and closing the back door. She jumped up and ran into the foyer, following the heavy footsteps as they progressed in that direction. In the foyer area she stopped. She noticed the sudden drop in temperature just before she saw the very large shape of the man she had seen on the stairs the night before. He appeared to be formed by transparent mist. She was determined to wait and see what the ghost did, but the figure merely faded away again.

Before she left the inn for the weekend, she spoke to the innkeeper and told him that she knew that the inn was haunted. At first he denied it but Adele was insistent. The innkeeper asked her why she was so determined that the inn was haunted and she told him her story.

Suddenly the man smiled and said, "Well, Adele, people have heard that before, but I wanted to make sure of what you had encountered."

About a month later Adele received a phone call from a woman who had stayed in the same room at the inn after she did. This woman had encountered the spirit, too, but it had left her very frightened.

The innkeeper, Harvey, later told Adele that after her visit the ghost man had been particularly active. Was he encouraged because Adele had acknowledged him? Or was he trying to reach the world of the living for some special reason?

Adele often gives private tours when people contact her to request one. In November of 1996, a young couple from Baltimore, Maryland come up for a private tour. Through Adele they learned of the hauntings at the Logan Inn which had been built in 1722, and arranged to stay Sunday night in the "haunted room." When Adele left the couple for the night, she told them that she would be interested to learn if anything happened to them while they stayed in the haunted room.

The next afternoon Adele received a frantic message on her machine from the young woman. She pleaded with Adele to call her back. Something had happened during the couple's brief stay at the Logan Inn; something that had left the young woman very upset.

Adele tried to reach them at the Logan Inn but they had already checked out without leaving any way for her to reach them. For three days Adele tried to connect with the couple but had little luck. At last she reached them and the young woman got on the phone. The young lady told her a fantastic tale.

After Adele had left them on Sunday evening, the young couple had gone out to eat dinner. When they returned, they had retired for the night.

The young woman found herself awake at about 1 a.m. despite the fact that she never woke up in the middle of the night.

She noted that the room was dark but the outside light filtered in enough so that one could see the furniture. As the young woman looked around trying to figure out what had awakened her, she noticed off to one side what appeared to be a large, dark figure. She was sure that she must be hallucinating and she closed her eyes to rid herself of the shape. When she opened them a second later, she was shocked to see that the room had instantly gone pitch black.

Suddenly the young woman felt something heavy drop on the bottom of the bed, across her feet. The young woman now understood what it meant to be frozen in terror. She tried to call out to her husband but could not. She tried to move, to push off the heavy, creeping weight, but she found that she could not move.

Seconds ticked by as it slipped further up across her feet. The young woman lay in the bed and waited what seemed an eternity as she struggled to move. The darkness was disturbed by an audible "swishing sound," then the weight was suddenly gone. The normal night light from the windows instantly filtered back into the room and she could move once more.

The young woman began beating at her husband who had slept peacefully through the experience. She had to tell someone what had happened; she needed to validate her experience.

Adele asked the young woman what she thought the figure was, but she did didn't know. The woman reasserted that it was a large, dark figure which had filled her with fear.

Adele knew the haunted room at the Logan Inn well for she had stayed in it herself, but without experiencing anything. She did believe this young woman, however, because the story was told with such conviction, and Adele could hear the fear still in her voice days after the incident.

There are many other stories that Adele Gamble has to tell, but she is saving them for her tour. Anyone interested in contacting her for tour information should call her at (215) 957-9988 or request information from the Pennsylvania Bureau of Tourism. Adele gives regular tours throughout the fall, and I can think of no better way to have fun for under ten dollars.

Adi-Kent Thomas Jeffrey's books on the hauntings in Delaware Valley are also available by contacting Adele.

The Northwest Corner

The move from Indiana had been difficult for Jim Hawks and his family, but now that it was over he had to admit that he was glad to be back home in Pennsylvania. Jim had made the move because of his father's death and his mother's subsequent illness. With all of his brothers and sisters in situations that they couldn't get out of, Jim had been left to pack up his family and go back to take care of the family farm and make the decisions necessary about their mother's health.

The cool evening air eased away the tension of the hot day as Jim sat on the porch swing listening to the night sounds of frogs and katydids. A light breeze came up and Jim laid his head back, closing his eyes.

The screeching of the screen door told Jim that he was not alone and he opened his eyes to see his wife, Kimberly, as she came toward him through the darkness. He stopped the swaying of the swing briefly while she sat down and snuggled against him. They didn't say a word, they just enjoyed the cool night air and the solitude of this time. Their teenage girls were settling down upstairs and Kimberly had settled his mother Doris before she came out to join him.

Slowly they began to hear a sound that did not fit into the quiet solitude of the lonely farm. It started low and seemed to drift toward them on the breeze. At first Jim thought that it was the sound of an animal crying, but Kimberly shifted forward, stopping the swing's motion.

"Do you hear that?" There was a tension in Kimberly's voice. "What is that?"

Jim shook his head and strained to listen. "Whatever it is, it's coming from around the corner there, to the northwest." Jim got up and went to the porch steps.

"It's a baby crying, Jim." Kimberly's voice caught in her throat.

Jim looked at her. "It can't be. There are no babies around here...." His voice trailed off as the cry broke the stillness of the air again. This time it was louder and there was no mistaking the fact that Kimberly was right. It was a baby crying.

Jim went down the porch steps, Kimberly close behind him. They followed the sound to the northwest corner of the old house but saw nothing. Jim and Kimberly stood there, listening to the crying. Kimberly put her hand on Jim's arm and leaned close.

"It give me the creeps," she whispered, shuddering.

As suddenly as the crying had started, it now stopped. Jim was glad that Kimberly had heard the sound, too, or he would have been tempted to believe that he had imagined it.

During the summer they heard the sound many times. It always came late in the evening when darkness had fallen and it always came from the northwest corner of the house. Kimberly had insisted that they not tell the girls, but when Dana, their oldest daughter, began talking about hearing the crying they found out that the girls had heard the sound, too.

Jim tried to broach the subject with his mother several times but she seemed to be uninterested. She insisted that they were imagining things. She had lived in the house for more than forty years and she swore that she had never heard any such sound coming from the northwest corner.

It was not until fall when Kimberly was digging up the flower bulbs that bordered the house that the grisly discovery was made. Kimberly had dug deeper at the northwest corner because she had difficulty finding the bulbs. Instead she found an old, rotting burlap sack. Curious about why the sack was buried in the flower beds, Kimberly had loosened the sack and then gave it a hard pull that tore the bag in two.

Suddenly the air was ripped by Kimberly's screams, causing Jim and the girls to dash from the house. There, at Kimberly's feet, was the skeleton of a small baby. It had been wrapped in newspaper, but the paper had rotted long ago leaving only the tiny, gray bones.

Jim stared at the tiny skeleton at his wife's feet and felt his face drain of blood. He had grown up in this house, had lived here most of his life. How long had that baby's body been buried at the northwest corner of his home?

Kimberly looked up at him with horrified eyes. Jim grabbed up the torn bag that was beneath the baby's bones and headed toward the house.

"Jim!" Kimberly shouted after him. She knew in her heart where he was going.

Jim took the porch steps two at a time. There was only one person who could explain this bag of baby bones: his mother.

Doris was lounging on the recliner in her bedroom watching television. She started when her son Jim burst into her room red-faced and waving a bundle of torn, filthy burlap. Suddenly fear clutched her heart. She knew that they had found the body. She knew that her secret was out.

"Mom, Kimberly just dug this up." Jim dumped the bag onto the floor, spilling out the tiny bones. "It's a baby, Mom. Why was it buried under the house? What was it doing there?"

Doris opened her mouth but no words came out. It had been thirty-five years since she had dug that hole late one night. Thirty-five years of thinking her secret safe. Thirty-five years of listening to that dead baby's cries. It had been enough. As she stared at the bones, her daughter-in-law and granddaughters filled the doorway.

"Mom, I want answers now!" Jim's voice made her flinch.

She looked at her son and his family with red-rimmed eyes. Wearily she tipped her chair forward into a sitting position. "You wouldn't remember this, Jim, but about thirty-five years ago your father and I were having some marital problems. I was seriously thinking of leaving him, but I had seven children and no skills so I hung on. That summer your father hired a drifter who was looking for work to help on the farm. He stayed in the tack shed where we had set up a cot.

"He was a fine-looking man, dark and young, and he paid me special attention. I was still thin back then and pretty. He was nice, not thinking that he owned me, and we had an affair. When your father found out, he nearly beat the man to death. He took him down the road and dumped his body off by the road. I suppose that he was still alive because I never heard that anyone found his body.

"Your father was furious with me and when he found out that I was pregnant he went mad. He was determined that no one would know. I never left the farm for nearly seven months. No one could come in if they stopped to visit, and I couldn't be seen outside. You kids were still very small so you knew nothing. I hid the pregnancy well. I had to or your father threatened to kill me.

"I gave birth to the baby late one afternoon in that tack shed where it had been conceived with the drifter. Your father had taken me there when the labor pains had begun. The last thing he said before he had locked me in there was, 'You'd better pray, woman, if that child looks like that man.'"

"I remember staring at that wee baby in the harsh glare of the late afternoon sun coming through the small window. The baby was dark like the drifter. All of you children had been fair like your father and myself.

"I was desperate. What would your father do when he saw the baby? Then the baby began crying. I tried to hush it but it refused to stop. I don't know what happened then except that I panicked. I couldn't stop the wails no matter how hard I tried and at last I pressed a pillow

231

over its face to make it be quiet.

"It was soon still and I felt a ray of hope. I'd tell your father that the baby had been stillborn. I'd wrap it in a bundle and then he'd never need look at it. It seemed like such a good idea at the time. I found some old newspapers on a shelf and wrapped it up in those. Then I shoved it into a burlap sack.

"Eventually your father came back. It was dark by then and I was nearly beside myself. I'd been locked up alone with that dead baby for hours, but I lied to your father. I told him my story. He wasn't satisfied. He dumped the bundle out of the sack and made me unwrap it. The tiny thing was cold and stiff. It had a bluish cast to it and I tried to pretend that it was a dead piglet, or something else, anything but my baby.

"It only took one look for your father to realize that it was not his child. The shock of dark hair gave testimony to my betrayal. His anger was frightening. He grabbed up the baby and shoved it back into the bag. Then he grabbed my arm and threw me toward the door. He followed with the burlap sack in one hand and a shovel from the shed in the other. We went to the northwest corner of the house and there he stuck the shovel into the ground. 'Dig,' he commanded.

"I dug the hole and buried the child. That night he beat me almost senseless and then locked me back into the shed. He told you kids that I was sick, but I just stayed in that shed for nearly a week until the bruises began to fade. After that he never hit me again.

"I nearly fainted when you all began talking about hearing the baby crying. No one else has ever heard it; no one but me. Every once in a while I'd wake up hearing those same thin wails and I knew that it was crying because it knew that I could never love it. It was crying for what I had done, for what it had lost." Doris raised damp eyes to her son.

Jim stared at her in horror. Somewhere in the back of his head he remembered a summer when his mother had disappeared for a while. He remembered crying for her and his father telling him that his mother was away because she was sick. Jim knew in his heart that his mother was speaking the horrible truth. His mother had murdered her own child.

Jim never told the authorities. His mother's punishment had been hearing that baby's wails for over thirty years. She died only a few months after the small body had been found. Jim had built a small box and they had returned the bones to their place beneath the northwest corner of the house. Then he built a small concrete flower box on top of the grave. Never again would the poor baby be disturbed.

Jim and his family didn't stay on there long. After his mother's death they never heard the sound of crying again. But after the house was sold the new owner mentioned to Jim once that occasionally they heard the sound of some small animal near the northwest corner of the house. The animal made a strange wailing cry like that of a baby.

Because of the criminal act involved the family asked that I not reveal their real name.

The Livingston Poltergeist
(York County and Middleway, West Virginia)

I first heard of this story many years ago and I believe that it is one of the most well-documented poltergeist cases in early America. The Rev. Prince Gallitzin (for whom the town of Prince Gallitzin is named) and Archbishop Carroll of Baltimore, Maryland both experienced this poltergeist and spoke and wrote about it later. Both of those eminent gentlemen believed that a real entity haunted and tormented the Livingston family. In addition to the authentication of both of these religious gentlemen, many others witnessed the phenomena, and no one came forward either at the time of the incidents nor later on to repudiate the story of Livingston family.

233

1790

Mr. Adam Livingston was a well respected gentleman in York County in the state of Pennsylvania. He was well known in the area and many folks wished that they were as lucky as he was. He had a large family of six children, a loving wife, health, land and property, and four slaves. By all accounts Mr. Livingston was an upstanding citizen who took his bounty in stride and who placed God before himself in all he did. He was of the Lutheran religion and practiced his faith devoutly. There was no one in the county less likely to feel God's sting than the Livingston family.

For several years Mr. Livingston continued to prosper in his York County home, but suddenly one year it was as though he had been touched like Job from the Bible. His cattle took ill and died, other livestock began to perish for no apparent reason and even his barns went up in flames. There were mysterious illnesses that struck at the family and slaves. Though no one died, the tribulations to the Livingston family were great.

Slowly Adam Livingston began to see his fortunes change for the worse. He lost some of his property and was forced to sell still more to pay off his debts. His neighbors began to whisper that he was cursed by bad luck.

The townspeople did not know how bad things truly were at the Livingston house. Strange rappings and odd noses filled the home and grounds day and night. A disembodied voice began to speak to the family aloud and it conversed with Adam in his dreams.

Worse yet, some force was rearranging the furniture, throwing fire out of the fireplace, and tossing clothing about. Even those acts were outdone when the entity began to physically attack the household. People were shoved by unseen hands.

The last straw came when the entity hacked up the Livingston's clothes and property. The clip-click of invisible scissors filled the house as item after item fell shredded beneath them. Belts, clothes, bedding, anything that could be cut was destroyed by the entity. Mr. Livingston was faced with a terrible dilemma. How could he let the townspeople and his church know that demons were plaguing him? Furthermore, what could he or his family have done to cause such an infestation?

At last the Livingstons could no longer deal with their problem, and Mr. Livingston proposed that the family move. Perhaps if they moved far enough away, the entity that was plaguing his family would leave them alone.

The Livingstons purchased a farm outside Charles Town, West Virginia, (which was part of Virginia at that time) and Adam moved his family southward to their new home. Unfortunately, Livingston's hopes of leaving the entity behind him were short-lived. In Charles Town the same evil forces seemed bent upon destroying him. He lost livestock and money. The strange illnesses continued, and even his crops began to fail despite the fact that everyone else had good crops.

The Voice followed the family to their new home and spoke aloud in front of investigators, friends, neighbors and family members. Adam reported that he still heard it speaking to him in dreams as well.

The terrible snipping of the phantom scissors filled the air of this new house as item after item fell shredded to the floor. Rapping sounds and rumbling noises shook the house, and other sounds they could not place rent the air both inside and outside of their home.

Adam Livingston searched for relief from this affliction through the church. He went to several local ministers and explained what was tormenting his family. The ministers, one after another, agreed to come to the Livingston home to pray and try to remove the demons.

In Charles Town word of the phenomena quickly spread. Local folks packed the farmhouse to hear the clicking of the scissors and to see the cut-up items. Others came with picnic lunches. While they sat and ate, they watched as chickens running about the barn yard were suddenly decapitated or their legs were cut from under them. Each time the terrible clip of the ghostly scissors could be heard. At other times, much to the public's delight, the horses were shorn and other animals were attacked by the phantom scissors.

Mr. Livingston and his family were emotionally drained by this time. Adam was on the verge of a nervous breakdown and his wife and children were pale and sickly. Adam no longer knew what he could do to stop the phenomena. He had prayed, in fact the entire household had prayed, devoutly for relief but none had come. He had sought out religious help several times, but the ministers only seemed to infuriate the entity and it grew still worse after the ministers had prayed.

The Voice derided Adam Livingston for his attempts to rid himself of the entity through the ministers. It told him that they could not help him.

One night, when Mr. Livingston thought he could bear the entity no more, he had a strange dream. He saw a robed religious figure standing before him. The Voice spoke to him, saying that this was the figure who could end his family's torment. Adam did not recognize the religion represented by the robes, but he would later discuss this dream with a peddler who would tell it that they sounded like the robes worn by Catholic priests. The salesman urged Adam to find a Catholic church somewhere and seek their help.

Adam did not know what he should do. He was a good Lutheran so how could he go to the Catholic church for help? Furthermore, after each visit from a minister the entity had grown agitated and angry and had taken it out upon his family, so how could he risk infuriating it even more?

The day after the peddler's visit, Livingston decided to take the risk and he set out in search of a Catholic church. He knew that his neighbors, the McSherrys, were Catholic, so he appealed to them. The family suggested that Adam attend a private Mass held in a home in Shepardstown the next Sunday.

The Mass was officiated over by a Father Cahill from Hagerstown, Maryland. Adam sought out the priest and explained his problem. Father Cahill was sure that this man was playing a joke on him, but when he spoke to the McSherry family whom he knew, he found out that Adam Livingston spoke the truth.

The priest decided to help and arranged to visit the Livingstons. Very shortly after Father Cahill entered the farmhouse, he witnessed the phenomena himself. He heard the clipping of the scissors and saw the damaged items fall to the ground. He saw the chickens decapitated; he heard knockings in the walls and on the ceilings. It is not known if Father Cahill heard the Voice, but it seems that if he did not hear it himself, he was convinced that it did exist from the testimony of others.

Father Cahill questioned the family closely about the manifestations, then he brought out a vial of Holy Water. He prayed aloud as he sprinkled the precious liquid throughout the house. A few days later he held a special Mass for the Livingstons.

After the Father's visit, the occurrences seemed to stop for a short time. The Livingston's were immensely grateful to the Catholic Church and they decided to convert to Catholicism. Adam became a zealot about the church and insisted that all of his family and many of his friends likewise convert. He was spurred on by the Voice which demanded more converts, more prayers, more penance and more devotion to the faith. The Voice was especially fond of demanding that the family pray for the lost souls in Purgatory.

The Voice told Adam to convert friends and distant family or else dire disasters would happen to them. Adam pleaded with the Voice for the sake of his friends and family. He begged to warn them, but the Voice said that warnings were futile. It said that they would not heed the Voice from the dead.

Sometime after the family converted to Catholicism, a ragged beggar came to the Livingston gate. He was shabbily dressed and was barefoot. The man pleaded for food and a place to rest. Adam Livingston and his family gave him both food and shelter. They offered him clean, decent clothing, and told him that he could remain in their home until he was rested and able to travel again.

After several days the man announced that he was sent to them to instruct them "in the way of my Father." He stayed with them for a while, imparting religious teachings.

When the beggar left, the family watched him pass through their front gate. They later said that he simply stepped through the gate, closed it and vanished.

In 1797 Father Prince Gallitzin traveled from the town he had founded, called Loretto in Pennsylvania, and went down to see the Livingstons. He verified the existence of the entity and the Voice, and he wrote of what he heard and saw. He came away convinced that a truly supernatural phenomena was haunting the Livingston family.

Though much of the destructive phenomena stopped after the family converted, the Voice lingered with them for several more years. Each time a member of the family backslid and left the Church, the Voice would stridently insist upon their return to the fold. It demanded that they seek out a priest and confess their sins. It demanded that they vow to be faithful in the future.

Throughout the years of torment and the comparatively restful years when only the Voice reigned, Adam kept in close contact with Father Cahill and Father Gallitzin. A few years after his conversion, Adam made a trip on foot from West Virginia to the Conewago Church in Hanover, Pennsylvania. He had traveled so far to see his now dear friend, Father Gallitzin.

In the last years of his life Adam made a will giving 35 acres of ground to the Church, in the care of Father Cahill. Father Cahill viewed the land as a living tribute to the conversion of Adam Livingston and his family. A little church was built there and can still be seen today.

The field where the church was placed is located approximately seven miles west of Charles Town and the area is named "Priest Field." Each year a special Mass is held there for Adam Livingston.

Sharing The House With Rebecca
(Roaring Spring, Blair County)

Throughout the years, ghost stories have come to me in many ways. Often I find my best stories when I'm not even looking. Perhaps this was most evident in this case. The story of "Rebecca" came to me by way of my mother's neighbor. The neighbor, who worked as a cleaning lady, told her of the haunted house she cleaned every Wednesday. My mother relayed the story to me, and I began contacting those involved. All of this story is based upon first-hand testimony of those who have lived, worked at, and visited this house.

The story of Rebecca is "odd" in one special way. Throughout time it has become common knowledge that animals react adversely to the presence of spirits. The history of parapsychology is filled with stories of cats that have hissed and howled as they tried to escape the presence of a spirit. Dogs have shown every response from mild fear to literally dying of fright. But the animals involved in this story had a different reaction: they seem to be fond of their ghost.

In the small Central Pennsylvania town of Roaring Spring there is a small house on an obscure street which has been the home of G.S. and his wife M.S. for the past eighteen years. When they purchased the house from a local family, they were told of the tragedy which took place there. The previous tenant, Rebecca, had died in the hallway between the master bedroom and the bathroom and had not been found for three days. The family that owned the house felt that the new owners should know the past history before it was told to them by their neighbors.

The story did not deter G.S. and his wife. It was a sad story, but not unusual. Furthermore, M.S.'s father had known and worked with Rebecca for many years; they had often joked around at work and M.S. had often heard her father tell stories about Rebecca. The one thing that M.S. and her husband never thought about or expected was that Rebecca might be haunting their new house.

After moving in, the couple never suspected a thing. But their pets often paused as if seeing or listening to someone. Then one hot, humid summer the air conditioning went on the blink. M.S. and her pets were nearly overcome by the tremendous heat which was made worse for them because they were not used to it. M.S. noticed that there seemed to be a very cold spot in the hallway, between the master bedroom and the bathroom, which she took advantage of. She spent the hot afternoon laying in the hall with her two cats and her dog. Only later would M.S. realize that the spot which was always so cold was the same place where Rebecca had died and lain unfound for three days.

The couple were always very busy, so it took several years to realize they shared their home with a ghost. If things were moved, then they thought the other person had done it. M.S. worked days and G.S. worked nights. They ran a small business from the house, as well, so it was always easy to find reasons why things had happened. But that all changed about six years ago....

At that time M.S. and G.S. noticed that the light switch in their bedroom had a life of its own. If they tried to turn the lights on in that room, a struggle of wills would ensue. On they'd flip the light, off it would instantly go. At first the couple thought it was a faulty switch. But M.S.'s uncle was an electrician and he could find nothing wrong it.

One day in frustration the couple called out to Rebecca to leave the light on. To their amazement the light switch simply flipped back to the On position. That's when they realized Rebecca was probably responsible for the other incidents.

It seemed that anything which would disturb or frighten the pets upset Rebecca as well. She often refuseed to leave lights on in the master bedroom if the pets were sleeping there.

M.S.'s father found out that Rebecca also refused to allow appliances turned on which might upset the pets. After his retirement, M.S.'s father volunteered to clean his daughter's home. He had heard the stories from his daughter, but he was not sure that he really believed them...until he tried to clean the house. M.S.'s father got out the vacuum cleaner and plugged it in. He flipped the switch but it flipped itself off again. Again he flipped it on, but immediately it flipped itself off once again. Time after time he turned on the machine only to have the switch immediately turn itself off.

At last M.S.'s father grew exasperated. "Okay, Rebecca," he called out to the room. "I know you're getting me back for all of the practical jokes I played on you at work. But I've got to get this floor vacuumed before M.S. gets home, so please let the vacuum on this time."

Before he could reach out to flip the switch back to the On position, Rebecca flipped it on herself.

Eventually the couple was forced to tell their friends of Rebecca's presence. She often made herself known when guests were visiting. So the couple found that it was easier to tell the truth than to try and come up with excuses for the strange behavior of the light switch in their room.

A few years ago M.S. and G.S. had a New Year's Eve party. Among their guests were a young couple named Leslie and Mark who had brought along their small daughter, Tabitha. Long before midnight, Tabitha fell asleep and M.S. told Leslie to put the little girl to bed in the master bedroom where she wouldn't be disturbed.

Leslie and Mark thought nothing of it until they were ready to leave for the night. As Mark felt his way through the dark room toward the bed, he called out to his wife to turn on the light. Leslie felt for the switch and flipped it. For a brief second the room was lit, but suddenly the switch flipped back off. Leslie thought that she must not have gotten the switch on fully, so she flipped it on again. Once more the light instantly flipped off. As she struggled to keep the light on, Mark paused beside the bed where he was trying to dress their young daughter to go outside.

"Everything okay in here?" G.S. asked, poking his head around the doorway.

"I can't seem to get this light to stay on," Leslie said, flipping the light on once more. Immediately the light switch flipped off again.

G.S. laughed as he stepped into the room. "No problem. I'll take care of it." He turned toward the room. "Now, Rebecca, let the light stay on. These folks have to get their baby ready to leave."

He reached out and flipped on the light. This time the room stayed lit.

G.S. proceeded to explain to the amazed young couple that their home was haunted, and that the ghost of Rebecca had been playing a trick on them.

Mark was very rattled by the very idea of a ghost playing tricks but Leslie was less upset. Leslie was later offered the job of cleaning the house every Wednesday and she accepted. Immediately she learned that Rebecca would have to be dealt with. She had trouble in the house until she began speaking to Rebecca herself.

Leslie also felt that Rebecca disliked her. Leslie believed it might be because she works for the same Emergency Management Unit which had taken away Rebecca's body years ago.

Rebecca played tricks on Leslie when she came to clean, but by far the worst one was tinkering with Leslie's car. Leslie noticed that every time she came to clean, her car would act up on the way home. It would buck and backfire. It sputtered and the engine died. At first Mark tried to figure out what was wrong, but after a while the car was okay by itself.

One morning Rebecca was being particularly troublesome and Leslie was in a hurry. She had to speak to Rebecca about the vacuum and the lights. When she was done, she had to hurry to pick up her little girl from school. In the car she dreaded turning the switch. What tricks would Rebecca play today?

Suddenly Leslie had an idea. If talking to Rebecca in the house worked, perhaps it might work in the car. "Rebecca," she said aloud to the air, "Please don't mess with my car today. I have to pick Tabitha up at school now, so I need my car to run well today."

With that Leslie turned on the engine and the car purred into life. She braced herself as she backed down the driveway but there was no backfiring. As she drove toward the school, she was pleasantly surprised to find that the car ran perfectly. Apparently Rebecca was being nice.

Through the years Leslie found that Rebecca still played tricks with her car, including changing the channels on the radio while the car is off. Rebecca had re-programmed the set channels on the radio several times, despite the fact that the channels can not be reset when the vehicle is off.

M.S. and G.S. were not surprised when they heard about the radio. Rebecca had very particular tastes in music and she often changed radio stations for them as well. In fact, Rebecca even turned on radios in the house and then switched the station to one that suited her better.

Recently Leslie reported reaching for the light switch in the master bedroom one day and feeling a cold spot pass through her hand. She said that it felt as if Rebecca had reached though her hand to turn off the light at the same time Leslie had reached to turn it on.

At first the haunting centered around the master bedroom, but now Rebecca played tricks in the kitchen. She would flip off and on the kitchen lights at will, and often refused to let M.S. use the food processor or other noisy appliances when the pets were sleeping.

Rebecca also opened and closed kitchen cabinets doors. Many times M.S. asked G.S. why he left some cabinet open or why he shut a particular cabinet she left open to air out. G.S. knew nothing about the cabinets and he confessed that he wondered why M.S. was letting certain doors open all of the time. M.S. told him in no uncertain terms that she did not leave them open. Apparently Rebecca opened them.

One night in February of 1997, M.S. woke up in the middle of the night because her two cats were playing noisily in the hallway outside the master bedroom. For a few moments M.S. laid in bed, watching the cats thumping about by the light from the hall which she always kept on. M.S. was just about to get up and scold the cats when they suddenly stopped in their tracks. At the same time they looked upward, then they hastily scattered. M.S. had seen them do that many times before when she had scolded them for some infraction, but this time there had been no one visible in the hall.

M.S. also noticed that when Rebecca's name is mentioned, her dog wagged its tail. It was as if the dog knew who they were talking about.

G.S.'s business partner had several experiences in the house which unnerved him at first. Sometimes the partner came into the basement of the house to work on their project when G.S. was not home. The business partner began experiencing all sorts of problems with the computer system. The computer screen would suddenly go blank, strange material would appear which should not have been on the system, and the man would hear music coming from the computer speakers despite the fact that he was not playing music on the computer!

At last, the business partner approached M.S. one day and asked half jokingly if the house was haunted. For a second M.S. paused, then she laughed. "Yes it is," she said. She told him about Rebecca and all that had happened at the house.

The man looked nonplused and she hurried on to explain that Rebecca is a good spirit. "I think she's just playing tricks on you because she's not sure you should be here. She seems to protect the house and doesn't like it when people are here without G.S. or myself."

M.S. turned and spoke to the room. "Rebecca, this man is G.S.'s business partner and he belongs here. Please quite playing tricks on him on the computer."

After that conversation the business partner reported that he has had almost no trouble with the computer system anymore.

M.S. reported that much of the hauntings had to do with the pets. "Mostly where the pets are, stuff is gonna happen."

Through the years the couple have noticed many things about the house that have convinced them that it is truly haunted. They have reported cold spots that move as well as that one spot in the hallway. There are balls of light or light streaks in the pictures they have taken of their pets. And, of course, the fact that Rebecca responds when spoken to is proof positive to them that Rebecca is truly there.

Recently G.S. and M.S. were in the basement music studio of the house with G.S.'s band, which includes Mark. While the band was taking a break from its practice, Leslie began staring at the ceiling. She leaned over and asked M.S. if she heard the noise above them, too. For a few seconds M.S. paused and listened. "It sounds like footsteps," she confided. Several other people heard the footsteps and commented upon them. They all knew that there was no one alive upstairs to make the sounds, but alive or not, Rebecca still makes living at their home very lively.

The name of the ghost in this story has been changed at the request of the family who now owns the home. Rebecca's family still lives in the same little town and the couple is afraid that the family will be upset. When they have approached the family in the past, trying to speak of Rebecca's spirit, her family seemed upset by the idea that their mother's spirit resided in her old home and not in Heaven.

The Girl In
The Red Shawl
(Philadelphia, Montgomery County)

By the winter of 1880, Dr. Silas Weir Mitchell had secured his reputation as both a physician and as a writer. He had worked for many years with people suffering from nervous conditions and had developed a workable treatment of rest for those suffering from nervous breakdowns. Aside from his groundbreaking work as a physician, he was also widely recognized for both his historical fiction novels and for his poetry. He was truly one of the most illustrious residents of Philadelphia.

At the age of fifty-one, Dr. Mitchell had begun to slow down a bit. He no longer made house calls, and he had been limiting his patients so that he would have time to pursue both his writing and his research. However, he was about to make one house call late one December night in 1880 which would change his outlook on life both as a physician and as a man. What happened to him that night influenced him so profoundly that he told the story of the little girl in the red shawl many times during the remainder of his life.

It had been snowing since early that December afternoon in 1880, and by nightfall Dr. Mitchell realized that what was bearing down on Philadelphia was an unrelenting blizzard. Dr. Mitchell worked for several hours before he deciding to retire for the night. The doctor put away his work, turned down the lights in his snug house, and climbed the stairs as he had each night for many years.

He had barely settled into his warm bed before a disturbing sound broke through the stillness. It was the ringing of his doorbell downstairs. Grumbling about who could possibly be out on such a bitter night, Dr. Mitchell stomped back down the stairs. He threw open the door, allowing the bitter night air to flood past him, and found himself staring at the slight figure of a little girl standing on his porch surrounded by swirling snow. The child seemed wraithlike. She wore only a thin, ragged dress and a worn red shawl, which she clutched tightly around her painfully thin shoulders.

"Good Lord, child, come in before you freeze." The doctor urged the child to step into the warmth of his hall. The child came in but she scarcely noticed the difference in temperature.

"You must come, doctor. My mother is very ill and she needs you." The child's voice was as painfully thin as her body.

Dr. Mitchell shook his head. It had been several years since he had gone out on house calls and tonight travel would be almost impossible. "Don't you have a regular doctor who could see your mother?" he asked.

The child shook her head no and stared intensely. "My mother's very sick and she needs you," she said again.

Something about the child's demeanor shook the doctor's resolve and he found himself wavering. Almost against his will, he agreed to go with the child in the ragged red shawl. He quickly dressed and retrieved his doctor's bag.

He opened the door and found that somehow the child had managed to slip past him unnoticed and she took the lead. The night was filled with blowing, icy snow and bone-chilling wind, yet the child never faltered. It was as if she did not have to struggle against the high winds while Dr. Mitchell stumbled through drifts, fighting the biting wind that threatened to blow him over.

Several times Dr. Mitchell lost sight of the child and paused, puzzled by which way to turn next. Each time the child suddenly appeared at his elbow and directed him on how best to reach her mother. The little girl led the doctor further into the city, into ever poorer sections of Philadelphia, until they were in the very slums. There the child quickly went into a large, old building that appeared abandoned. Dr. Mitchell stumbled on after her into the slight protection of the cold brick tenement. The only relief from the night was the windbreak that the brick structure provided since there was no heat inside the building.

The child took the stairs past the first floor, then the second. On the third floor landing she paused for him to catch up, then she led him to a shabby room down the hall. The little girl paused beside the room's doorway. "This way," she whispered. "My mother's in there."

The doctor did not pause to see where the child went but hurried straight into the room. For a few seconds he paused in the filthy, cold room. The room was bare except for a pile of dirty, ragged quilts on the floor. A single candle nub flickered, giving only faint light. Something stirred within the dirty nest of quilts, and the doctor hurried forward. There he found a woman obviously suffering from pneumonia, who thrashed and moaned in a deadly delirium. Dr. Mitchell knew that he was going to have to fight death hard if he was going to save this woman's life.

He glanced up to see the little girl standing in the doorway, watching him intently. "I need a phone," he said. "I must get your mother to a hospital as quickly as possible."

"There is no phone here," the child said, already moving away, "but I will take you to one."

The doctor dashed after the child and followed as she led him to another building. She stayed outside as he quickly made the phone call to a local hospital. The matron promised to do what she could to hurry an ambulance, but it would be several hours at least before one could reach the tenement through the blizzard. The doctor knew that he would have to use all of his knowledge if he was to keep the woman alive until help could come.

He hurried back to the woman's pathetic room. During his ministrations he found himself pausing to study the woman's face. He was sure he knew this woman. Suddenly he remembered who she was. She had been a maid in his home many years ago.

As he worked he watched for the child to return, but the little girl was gone. He hoped that she had found some relatively warm corner to rest in. She had been a very brave child to come through such a terrible night in search of help for her mother. In truth, if her mother lived it would be as much because of the child's courage as his own skill as a physician.

Toward morning the woman began to stir again but this time she woke and was coherent. "Dr. Mitchell," she whispered. "I don't understand. How did you get here?"

The doctor eased the woman back into her nest of quilts. "Just rest," he soothed. "Just rest."

"But how?" the woman persisted. "How did you find me?"

"It was your daughter, my dear," he said. " She came to my house last night and insisted that I follow her here. She was very strong and courageous. You must be very proud of her."

As the doctor spoke, the woman shook her head faintly. "I don't understand." Her voice broke into a ragged sob. "My daughter died a month ago."

The doctor stared at the sick woman in astonishment. "That's impossible. She came last night and told me that you were sick. I followed her here. How else could I have known that you were ill? How could I have found you?"

The woman stared away from the doctor at a door across the room. "I don't know what you are talking about, Dr. Mitchell, but my daughter is dead. All I have left of her is in that closet."

The doctor stood and walked to the closet on numb legs. He opened the door and found that all the closet housed was a single hanger on which was hung a ragged dress and a worn red shawl. These were the clothes that the child had worn throughout the night. With shaking fingers he reached out to touch the garments. They were dry, but that was impossible. His own clothes were still damp from the stinging snow he had trudged through.

Suddenly he knew with perfect conviction that he had followed a ghost child clothed in a red shawl that night. He had followed a little girl who had come back from the dead to save her mother's life. Everything about that night suddenly made sense. Now he knew why the child had not struggled against the wind and snow. Now he remembered how she had suddenly appeared when he had been confused and urged him, "This way, Doctor. This way." Now he knew that love survived even death. It was a lesson taught to him by a dead little girl in a worn red shawl.

The Royer House
(Royer, Blair County)

D aniel Royer and his three sons made a name for themselves
in Central Pennsylvania during the first part of the 1800s.
Their fortunes were made in the iron ore works, which were so important during the industrial revolution, and for the vast railroads which
were growing rapidly at that time.

Over the decades, the Royers moved from the area. While their
descendants are gone, the stately homes from this earlier era remain as
mute testimony that the Royers once were here. The homes also remind
local residents that some of the long-dead Royers and their employees
might still be around....

Though there were three Royer brothers who each built homes
in the area, the one house that still stands in the village of Royer is known
officially as the Royer House. Samuel Royer, who became the supervisor of the Springfield Furnace in 1814, built this home in approximately
1815. The house was surrounded by a small schoolhouse, church, grist
mill, store, and the cottages of the ironworks' employees. This became
the village of Royer. Now located at the edge of Royer, sits the gray stone
Royer House with, if the stories are true, some of the home's past ten-
ants still in residence.

According to legend, before Samuel moved into the house, another supervisor lived there briefly. This man was very jealous and fix-
ated on his wife. He was less than pleased when she told him that they
would be having a baby.

The supervisor was even jealous of his own child once it was born,
and for the longest time his wife refused to leave him alone with the baby.
She felt that his anger and dislike of the baby bordered on insanity, but

Front View of the Royer House. It is this door beneath the small porch where the woman in red is said to answer the door.

over the first few months of the child's life the supervisor worked to prove that he was trustworthy so that his wife would respond to him better. In truth, he disliked the child. It took up too much of his wife's precious time and attention—time and attention that he wanted for himself.

One day, when the baby was several months old, the supervisor's wife was called away for an emergency. The supervisor promised to take care of the child so, with misgivings, she left to help midwife for a local woman until a doctor could be called in. In those days finding the doctor could be very difficult, especially if he was on rounds in the winding countryside. It was hours until the doctor relieved her so that she could return home to her child.

The big stone house was quiet as she entered. She searched the first and second floors. No one seemed home and the baby was missing from the nursery. Calling out in panic, she heard a reply from above. Her husband heard her frantic calls and came down from the attic. He was subdued and remote. He wouldn't answer her directly about the baby's whereabouts.

The supervisor's wife was growing frantic. Where was her baby?

Finally her husband confessed that he'd taken care of it; that the child would not come between them again because it was dead. He had killed it. And he told her he had hung the child in the attic.

It couldn't be true. His wife tried to push past him into the up-

249

per regions of the house. They wrestled and he won, subduing her. Now she tried to calm herself as he held her, telling her how wonderful their lives would once again be without the baby to care for. Her mind was racing with choices. Perhaps the child was not really dead. But when she questioned him, he claimed he'd hidden child's body somewhere in the walls of the house.

When the young mother tried to get away for help, there was a desperate struggle and she was strangled. Her husband realized that, while he might have explained away the child's death, he couldn't cover up two deaths. So he went to the master bedroom, took out his gun, and killed himself.

At the time this would have happened the Royer family was very rich and may have struggled to suppress the sordid tale. History does not officially admit that this story is true, but the story has persisted with the locals for years. Before the house was abandoned in the 1960s, several families came away with odd stories to tell. They claimed to have seen a baby in a cradle in the attic—a baby that disappeared when approached.

Other people have claimed that a distraught young woman has appeared to them, crying and pleading for their help in finding her baby. She is very agitated and follows them, begging for their help. She pleads for them to find her child's body and give it a proper burial.

Visitors to the house were often surprised and frightened to find their knocks at the front door were answered by a lady in red ball gown. This woman, in late 1800s period dress, is decked out in a fancy dress with a long train trailing behind her. She would answer the door and then simply disappear before the eyes of the visitors.

Local tradition has it that this is the ghost of yet another Royer housewife. This woman and her husband fought bitterly for years. In a last desperate attempt to keep his wife from leaving, the husband proposed that they make a truce. He began treating her better and bringing her little gifts. His dazzled wife was grateful for the second chance and so she was more than obliging when her husband suggested a ball to celebrate their reconciliation. She was even willing to wear the bright red ball gown he had given her even though it was fitted with a long train that made dancing nearly impossible.

The night of the ball a more romantic, solicitous couple could not be found than the host and hostess. They spent the better part of the evening cuddling together and passing among their guests. The guests left muttering about the miracle that had been wrought in this apparently doomed marriage. It was such a blessing since the scandal of a divorce could have cost the entire family greatly.

After the ball was over the host and hostess retired, sending away their help. The mess could be dealt with in the morning.

Upstairs the host set his plan in motion. There had never been a reconciliation in his heart, but he knew how much money the scandal of a divorce could have cost him. He had also known that he would not live the rest of his life with his wife, and so he had set about wooing her into believing that he had wanted a second chance for their marriage. All of this had been done in preparation for this night. Now the time was at hand.

As his wife stepped into the hallway of the second floor still struggling with the cumbersome train, he stepped into the hall and asked her to fetch him a brandy. His wife was tired, and yet she smiled sweetly and bundled up the train of the red gown so that she could negotiate the stairs once more. This had been such a pleasant night that she was loath to spoil it.

The stairs of the Royer house were designed in an era when beauty was as important as function. The staircase loops through the center of the house in a double spiral, the banister threaded with marble, and ends in the small entry hall just before the front door.

Back view of the Royer house.

As his wife started down the stairs, the husband moved like lightning down the hall and down the steps, throwing his weight against her back. Frantically she clawed the marble banister and her feet tangled in the train of her gown. She fell and rolled down the stairs.

At the bottom of the steps she lay battered and winded, struggling to cope with what had just happened. Her husband realized his plan hadn't quite worked, so before she had time to move, he bounded down the stairs, picked up a poker, and smashed it across her head.

Despite his carefully laid plans to make his wife's death a tragic accident, the husband was eventually arrested and confessed to the murder. He explained how he had planned the accident. He had deliberately sent his wife a dress that would be easy to trip in. How he had wanted those at the ball to see her struggle with the gown, and to see how attentive he was to her.

History is not clear about what became of the husband, but for many surprised people the lady in red is very real. She answers doors, glides up and down the stairs and some even claimed to see her reenact the fatal fall down the stairs nearly a hundred years ago.

Death seemed to stalk this property. Beside the stone mansion house is a spring house where a young woman is said to appear to men. She tries to lure them to the spring in hopes of pushing them into the water to die.

There have been persistent rumors that someone hung themselves in the spring house, but no one knows the name of this suicide.

In a strange twist, a young woman in the late 1930s drove her car into the spring at the edge of the property and committed suicide. No one ever found out who the woman was, or why a woman with out-of-state license plates would drive all of that distance just to commit suicide.

Suicides seem to haunt this land. Behind the house once stood a tenant house. In the early 1900s a Mr. and Mrs. Hamilton (their real names) of Williamsburg rented the tenant house. Soon after they moved in, they noticed that something was wrong with their new home.

Mrs. Hamilton complained that things would disappear from their accustomed places only to be found elsewhere in the house. She also complained about hearing persistent footsteps on the stairs.

Over the course of time, they noticed a pattern: Once every few months, at the same time each night, the bedroom door would fly open, waking the Hamiltons. The couple decided to try an experiment. When

The spring house beside the Royer house. The spring house is rumored to be haunted by the spirit who hanged himself there.

it was time, Mr. Hamilton, a blacksmith, drove a large nail into the door lock. Then the couple stayed up, waiting to see what would happen.

The appointed time came. Steps thumped up the stairs to the door. For a second they thought that the nail had stopped whatever was out there, but then the nail literally flew from the lock and the door crashed open. For the rest of their short stay in the tenant house, they put up with the mysterious steps, the crashing door, and the moving objects.

In time the Hamiltons found out that the house had been the scene of a suicide. The original tenant farmer had hung himself either in the bedroom or in the room directly below it. The Hamiltons came to grips with the fact that the dead farmer still shared the house with them.

It seems that something happened in that gray stone house that history, for whatever reason, has forgotten. But it's clear that for over a hundred years the beautiful house and the surrounding property have been the scene of hauntings and tragedy.

The Russell House
(Bedford, Bedford County)

In the early 1970s, Bedford County found itself outgrowing the facilities built to house its county government. It was faced with a dilemma. Should it tear down the beautiful, historic buildings that surrounded the courthouse and town's square to build new offices? Or should it build offices far away from the seat of county governmental activity? They chose to purchase and refit a couple of the nearby historic homes so that they could be used as office space. One of the buildings they bought was the former Pate Funeral Parlor, which was known historically as the Russell House.

The Russell House is a 20-room mansion built in approximately 1815 for James M. Russell, an Irish immigrant. It was designed by Solomon Filler a popular architect of his time. It is a beautiful structure with several of Filler's signature features. Its red brick was burned in the local kilns and was laid in Flemish bond in front; the sides and rear are finished in American bond. The house features double chimneys connected by slate slabs and fireplaces with well-proportioned mantels. The stairwell in the front hall rises gracefully to the third floor, with stringers decorated with S-shaped moldings, and rectangular spindles topped by a walnut railing that ends in a flourish at the foot of the stairs.

The entrance hall door is topped by a graceful fan-shaped window glass. The hallways and several rooms are distinguished by graceful arches supported by slender fluted columns instead of bare crossbeams. Throughout the house are charming little hidey-holes tucked into the brick walls. The rooms are high ceilinged and lighted by full many-paned windows. In all, the effect Fuller achieved was one of grace and timeless elegance.

The house was a private residence for many years before it was leased by Mr. and Mrs. Warren A. Snyder, who opened a hotel they called the "Colonial House." Many of the residents of the Colonial House were permanent guests who lived there for years. They included an insurance agent, two state policemen, a spinster school teacher, and a dentist. There was also office space offered in the front of the house which housed the dentist's and the insurance agent's office.

After the Snyders shut down their boarding house, the building remained empty for some time until Fred C. Pate purchased the house and lot. Mr. Pate opened a funeral parlor and also ran a furniture and rug-selling business from the lower levels. The upstairs became the living quarters of his family.

When his one son went into the family business and married, Mr. Pate decided that two families should not live under one roof. So he built a smaller house behind the Russell House where he and his second wife lived. The main house remained the home of his son's growing family for many years.

Eventually the family grew up and moved on. Mrs. Pate found herself alone in the large house and decided to offer parts of it as office space. In 1972, Mrs. Pate sold the house to the county and retired to the smaller house in back.

In the early 1970s, the county moved several departments into the new offices in the Russell House. How long it was before the employees realized there was something strange about their new accommodations no one knows. Slowly the employees first noticed that items, which were left safely in their places when the building was locked at night, would be found somewhere else when needed the next time. Then things would fall over by themselves, or footsteps or unexplained creaks from the old house would sound repeatedly while the employees worked.

The office workers were not the only ones who noticed that there was something slightly different about the Russell House. Even the cleaning woman told stories of having her upright vacuum cleaner knocked over when she left it standing to plug it in.

By February of 1984, the stories were common knowledge, so much so that the county maintenance man responsible for the Russell House was being called in to explain exactly what was happening.

The second floor housed the office of the county auditors. There were three ladies who worked in that office full-time. The women be-

The Russell house, now a Bedford County Annex building.

gan complaining that items were being moved, that objects seemed to "jump" when they tried to reach for them. They told stories about their swivel chairs twirling while they stood watching them. The women were growing increasingly nervous and upset.

The women reported that an adding machine they used would often produce numbers on the paper tape which they hadn't pushed. At first this problem was attributed to a malfunction in the machine, and it was sent out to be repaired. However, the company that examined the machine could find nothing wrong with it.

The machine was returned to it's place but continued to tote up strange calculations that had nothing to do with county business. The auditors were given a new machine to replace the unreliable adding machine, but it, too, began calculating strange numbers when no one was using it.

Next the auditors decided that the problem must be with the electricity. But no matter which outlet was used, the machine mysteriously rang up numbers when no one was using it. Eventually the adding machine had to be kept unplugged.

One morning, as one of the auditors got close to the locked door of the office, she heard the machine busily punching numbers and assumed that one of her fellow employees had come in early and was already working. When she entered the office she found that it was empty, and that the machine was both unplugged and turned off. But the paper tape showed that a string of numbers had been computed since they had left the night before.

The county maintenance person responsible for the offices, after hearing their stories, decided that someone was playing a practical joke on the auditors. He changed the locks on the doors in their area and gave them the only keys. He did not even keep a key himself.

Despite his efforts, the incidents of swiveling chairs and "jumping" items seemed to continue. It was quite unnerving for the ladies to reach for an item, and have it jump beyond their grasp while they watched open-mouthed.

The women had pushed their desks together so that two were side-by-side with the third pushed in to face the other two. This meant that all three women could see each other at all times, and it also meant that they would be witnesses for each other as the strange phenomenon continued.

Repeatedly during the next several months, the maintenance man received requests to check the electricity and to please do something about the lack of heat in the county auditors area, for they were always cold. The maintenance man had heard similar complaints from others who had worked in the same space previously, but now the prevalent coldness seemed to be chronic. He admitted that despite his best efforts, he just could not keep that area warm.

One day as the ladies worked, an electric pencil sharpener which they shared came to buzzing life while no one used it. For a stunned second the ladies stared at the sharpener, but reason soon took over and one of them traced down its cord and pulled the plug. The sharpener died as the current was withdrawn. Smiling at the reasonableness of the situation, she began to explain to the others that the sharpener must have developed a short somewhere. Suddenly the sharpener came bursting back to life while it was unplugged!

After that the unplugged sharpener came on sporadically.

One day the wastepaper basket in the auditors' office tipped over, dumping the contents. As the ladies picked up the trash, they came across some pictures of a deceased former owner of the house. No one had ever seen the pictures before, and no one knew where they had come from.

Whatever was haunting the Russell House seemed to enjoy its

The cottage built by the Pate family (left background), behind the Russell house.

View of Russell house showing the second floor windows, which is the area at the center of the hauntings.

jokes. Several times, while people witnessed it, the sharpener raised itself about two inches from the communal desk area and bounced itself up and down eight or nine times. This movement was made all the more unnerving by the fact that the pencil sharpener was held down by suction cups.

During this time the auditors also had trouble keeping the heavy cable cords that ran from the wall jacks to the telephones in place. One day the cords kept moving, tripping them, and the one female worker got angry. They pulled the desks apart and wedged the cords firmly between them before pushing the desks tightly together again. On top of that, a heavy statue was placed over the cords to further weight them down.

"Okay, let's see you move that," the woman said aloud.

While they watched, the statue slid sideways and pivoted partly off the cords.

The maintenance man was called in about the moving phone cords. Exasperated by complaints and stories of things he couldn't control, he called out the name of the dead man whose pictures had been found in the trash in that room. He called out the man's name three times when suddenly he noticed a telephone cable pick itself up and flip over. This was enough for the man and he quickly left the room.

Stories of the haunted office filtered out to the other office staffs. Eventually the stories reached the ears of Sharyn Maust, the reporter for the local paper, The Bedford Gazette, assigned to the county beat. Ms. Maust began gathering the stories for what she thought might be a fun feature for her paper.

In the article she subsequently printed there was a report that the maintenance man had taken a Bible to the office and left it on the desk where most of the activity seemed to be occurring. According to what she was told, apparently this worked and even the adding machine began functioning properly. (When I spoke to the maintenance man, he denied this story and confirmed another rumor about an exorcism having taken place in the building because the hauntings would not stop and were disrupting county business.)

Other areas of the house apparently were haunted, too. In the kitchen next to the haunted office the oven door began opening by itself, a broom and dustpan appeared from nowhere, and a window began opening itself.

A first floor secretary told a story of staying alone late one evening to finish up some important work. As she typed, she glimpsed a figure walk past her open door. She knew that the building was locked and she should have been alone there, so she got up and ran into the hall.

As the woman entered the hall, she caught sight of an office door closing at the end of the hall. Quickly she hurried down to the door and grabbed the knob. She turned the knob slightly but it resisted her attempts. The door was locked, so she took the appropriate key from the ring in her pocket and opened the door. There was no one inside the room, and it was a sealed room with no means of egress other than the door she had been standing beside.

At last the county commissioners heard about the problems with their new offices in the Russell House. One commissioner decided that something must be done. He contacted a person he knew who did exorcisms or "laid spirits to rest." The person was brought in and subsequently there have been no new disturbances in the house.

Who was the mischievous spirit that haunted the Russell House? No one knows for sure, but when I spoke to Sarah Pate-Boyce, whose father and grandfather ran Pate's Funeral Parlor from part of the Russell House, she confirmed that there had been "strange noises" and "various funny incidents" when she lived in the upper floors of the house. I told her of what the office workers had experienced and she laughed but said that she wasn't surprised.

Mrs. Pate-Boyce is an lively elderly lady who now resides in the smaller house behind the Russell House which her grandfather had built. She told me that because her family ran so many businesses in the Russell House, she and her two sisters had been carefully instructed to not speak of anything "strange or scary" in the house—it would have been bad for the trade.

Has the spirit that haunted the Russell House left? No one knows for sure. The maintenance man who was present during this time still works for the county. He said that the hauntings did not abruptly cease after the exorcism but rather seemed to die out slowly. Has the spirit in the house simply decided to rest for a while, or has it merely stopped because it realized that it's presence was unnerving and unwanted in the house? Or has the Russell House seen the last of it's ghost? Only time will tell.

Signs & Portents

Through the years I've heard many storie s in Pennsylvania about signs and portents. Some of these are grouped together here because I find that people always tell these stories together. One person will say, "You won't believe this but..." and when they finish their story someone else pipes up with, "You know that reminds me of the time when...." And so it goes until everyone with a similar story has told it. Most families have such stories and they are usually drawn from the deaths of loved ones.

Broken Skillets And Baying Dogs (Williamsburg, Blair County)

Jeanette stood at the old kitchen sink, scrubbing a pile of cast iron skillets. It was a hot summer day in 1958 and the day was made even hotter by the heat from the cookstove. The stove was their only way to cook food or heat water, so despite the horrible heat they had to keep it fired throughout the summer.

Right now, though, Jeanette was just trying to concentrate on her scrubbing and not think too much about the doctor. In the other room he was speaking to her mother, Hannah, and her aunt, Sarah. Her father, Bull, had been ill for a long time, but last night he had a spell that was worse than any of the previous ones. The doctor said that his heart was just worn out and that it was only a matter of days until he died.

The curtain that partitioned off the living room doorway from the kitchen fluttered open as her Aunt Sarah came through. Sarah was a squat barrel of a woman much like Jeanette's own mother. She wore

261

her dark hair in a braided crown around her head and now there were wisps of the salt-and-pepper hair slipping from her braid. She looked hot and tired.

"What did the doctor say," Jeanette asked, rinsing off the skillets and wiping them off with a damp towel.

Sarah picked up a cardboard fan with a picture of Christ praying on it and began fanning her red, sweaty face. "It ain't good, Jeanette. 'Fraid this'll be the day. Poor Hannah is near beside herself trying to hide the fact from him." Sarah sniffed, "You ask me, she'd be better off telling him the truth and sending for the preacher. Give the man a chance to settle things, I say."

"Aunt Sarah!" Jeanette exploded. "You hold your tongue. Ma's got enough to tend to." Jeanette threw her aunt a deadly look.

Sarah waved her niece away. She was exhausted. The night before she had barely gotten any sleep. That dog of Bull's had been howling day and night for nearly three days and last night it hadn't stopped for a moment.

Jeanette took the skillets and sat them on the cookstove to finish drying. "Aunt Sarah, did the doctor really say that Papa would die today?" Jeanette tried to keep her voice from cracking but she just couldn't. She was the oldest of the fourteen kids still home and the weight of caring for her remaining eleven brothers and sisters had fallen on her shoulders for the past few months. She was barely sixteen, but she had been mother, housekeeper, and even nurse at times. Her mother had always been a slovenly housekeeper at best, but since her father's illness the house had gone from bad to worse.

They lived in a large, ramshackle house that had seen better days. There were holes in the floors and walls. Water stains marked every ceiling in the house, and the beds were mere mattresses laid on homemade frames and covered by dirty, ratty blankets that they had gotten from the mission barrels at church. Now, with her father facing death, things would be even worse.

A sudden loud crack broke the humid stillness of the afternoon. Jeanette gave a little shriek and her Aunt Sarah jumped up knocking over her chair. Both women looked at the cookstove. There, atop the stove, one of the cast iron skillets had cracked in half. Jeanette snatched a rag to grab it up, but her aunt shouted at her to stop.

Confused, Jeanette stared at her aunt. She had never seen a cast iron skillet break in two before. Sarah was pale, her eyes were riveted to the broken skillet. "Don't touch that, girl," she hissed. "That means death."

"Jeanette, I tell you that broken skillet means death. I only saw that happen once before and it was just hours before the sick person in that house died. And—" She hesitated, gulping hot air and running a shaking hand across her forehead. "And that dog of your father's been bawling for three nights now. A baying dog means death in the house, too. That dog can sense death a-coming and is mourning already."

Jeanette heard all she could. Bawling dogs and broken skillets meant that it was hot and they had a faulty skillet, that was all. She picked up the two pieces of skillet and dumped them into the coal bucket.

The rest of the day was spent in a haze of heat and work. Jeanette washed clothes by hand in an old rinse tub behind the house. Later she walked to the store with a few cents in her pocket and bought some scraps from the butcher. She took the fat home, browned it off in a large skillet, and made a batch of flour-browned gravy for supper. It wasn't much but it filled the hollow that nagged at their stomachs.

When Jeanette went to bed that night, she was so tired that she gave little thought to her aunt and her superstitious ways. Her last thought was that come morning she was going to dress in her best dress and go look for work. Someone had to earn some money before they all starved.

It was barely midnight when something woke Jeanette. She lay in her grimy bed and listened. Something was wrong, but what? The dog, her mind whispered. The big, black dog behind the house had quit bawling. When she had gone to sleep it had been in full swing, howling and crying as it had for the three nights before.

There was something about the stillness of the air that frightened her. Jeanette rolled over, careful not to disturb her little sister that shared her bed, and got up. She found her mother and aunt in the kitchen. They were sitting just inside the open kitchen door. Her mother was crying softly and her aunt was just sitting there making small clucking, comforting sounds.

Wiping her eyes, Hannah looked up at her daughter. "Go back to bed, Jeanette. It's all over now. Your father passed on a few moments ago."

Jeanette stared at her mother. Her voice was lost. All she could think of was that baying black dog that was now oddly silent despite the warmth she had blamed for causing the dog to cry. Her mind flashed to the cookstove top with the broken skillet sitting on it. Her aunt's words echoed in her head. "Broken skillets and baying dogs mean death..."

Papa's Picture
(Williamsburg, Blair County)

It was late and Helen and Chet were just starting up the stairs when they heard the distinct thunk in the living room. Helen paused on the stairs and turned to Chet.

"What was that?" She could not help feeling a bit apprehensive. There was something about the stillness of the darkness around them for they had turned off the lights only seconds before the sound had come.

She heard Chet sigh. He had spent a long day in the fields and he only wanted to go to bed. "I'll go check."

She heard Chet fumble down a few steps and then the light winked on. She followed her husband back downstairs. There was nothing amiss in the kitchen. They walked through it into the dining room. There, too, everything was neatly put away just as they had left it earlier. Helen glanced at the clock that ticked softly, it was only a few seconds before it would be chiming the tenth hour.

Chet snapped on the hall light; there they found the source of the thump. Laying on the floor just beside the entry way was a large oil painting of a country scene that had come from Helen's family.

The picture had a bit of a history. Helen's mother was an exceptionally beautiful young woman named Anna, who had fallen in love with the younger of two brothers, Edward Koke. There had been a bitter rivalry for the young beauty's hand but when John Koke realized that Anna was going to marry Edward, he had been gracious in his defeat. Still, he had never married and often tried to make gifts to the young couple of things which he knew would bring his Anna joy.

According to the story, the three of them were at a street fair in town. They strolled around, tasting different dishes and seeing the sights. Along the sidewalks vendors had set up stalls to hawk their wares. Among them was a young man was trying to sell his paintings.

Anna had fallen in love with the painting immediately. Edward did not have enough money to purchase it so John took this chance to buy it and make it a gift. Edward was furious at the very notion and forbid Anna to take the painting. Sadly Anna refused the gift and left with her husband, but John did not forget that look of joy and then longing that had filled his beloved Anna's eyes.

John purchased the painting and later convinced his parents to give the painting to the young couple as a gift. Edward recognized the painting as soon as it was unwrapped and knew that John had tricked them into accepting it. His anger and jealousy took over and he punished Anna as though she had been part of the conspiracy. He told her that she would have to burn the painting.

To Anna, destroying the beautiful thing would have been sacrilege. She cried and pleaded and finally she and Edward reached a compromise. Anna could keep the painting in case Edward's parents ever asked about it, but she had to keep it shrouded in the attic. She had to promise never to hang it as long as Edward lived. Anna was true to her word, but Edward died only five years later, leaving her with a son to raise.

John waited nearly two years before he began openly courting Anna, and despite the scandal that it caused in the small town, two years after Edward died John married his Anna. Only then did Anna remember the painting and brought it downstairs to be hung. From then until Helen had married, that painting had hung in her parent's home. At her wedding, Anna and John gave Helen the painting.

Chet picked up the painting and checked its wire. When he saw that the wire was still whole, Chet examined the wall, feeling for the hole where the nail must have fallen from. Instead he felt the nail still securely stuck into the wall.

"Why did it fall?" Helen asked.

Chet shrugged. Helen glanced at the windows which she remembered closing earlier that evening. "I shut the windows so it couldn't have been a breeze."

Chet lifted the painting and replaced it on it's nail. "Well, whatever caused it, I'll put it back now."

Again Helen and Chet turned off the downstairs lights and climbed the stairs to bed. Just as they reached the top of the steps they heard the loud thunk again.

Frowning, Chet turned around. "Now what," he muttered, stumbling back down the stairs.

The thunk had left Helen with chills. Somehow she knew that it was the painting again. Quickly she followed her husband back down the stairs. There lay the painting just as they had found it before. Again Chet checked the wire and the nail, but they were fine. He heaved the painting back into place, shook the painting to be sure it was firm, and then stood back.

"There," he said, "that painting isn't going anywhere now."

The couple climbed the stairs once more, but just before they reached the landing there was a thunk below them again. Now Chet was angry. Someone was playing a trick or something and he was too tired to play games.

Helen, however, felt chills pass through her. Something was very wrong but she couldn't understand what all of this meant.

In the living room they once more found the painting on the floor and Chet hung it yet again. Cursing now, Chet turned off the lights and followed Helen up the steps once more. They had barely gone up four steps when there was a shrill ringing from the kitchen. The phone, at this time of night?

Chet and Helen stumbled down the steps again. Helen turned on the lights while Chet ran for the phone. He recognized the voice of his sister-in-law. Something must be wrong or she would not have called so late, and hadn't he heard her voice shake?

"What's wrong, Mary?" Chet tried to keep the fear out of his voice, but he caught Helen's alarmed look.

Mary began to cry softly. "Please tell Helen that Papa just died."

"When?" Chet's breath was forced out. John had been both a loving father to his wife and children. Helen would be devastated by the loss. How was he supposed to tell her?

Mary's sobs broke off and suddenly there was silence for a second, then Mary's husband Charlie came on the line.

"Hello, Chet? Did you understand Mary? We're still at the house. Mary insisted that we call immediately. Sorry. I wanted to wait until morning, but she said that Helen had a right to know."

Chet repeated his question.

"Died about a minute till ten, so the doctor said. We were in the living room waiting and the clock struck ten just about the time that the doctor came out to tell us."

Chet spoke with Charlie for a few more seconds about making some arrangements to see them in the morning, then hung up. He turned to Helen who was hovering just behind him.

"What's going on Chet?" Her voice was filled with apprehension.

"Helen, your Papa died a little bit ago. Charlie said it was about ten o'clock. He just got Mary calmed down enough to call."

Helen reached for a kitchen chair and sat down heavily. Her eyes were dry yet, but he could see her pain. "It was just about ten o'clock the first time Papa's painting fell. It was a sign; he was saying good-bye."

As her voice died off, the painting crashed to the floor for the last time.

Chet left the painting propped against the wall until morning, then he hung it once more. That painting was to hang there on the same wire and nail for nearly thirty more years before it was taken down, and every time that Helen looked at it she remembered how her beloved Papa had come to say his last good-bye.

Three Mason Jars
(Acosta, Somerset County)

It was a cool autumn morning in 1937 when Helen Koke made her way through the hall of her parent's home to the back half of the house where her older brother John lay near death. Helen was only fourteen years old, but her life had been marked by brushes with tragedy...and the occult

John was her mother's child from a first marriage and so was much older than Helen. He had bitterly resented the fact that his mother had married again soon after his father's death, but he did dote upon his two baby sisters. Now Mary, the oldest girl, was married and so he was left with just Helen and his mother. His stepfather had died when Helen was just a baby, leaving the family to live on his small savings.

John turned to science and the occult for comfort after his mother's new marriage. He built a laboratory where he pursued experiments and later on dedicated all of his time to studying and practicing witchcraft.

Helen had both loved and feared her older brother as she grew up. He was a morose, dark man who often rewarded her happy chatter with one of his rare smiles. But it was what he did in that laboratory that frightened her. Ever since she could remember there had been strange sometimes horrible smells coming from behind the doors. She would often have to tell John to quit whatever he was doing when it disturbed the rest of the household. More times than she could remember dishes had been levitated, furniture had moved by itself, and shadows would separate from the wall to walk down the halls.

When this would happen, she would call up the stairs for John to stop and the dishes would fall, the furniture would cease moving, and the shadows would somehow melt back into the walls.

Now John's strange experiments had gone too far, and she knew that their mother blamed them for John's sickness. He had pneumonia from staying out in bad weather to work on some spell. Ultimately Helen's mother believed that it was her own fault that John was so ill. She knew that her marriage had driven the desperate, lonely boy into the world of the occult and that the occult now drove him on.

Helen came to the thick doors that marked the end of the family's section of the upstairs and the beginning of John's. The first room was the laboratory filled with bottles, test tubes, and a great book, that always rested open to John's current work, on the large table in the center of the room. There were shelves everywhere, filled with mason jars labeled in John's neat hand with all kinds of chemicals, herbs, and other things that Helen dreaded to look at.

Helen had to pass through the laboratory to go into the bedroom beyond, where John lay so ill. She carried the medicine that the doctor prescribed, and a tray with a light meal of hot tea and lightly toasted bread. John had not eaten well for days and she'd been instructed by her mother not to bring the tray back until John finished the meal.

Helen pushed open the doors with her hip and slid through backward. The doors swung open briefly and she had the unpleasant feeling that she was being swallowed. No matter how warm the rest of the house was, those rooms were always cold and there was something unpleasantly damp in the air there. She kept her eyes fixed upon the door at the other end of the room, and made for that door quickly.

John heard his little sister coming and struggled to sit up in bed. She was so pretty he thought. She was a tall, thin girl with long, dark hair and a delicately featured face. But her brown eyes were stained with worry and he was sorry that he was the cause. Now he was worried for the little girl. He knew that he was about to die, he could feel it closing in, and that would leave Helen alone with an invalid mother who most probably would follow him shortly.

Helen threw him a sunny, fake smile. "Mama sent you something to eat and I'm not to return until you finish it. I have work to do, so you'd better eat every bite." Her voice held mock severity.

He looked at the tray and felt his stomach roil. Food would make him sick.

"I'm not really hungry, Helen," he began, then he saw the tears glistening in her dark eyes. "But I'll eat if you can help me."

With her help, John managed most of the tea and a small portion of the toast. At last he could keep up the pretense no more. Pushing away her hand gently he fell back against the pillows exhausted. A fit of coughing shook him. He reached for a cloth to hide the blood that he knew was about to come. He had been coughing up blood for nearly two days now.

He thought that he had hidden it from Helen, but she grabbed his hand. Taking it from his limp fingers, she opened the cloth to see the blood. When he opened his eyes, Helen was standing beside him shaking him, and he could feel the warm, wetness of her tears.

"Helen," he whispered, raising one emaciated hand to her cheek to wipe her tears. "Helen, listen." Exhausted, he dropped his hand. It took him long moments to gather his strength for another try.

"Helen, I'm going to die." She began to shake her head, but he squeezed her hand tightly and she was quiet. "It will be soon, little one, and you must not be frightened...." His voice dropped off as he gasped for air. The coughing was coming upon him again.

Suddenly there was a terrible crashing from the laboratory. Helen jumped and John struggled to stop coughing. He felt something cold enter his room. This was the sign he had been waiting for.

John grasped Helen's frail hand in his own, struggling before his breath came. "Go see what fell and tell me which jars broke...it's important."

Though she was frightened, Helen scrambled up and ran to the laboratory to find out what had broken. The laboratory was a shambles. It looked like a big wind had swept through the room. A shelf of mason jars had fallen over, as though someone had swept them from their shelf with a swipe of an arm. She picked through the clutter of glass for the labels and found that only three jars were shattered. These three labels she carefully picked up and took back to John.

John looked even worse, if it was possible, Helen thought as she handed him the labels. He took them with shaking fingers and read the names silently. Now he was looking at her sadly.

"Helen, I must leave you now," he whispered. He held up the labels which she took. "These are my sign, my death has come." John seemed to hesitate a moment and then he muttered, "I chose my fate..." With those words a look of surprise marked his face and then he was gone.

Helen shook her brother but he did not respond. She felt panic swell and bolted for the door. By the time she was downstairs she was almost hysterical. She shot past her mother and ran down the street. She needed help. She needed the doctor.

When the doctor arrived, he found John's body resting on the bed. Helen had gone back after calling for him and had covered up her brother and shut his eyes. She had taken the slips of label from the mason jars and tucked them into her pocket. They had been John's sign that death had come. She was never to understand exactly what they meant to John, but she did know that to John they were a message that he was to die.

The Ghost House Of St. Mary's
(Ganister, Blair County)

The small village of Ganister is caught up in it's past. The village is no more than a shell of what it once was. The railroad and the famous Ganister rock stone quarries once made Ganister a prosperous village where people could both live and work. Now the railroad is gone; even the traces of those well worn tracks are but faint scars upon the landscape. The stone quarries, too, have long since ceased to be worked.

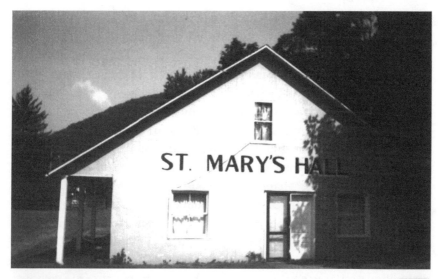

Top photo, St. Mary's Hall. Behind this building is the quarry where the disappearing house has been seen. Bottom photo, the ridge at St. Mary's quarry where the disappearing house is said to appear.

The story has it that a quarrier hit an underground lake and the water rose so fast that the workers had to abandon their machinery to save their lives. Great pumps were brought in to pump out the water from the quarry holes, but the lake was too deep. It soon became obvious that the quarry hole had to be abandoned. One of the quarries is known as the Blue Hole and has a sinister reputation. It is the single

271

most suicide prone area around Williamsburg. People have come from out of state just to die there at the lonely water hole.

There are other, lesser known quarry holes in the area, St. Mary's is one of these. The quarry hole received it's name because it is near the St. Mary's church. Local people often went to the hole in the summer to swim and picnic. It was not tainted by the bad reputation that the Blue Hole had. No gangs hung out there, and kids did not use it as a place to drink and have sex. The St. Mary's quarry did not have the same treacherous undercurrents that had cost so many lives in the Blue Hole. It was a nice place to cool off and watch your kids have fun, and it was free.

From time to time, however, something very strange did happen at the St. Mary's quarry hole. Some of the picnickers and hikers who came to enjoy the sun and the view were treated to the chilling sight of the vanishing house. More than one local person has seen an old house sitting on the top rim of the quarry, but there is no house up there. There are no houses for miles around the quarry hole at all. Those who have seen the old house have often tried to find it by climbing either the rocky ledges or by taking the more circular route across the wooded mountains. They make it to the spot where the house should be, but there is nothing there.

Local rumor has it that there was once a house where the vanishing house is now sighted. No one really knows whatever became of the old house. Was it torn down or did it burn? What could have happened in the ghost house to make it reappear on the edge of the rough ledge to the quarry? Perhaps the biggest question of all is how could a house suddenly appear, looking very solid and real, and yet disappear before the sighters can reach it? Why? The ghost house causes more questions than answers.

There are fewer locals now who frequent the quarry hole. Perhaps they have found other places to cool off on hot summer days, or perhaps it is because they don't wish to see the ghost house looming over them as they go about their human activities.

Bondage Of The Wolf's Skin
(Bedford County)

The story of the black wolf's skin is now so old that the names of those involved have long been forgotten so I was forced to name the characters in order to tell this story in a coherent manner. However, Wolf Camp Run is still the name of the small stream that flows from Juniata Township into Londonderry Township and eventually pours its waters into Little Wills Creek north of Hyndman.

1700s

Jerome Hanley enjoyed frontier life in the wilds of Pennsylvania's Appalachian mountains. He lived with his sister Sarah and her family because he was not particularly hardworking and she would allow him to stay for free. Jerome's one occupation was hunting wolves.

Though he had regular trapping routes, one of Jerome's favorite places to hunt for wolves was from the second story of an abandoned mill downstream about a mile from his home. There he lazily would sit at a window and wait for the wolves to cross from one hill to another. The mill also was an excellent place to hunt from because many of the local residents considered it haunted. They avoided the area, leaving him with easy hunting and plenty of game.

As he approached the mill late one afternoon, he saw a large black wolf ahead of him. The pelt of this animal would bring an excellent price in Bedford he judged, so he gave pursuit. While he stalked the creature, the wolf sensed him and took off on a dead run. Jerome gave up stealth and began an all-out chase. The wolf ran on toward the mill and rushed inside, seeking a hiding place. Jerome had the wolf trapped; there was only one door open in the mill and so he stationed himself outside of that door and waited. The afternoon wore on and Jerome was getting restless, but he did not want to face a trapped wolf in the confines of the mill so he continued to wait.

As dusk settled, a movement at the doorway caught his eye, and Jerome raised his musket sure now of his kill. Seconds later he dropped the weapon in stunned silence. Standing in the doorway was a pretty young woman and she was completely naked. Confused Jerome stood up and started forward. The woman saw him coming and, giving a small cry of embarrassment, hastened back into the shadowy interior of the mill.

"Stay there, sir, I implore you!" the girl called out in a frightened voice.

Jerome stopped. "What are you doing here, and like that, Ma'am?"

"I was swimming here with some friends and they played a terrible trick on me. They left and took my clothes with them. Can you help me, please?" The woman stepped slightly out of the shadowed doorway as she pleaded with him. Her hands struggled vainly to cover her body.

Jerome shrugged out of his rough shirt and tossed it to her feet. "Here, put this on and I'll try to get you to my sister's. She'll help you get some clothes."

The young woman snatched up the garment and disappeared into the shadows once more. In a few seconds she reappeared tugging at the hem of the shirt. It fell far below her hips. "I thank you," she whispered as she stepped out into the nearly full moonlight.

Jerome was stunned by what he saw. This girl was not merely pretty, she was beautiful. A mane of black hair framed the perfect oval of her pale face. Her eyes seemed nearly gray in the golden light, and her features were delicately placed. She barely reached his chin, and Jerome could not help sneaking glances at her as she followed him.

At his sister's home Jerome faced a dilemma. How was he going to get Sarah outside to help this woman? He dared not take her inside while she was still nearly naked. Sarah would not appreciate that. He finally decided to take her to the tack shed and leave her there while he fetched his sister.

"What's your name?" he asked. "I don't even know your name."

"Elizabeth King," she whispered. "We were just traveling through here when we saw the mill with the stream running along side; we decided to stop and take a cooling swim." Her eyes clouded with unshed tears. "I don't know why they would have left me like this."

Jerome's heart went out to this abandoned girl. "Just wait here a minute and I'll be back. I'll bring my sister, Sarah. She'll know what to do, I promise."

Jerome was as good as his word. Sarah lit a battered lantern while she listened to her brother's incredible story and followed him to the tack shed.

"Goodness," Sarah gasped as she stepped into the shed and came face to face with the furiously blushing Elizabeth. "You really are naked."

Elizabeth tried to hide her embarrassment by rushing into explanations, but Sarah held up her hand to silence the young woman. Turning to her brother she said, "Go back into the house and get my black mourning dress from the chest in my room. Tell Rodney what's going on, and tell him to keep the children inside and put them to bed. This girl," she glanced at Elizabeth kindly, "won't need their gawking eyes when we get her inside."

Jerome hurried inside leaving the two ladies alone.

"I hope you don't mind wearing a mourning dress, but it's about the only thing I have that might fit you." Sarah rubbed a work-roughened hand across her plump stomach. "Four children are bound to spread a woman out a bit."

Elizabeth smiled uncertainly. "I just thank you for helping me at all. I know what it must look like, but your brother has been a perfect gentleman. I'm just ..." her voice trailed off into a tiny sob.

Sarah rushed forward to hug the young woman. "You're gonna be all right now."

"But what am I going to do? Where will I go? I don't have anything; I don't even know where my friends are now."

Sarah sniffed. "Friends! You don't have to worry about all of that tonight, though. We'll get you in the house and get you something to eat. With some food and some rest things are bound to look better. We'll work something out."

Elizabeth pulled back slightly. "Do you mean that I can stay here with you until I decide what to do?"

"I suppose so," Sarah said, feeling slightly unsure of how long she really would want this darkly beautiful woman around.

Jerome came back at that moment. He handed the black dress in through the door but remained outside. "Rodney said that he'd have the children in bed in a few minutes," he told his sister.

Sarah turned her back as Elizabeth quickly shucked the rough shirt that had covered her and slipped into the black dress. It hung loosely on her tiny frame and fell in a puddle over her bare feet. Sarah turned and sighed. "I suppose that tomorrow we'll have to put in a few tucks. And hem it up some, too."

Elizabeth picked up the shirt and stepped outside into the cool darkness. Jerome was standing beside the door shuffling his feet. "That's better." He grinned.

"Thank you for your shirt, and all of your help." Elizabeth whispered softly as she pressed the shirt back into his hands.

Jerome slipped the shirt back on over his stained long john shirt and followed the women into the cabin. Sarah briefly introduced Elizabeth to Rodney, then set about slicing bread and brewing a pot of strong tea. Jerome fetched a crock of butter from the cooling cellar and a jar of canned venison to make thick sandwiches. He was starving, he suddenly realized. It had been a long time since breakfast.

As Elizabeth and Jerome ate, they filled Rodney in on how they had met. Elizabeth finished it up by saying that Sarah had promised to let her stay until she could decide what to do. At that, Rodney eyed his plump wife curiously. It was late spring and there was a lot of work to be done. Rodney hoped Sarah realized that she wouldn't have time to play hostess to this strange young woman.

As though reading his thoughts, Elizabeth said, "Don't worry, Rodney, I don't plan to stay long, and I'm a lot stronger than I look. I'll work for my keep."

After everyone settled for the night, Jerome slipped out. The moon was full and so he wandered back through the woods toward the mill. His mind constantly went back to Elizabeth and her story. Why would anyone leave a young woman alone and unprotected in a secluded place like the old mill? Why hadn't he seen any tracks around the mill while he waited? Most of all, he wondered what had become of the great black wolf that he had chased into the building.

At the mill Jerome became even more puzzled. There on the stone floor of the mill was the hide of a large black wolf! His mind buzzed with unanswered questions, but he wouldn't allow himself to examine

276

them too closely. Instead, he tacked the raw hide to the old wooden wall to dry. He promised himself that he'd come back for it later, but deep inside he really wasn't sure that he wanted it anymore.

When Jerome met Elizabeth the next day, he could not believe the change. In the pale moonlight she had looked alluring, ethereal, out in the daylight she was older, deathly pale, and not nearly as enchanting as he had previously thought. Still, Jerome felt drawn to this woman and they began to court. Sarah allowed Elizabeth to stay, and she did indeed work hard for her keep. Eventually Jerome and Elizabeth were married in the Bedford County Courthouse.

After their marriage, Jerome set about building a little cabin for them near Little Wills Creek where Wolf Camp Run ended. This was near an old Indian trail that had been used for many years. Though Jerome had high hopes for his new marriage, within a year his life seemed unbearable. Elizabeth harped endlessly about feeling tired and bound to Jerome. She ranted about being tied to him and his home, and he did not seem to be able to do anything that suited her.

One morning, in sheer desperation to get away from his shrewish wife, Jerome wandered the woods. Near the Indian trail he met a group of nearly sixty Indians who had a white prisoner with them. They told Jerome that the white man had killed their chief and they were going to find General Washington so that they could get permission to execute the white man according to their laws. The prisoner was a man in his late twenties. Jerome watched the Indians on their way and continued wandering until he found himself in the woods near his sister's home. He went into the abandoned mill to sit and think and found the long-forgotten wolf hide still nailed to the mill wall. It brought back memories of his first meeting with Elizabeth and in anger he tore it down, tossing it into the stream.

Jerome finally went home late that evening expecting Elizabeth to harp about his long absence. She hated it when he hunted or fished, she hated it when he farmed, and lately she seemed to hate everything he did. But at the cabin Jerome could find no one. He finally rushed to a neighbor's home, worried that something had happened to his wife. There he heard a strange story.

The neighbors told him that while Elizabeth was working in the garden that afternoon, a group of Indians wandered along the road in front of his cabin. They were they same group of Indians in search of General Washington that Jerome had met earlier. As soon as Elizabeth saw the men she gave a cry and rushed into the road to find out what was going on. She questioned the Indians closely about the prisoner and what would happen to him—and grew more agitated as they talked. Suddenly she kissed the stunned prisoner and told the Indians that she was this man's wife. She had insisted on leaving everything behind to go with them. The neighbors, summoned by the confusion, listened and watched but no one could dissuade her from going to see the general with this man.

Jerome could not believe what he had been told. Why would his wife leave? Quietly Jerome told the neighbors his story about how he had met Elizabeth the first time. He told about the black wolf and the hide he had found and bound to the wall of the abandoned mill. As he spoke, he realized that Elizabeth must have left him shortly after he had finally pulled up the old wolf hide from the mill wall.

Horrified, he wondered if there was some connection between the two? There had to be. Jerome became convinced that it was the wolf's hide which had bound his wife to him. And that by tearing it from the wall he had released her to leave him. Somehow his wife and that wolf had been one and the same....

The White Woman Of Wopsanonic Station

Trains and railroading built much of historic Pennsylvania. It is no wonder then that many of the haunted areas in the state deal with trains, railroad stations, and train tracks. There are stories of haunted tracks, of spectral lights, and even of a railroader who still waves his lantern for trains that no longer run their routes. But of all the railroad stories, none is sadder than that of the woman who haunted the

Wopsanonic Train Station until it was torn down. The name of the woman has long been lost, but her story is still whispered by historians when they are in a morose mood, and by locals who dare to wander past the wild, abandoned lot on top of the Buckhorn mountain where the woman once walked.

The war between the states was hard on many people, but perhaps one of the persons who were hurt worst by the bloody conflict was a young woman named Lydia Kincade. Once she was blissfully happy, planning her wedding to John Baxter, whom she loved more than life itself. But that was before the conflict had started. John had felt compelled to join up on the Union side, and so Lydia found herself in the unenviable position of waiting for John to return from the war to marry her. She pleaded with him not to go, but his patriotic duty called. John promised her, though, that he would return soon on one of the trains that stopped at the local station, known as the Wopsanonic Train Station.

For Lydia the days after John's departure were lonely and fearful. Horrible stories drifted back to her tranquil home about the war, but she listened to every detail just so that she could know what her John was going through. Soon, though, the tales got worse, and local boys began coming home maimed or shattered in both body and soul. Worse were the long pine boxes draped in flags or black cloths. Lydia tried to be optimistic and would often find herself dressing up and walking to the Wopsanonic station just to sit in the back of the large station room and watch the people coming and going. It brought her a strange kind of comfort to see others returned to their loved ones.

She'd watch joyful reunions and tearful homecomings alike with tears in her own eyes and John's face held tightly in her heart. He would come home to her she told herself, and she would not allow the darker thought to flutter through her fearful heart. She knew that others got messages from the front that their sons, husbands, fathers, and lovers had died, but Lydia thought she could love John back home. Their love just could not, would not, die.

For Lydia the slide into insanity was a quiet one. She simply preferred her own romantic world where John was on the next train, running out of the hissing iron beast when it stopped to sweep her up in his strong arms, to the horrible reality of the ever-growing number of pine boxes mournfully collected on the train platform. She stopped seeing the boxes, the maimed and mutilated returning from the battle front. She no longer hung onto every word told by those just returned. She stopped hearing of friends now dead. In her world, shattered bodies and shattered minds did not exist. Only John was real and she thought she often glimpsed him when the trains first pulled in, but she could never find him again in the crush of the station house.

Lydia dressed each morning in her finest frock, a white confection of linen and lace with a wispy hat that trailed a lacy veil over her face. She did up her dark hair in John's favorite style and set off for the train station. Her family tried to stop her, tried to force her to face the reality, but Lydia would only bury herself deeper in her fantasy world with a faint smile and a few murmured words. "I really do have to hurry. Johnny's coming home today, and I can't let him see me like this." She'd bustle about and then slip off to the train station when she was no longer watched.

John's family also tried to reach out to Lydia. They, too, shared her fears and pain for they were waiting for word as well. But Lyida simply would not be reached. She would just smile and say, "Johnny would be angry if he could hear you talking like this."

At the train station the old station master and the young clerk grew to expect Lyida, who waited quietly in the back for Johnny to come. She never gave them any trouble, so they just shook their heads sadly as she came in each day. "You know he's coming home today," she'd happily confide in a whisper before she found her accustomed seat.

When news finally came, John's family tried to tell Lydia that John had died in a skirmish in some far off place that they had never heard of. Lydia listened closely to what they said, and for a moment they thought that they had reached her, because tears slid unchecked down her pale cheeks. But the next morning Lydia got up and went back to the train station, and the morning after that, and the morning after that one. She refused to listen if anyone tried to tell her John was not coming home again.

Perhaps Lydia was not completely insane after all, for not long afterwards she grew ill. Those who knew her said that she just seemed to dry up and die. She was buried in the same white dress she often wore to the train station.

For the station master, who had so often taken pity on Lydia and offered her a cup of tea or a piece of his sandwich, it seemed like the sad affair was finally over. He thought that she was happier now, perhaps she had even found her John in Heaven. Still, each time he glanced into the back room where Lydia had kept her vigil, he remembered the beautiful, sad girl and shook his head. In time her memory would fade he thought, but for now he could not help remembering.

Several months went by, and one day the station master happened to glance into the back room in passing, and his heart nearly stopped. There, in Lydia's chair, was a woman draped in a white gown, a wispy hat upon her head hiding her face from view.

The station master tried to convince himself that it was just a female passenger who had missed the last train. He debated with himself and then he finally forced himself to walk into the darkened back room to speak to her.

"Can I help you, Miss?"

The girl looked up and smiled vaguely. The station master staggered backward. Lydia didn't say a word, but she took off her hat and laid it in her lap just as she had done so many times in life. The station master ran out and got his clerk to look into the room. He, too, saw Lydia waiting for John just as she had for so long.

Lydia was often seen after that. She always waited in the back room, sitting primly, holding her hat, and watching intently as passengers came and went. She caused no more trouble in death than she did in life. Still, she frightened more than one passenger who tried to strike up a conversation with her. She never spoke, but she'd often smile sadly at them and then just fade away.

Eventually the Wopsanonic station shut off the back room of the waiting area. Lydia now kept her vigil alone. They say that she kept it until the station was abandoned and perhaps she keeps it even now, sitting in the ruins of the torn-down station, spending eternity in the same dream world she had created in her life.

There is another version of this story where the woman in white haunted the train station because she was looking for her child. The child had supposedly died in a train wreck along that rail line and the mother had died, too, soon after from grief. After the mother's death people claimed to see her sitting in the station waiting for trains to arrive. Others claimed that she would stand on the platform watching everyone emerge from each train as she waited for her dead child that never arrived.

Bibliography

Baker Mansion

1) *Strange And Amazing Stories of Raystown Country*, p. 16, "Altoona's Baker Mansion" by Jon Baughman, published by The Broad Top Bulletin, Saxton PA 16678, Copyright 1987.

2) "Auras of History, Supernatural Permeate Baker Mansion" by Nancy Coleman, *The Tribune-Democrat*, March 22, 1981 (Sunday Edition).

3) "America's Ten Most Haunted Houses" by Rosemarie Robtham, *Life Magazine*, Nov. 1980 issue.

4) "Life Staffers H(a)unt for Ghost at Mansion" by Jeff Mulhollem , *Altoona Mirror*, Sept. 5, 1980.

5) Blair County Historical Society.

6) Baker's Mansion Museum Archives and Staff.

The Witch of Rehmeyer's Hollow

1) "PA's Haunted History," provided by PA Dept. of Commerce, *Patriot News*, Oct. 29, 1978 (Sunday Edition).

2) *Hex* by Arthur H. Lewis.

The Monster Of Broad Top

1) *Tales of the Broad Top*, p. 12, "Does A Giant Snake Haunt The Broad Top?" by Ron Morgan and Jon Baughman, Published by The Broad Top Bulletin, Saxton, PA 16678.

2) *Strange And Amazing Stories of Raystown Country*, p. 18, "The Giant Snake of the Broad Top" by Jon Baughman, published by The Broad Top Bulletin, Saxton, PA 16678, Copyright 1987.

The Legend Of Captain Jack

1) *Tales From The Allegheny Foothills*, Vol. V, "Captain Jack" by Vaughn E. Whisker, published in 1976 by the Bedford Gazette, Bedford, PA 15522.

2) *History of the Early Settlement of the Juniata Valley*, "Captain Jack, " p.134, and "Jack's Narrows," p.388, by U. J. Jones and Floyd G. Hoenstine, Copyright 1940, published by *The Telegraph Press*, Harrisburg, PA.

Dreaming Of The Lost Cox Children

1) *Strange And Amazing Stories of Raystown Country*, p. 29, "The Lost Children of the Alleghenies" by Jon Baughman, published by *The Broad Top Bulletin*, Saxton, PA, 16678, Copyright 1987.

2) "The Lost Cox Children," Blair County *Shoppers Guide*, Duncansville, PA, July 23, 1980.

3) "In the Hollow of the Lost Children, My Father Wept" by Bill Drobnich, *The Shoppers Guide*, Aug. 1, 1993.

4) *Bygone Days In The Cove*, Vol. 9, p.49, "Pavia and the Lost Cox Children" by Miss Ella M. Snowberger, published by *The Morrisons Cove Herald*, Martinsburg, PA, Jan. 1, 1941.

The Hauntings Of Elmhurst

1) Cambria County Historical Society Records.

2) "Gibson Girl Didn't Like House—Or Mother-in-law" by Nancy Coleman, Johnstown Tribune-Democrat, Saturday, Oct. 23, 1976.

3) "We Have Met The Elmhurst Ghosts And They Are Friends" by Nancy Coleman, Johnstown Tribune -Democrat, Weekly Edition, Nov. 2, 1978.

4) "The Gibson Girl" by Don Matthews, Jr., The Tribune-Democrat, Dec. 4, 1979.

5) Grolier Electronic Encyclopedia Systems

The Strange Case Of Fithian Minuit:

1) "Ghostly Guide to Bizarre Points of Interest," provided by PA State Dept. of Commerce, Sunday Patriot-News, Oct. 29, 1978.

2) Grolier Electronic Encyclopedia Systems

The Ghost Ships Of Lake Erie

1) "Ghostly Guide to Bizarre Points of Interest ," provided by PA State Dept. of Commerce, Sunday Patriot-News, Oct. 29, 1978.

2) Erie Historical Museum and Planetarium, 356 W. 6th Street, Erie, PA 16507.

3) "The Lake Erie Quadrangle," Waters Of Repose by David Stone & David Frew, published by the Erie County Historical Society, 417 State St., Erie, PA 16501.

Haunted Pennsylvania

The Black Horse Inn
1) *Tales From The Allegheny Foothills*, Vol. VIII (April 1979),
"Black Horse Inn" by Vaughn E. Whisker.

The General Wayne Inn
1) *Unsolved Mysteries*, NBC Television.
2) National Register of Historic Places
3) Anthony Wayne Historical Association, Inc.
4) Private Records of the General Wayne Inn
5) *Main Line Jewish Expression*, Thursday, April 12, 1979
6) "America's Oldest Restaurant Has 27th Anniversary"
by J. Robe Mendte, *The Main Line Chronicle*.
7) County Commissioners Office, Norristown, PA, December 7, 1899
8) "Spirits At General Wayne" from the column
"Barhopping" by Floyd Murray,
Delaware County Daily Times, Friday, Oct. 18, 1996.
9) "Historic Local Inn" by Sally Branca,
Main Line Times, Thursday, July 29, 1976.
10) "Unhappy Hessian Ghost Wants Olyphant
Psychic to Find Grave" by Eileen Dutka,
The Scrantonian, Sunday, Feb. 12, 1978.
11) *The Ten Creepiest Places In America*
by Allan Zullo, published by Troll Books.
12) *"Main Line Inns & Taverns # 27,"*
General Wayne Inn, by Robert Mendte.
13) *"Main Line Inns & Taverns # 1,"* Part VII of Series,
Black Horse and Gen. Wayne Center of Stirring Events
During Revolutionary History.
14) "General Wayne Inn, New Research Distinguished Facts From
Legends" (from a continuation) by Robert J. Mendte,
Main Line Chronicle, Sept. 9, 1971.
15) Ludington Public library & Information Center, Bryn Mawr &
Lancaster Ave., Bryn Mawr, PA 19010-3471

Haunted Gettysburg
1) *Ghosts of Gettysburg and Ghosts of Gettysburg II*,
Documentaries on History Channel by Greystone Communications.
2) *Ghosts of Gettysburg I, II, III*, by Mark Nesbitt,
Thomas Publications.

The Ghost Hounds
1) "Ghostly Guide to Bizarre Points of Interest," provided by PA State Dept. of Commerce, Sunday *Patriot-News*, Oct. 29, 1978.

Jean Bonnet Tavern
1) National Register of Historic Places.

The Death of Lily
1) *Bygone Days In The Cove*, Volumes 1-11 by Miss Ella M. Snowberger, published by *The Morrisons Cove Herald*, Martinsburg, PA.

The Innocent Hand
1) "Ghostly Guide to Bizarre Points of Interest," provided by PA State Dept. of Commerce, Sunday *Patriot-News*, Oct. 29, 1978.

"Mad" Anthony Wayne
1) Grolier's Electronic Encyclopedias
2) Erie Historical Museum and Planetarium, 356 W. 6th St., Erie, PA 16507.
3) "Ghostly Guide to Bizarre Points of Interest," provided by: PA State Dept. of Commerce, Sunday *Patriot-News*, Oct. 29, 1978.

The New Hope Hauntings
1) *Ghost Tours* by Adele Gamble, New Hope, PA.

The Livingston Poltergeist
1) *Haunts Of Adams And Other Counties* by Sally M. Barach, published by: A.G. Halldin Publishing Company, Indiana, PA 15701-0667.

The Girl In The Red Shawl
1) *More Ghosts In The Valley* by Adi-Kent Thomas Jeffrey, published by: Hampton Publishing.
2) *Strange Unsolved Mysteries* by Margaret Ronan, published by Scholastic Book Services.

The Russell House
1) "County Ghost?" by Sharyn Maust, Bedford Gazette, Bedford, PA.
2) "Russell House Series, Parts I & II" by Winona Garbrick,
Bedford County Press, Everett, PA.
3) Pioneer Historical Society, 242 E. John St., Bedford, PA 15522.

Bondage Of The Wolf Skin
1) *Tales From The Allegheny Foothills, Vol. VII* (June 1978),
by Vaughn E. Whisker, published by Bedford Gazette,
Bedford, PA 15522.

White Woman Of The Wopsanonic Station
1) *"Some Legends Leave You White As A..."* by M. Michele Dula,
The Johnstown Tribune-Democrat , Aug. 2, 1981.

Now Online!

Toad Hall, Inc.

"We Leap to a Different Lily Pad"

Visit Our Web Site

http://www.toadhallinc.com

Toad Hall, Inc. is a multi-media company geared to presenting information in the new age of electronics, television, movies and publications. With our state-of-the-art equipment, we have entered the world of the Internet in bringing our clients' work to the public and the public to our clients' work.

Our Divisions Include:
A Literary Agency
How-To and Reference Books
Metaphysical and
Paranormal - Nonfiction
Crafts Books
Non-Traditional Fiction